Street's Cruising Guide to the Eastern Caribbean, Volume III—
Martinique to Trinidad

Books by Donald M. Street, Jr.

A Cruising Guide to the Lesser Antilles (1966, rev. ed 1974)
A Yachting Guide to the Grenadines (1970)
The Ocean Sailing Yacht, Volume I (1973)
The Ocean Sailing Yacht, Volume II (1978)
Seawise (1979)
Street's Cruising Guide to the Eastern Caribbean (1980) in five volumes

Street's Cruising Guide to the Eastern Caribbean, Volume III— Martinique to Trinidad

Donald M. Street, Jr.

Sketch charts by Morgan B. MacDonald III
and Alan Wilkenson of Imray, Norie, Laurie and Wilson Ltd.
Topographical views by James Mitchell

W · W · NORTON & COMPANY

NEW YORK   LONDON

The text of this book is composed in Caledonia, with
display type set in Bulmer. Composition by Vail-Ballou Press, Inc.
Manufacturing by Kingsport Press
Book design by M. Franklin-Plympton

ISBN 0-393-03319-8

W. W. Norton & Company, Inc., 500 Fifth Avenue, New York,
N. Y. 10110
W. W. Norton & Company Ltd., 37 Great Russell Street, London
WC1B 3NU

1 2 3 4 5 6 7 8 9 0

Dedication

The idea for this cruising guide was originally conceived in 1963, and it was only through the hard work, perseverance, courage, and self-sacrifice of my late wife, Marilyn, that the original book got off the ground.

Fortunately for myself and my daughter, Dory, I met Patricia Boucher, now my wife, on the beach in Tyrell Bay. She has presented me with three active sons, yet has had time to help in business, sailing *Iolaire*, and exploring. Although she had hardly sailed before our marriage, she has taken to sailing like a duck to water. Her love of sailing was largely instrumental in my decision to keep *Iolaire* when I was thinking of selling her to reduce expenses.

It is only because of Trich's hard work keeping our various business enterprises going in my absence that I have been able to keep the third love of my life, *Iolaire*.

Iolaire has been my mistress for thirty years; at age eighty-two she is still the type of boat Michael Dufour would appreciate: she is "fast, beautiful, and responsive—like a good-looking woman." She first arrived in the Islands in 1947, remained for a few years, and cruised back to Europe in 1949, from Jamaica to England direct. In 1950, under the ownership of R. H. Somerset, she won her division's R.O.R.C. Season's Points Championship at the age of forty-five, returned to the Islands in 1951, cruised there during the winter of 1951–1952, sailed in the Bermuda Race in 1952, then cruised back to Europe and the Mediterranean. In 1954, she returned to the Islands, where I purchased her in 1957.

In 1975, we celebrated *Iolaire*'s seventieth birthday by cruising to Europe via Bermuda, New London, New York, Boston, Halifax, and then having a fifteen-day passage to Ireland. We cruised on to Cowes, took part in the fiftieth anniversary of the first Fastnet Race, and then raced to La Rochelle, La Trinité, Benodet, and back to the Solent—four races, totaling 1,300 miles, in twenty-one days.

After Calasis, we went up the Thames to St. Katherine's Dock in the Pool of London under Tower Bridge, then back down the Thames and up the Colne River in Essex, where we lay alongside the dock in Rowhedge, where *Iolaire* had been built seventy years before. Then to Plymouth, Glandore in Ireland, Madeira, the Canaries, and back across the Atlantic in eighteen and one-half days to Antigua.

We arrived in Antigua seven months and seven days after our departure, having sailed 13,000 miles and raced 1,300 miles, all without an engine, visiting all the places people had said we'd never make except under power.

We decided that *Iolaire* should celebrate her eightieth birthday in 1985 by retiring from round-the-buoy racing. Her swan song in Antigua Week of 1985 was wonderful—third in the cruising division (seventeen boats), first in the boats twenty years old or older.

Then we took *Iolaire* on a 12,000-mile, double trans-Atlantic jaunt. In seven months we visited Bermuda, five of the Azores islands, Ireland, Vigo in Spain, the Salvage Islands and the Madeiran Archipelago, five of the Canary Islands, and three of the Cape Verdian Islands; then we rolled on home in fourteen days and four hours from the Cape Verdes to Antigua—not a record but a good fast passage for a heavy-displacement cruising boat.

Iolaire has nine trans-Atlantic passages under her belt, and I have sailed her a minimum of 120,000 miles; who knows how many miles she has sailed altogether.

There is little of the Caribbean whose waters have not been furrowed by her hull, and, as some of my good friends will point out, few rocks that have not been dented by her keel!

To my three loves—Marilyn, Trich, and *Iolaire*—I dedicate this book.

D.M.S.

Contents: Volume III

Contents of the other volumes in Street's *Cruising Guide to the Eastern Caribbean*

Contents:
Volume I

Contents:
Volume II, Part One

Contents: Volume II, Part Two

Contents:
Volume IV–Venezuela

Sketch Charts

Publisher's Note

D. M. Street, Jr., a veteran Caribbean sailor, is also known as an author and the compiler of Imray-Iolaire charts of that area, and as a worldwide yacht insurance broker who places policies with Lloyd's of London.

Mr. Street also serves as a design consultant on new construction, most notably recently on *Lone Star*, a 54-foot wooden ketch, built by Mashford Brothers of Plymouth, England. He also serves as design consultant on rerigging existing yachts and finding good cruising boats for people who want a proper yacht. His latest project is to do a sailing and seamanship video series with SEA TV.

Street is mainly known as a cruising skipper, but he has raced with success on *Iolaire* and other boats. *Iolaire* has retired from round-the-buoy racing at age 82, but the skipper has not and can be found at the various Caribbean regattas skippering, or sailing as tactician with local knowledge, on other boats.

His contributions to sailing in the Eastern Caribbean consist of his cruising guides and the Imray-Iolaire charts. Thirty-seven Imray-Iolaire charts have replaced roughly 200 French, U.S., British, Dutch, and a few Spanish charts and are all that are needed to cruise the Eastern Caribbean.

As an author, he is prolific. His original *Cruising Guide to the Lesser Antilles* was published in 1966, *A Yachting Guide to the Grenadines* in 1970, and an updated and expanded *Cruising Guide to the Eastern Caribbean* in 1974, with continued expansions and updates in the 1980s. The title of the last is now *Street's Cruising Guide to the Eastern Caribbean*, a five-volume work that covers an arc of islands 1,000 miles long.

He has also written *The Ocean Sailing Yacht*, Volume I (1973) and Volume II (1978). *Seawise*, a collection of articles, came out in 1976. He is presently at work at completely rewriting Volume I of *Street's Cruising Guide to the Eastern Caribbean* in light of the information obtained on his seven trans-Atlantic passages and hundreds of interviews. The new book will be titled *Street's Trans-Atlantic Crossing Guide and Introduction to the Eastern Caribbean*. He is also working on a series of books, *Street on Sails, Street on Seamanship and Storms,* and *Street on Small Boat Handling*, a collection of updated articles that have appeared over the last twenty years; and *Iolaire and I*, the story of *Iolaire*'s eighty-two years and Street's lifetime of adventures and misadventures in the yachting world.

He regularly writes for *Sail, Cruising World, Sailing, Wooden Boat, Tell-Tale Compass, Yachting, Yachting World,* and *Yachting Monthly,* and for publications in Sweden, Germany, Italy, Ireland, Australia, and New Zealand.

For well over twenty years, Street owned land and houses in Grenada, but unfortunately the houses are no more. They were taken over by the People's Revolutionary Army in May 1979 as part of its military base. The houses did not survive the U.S. liberation in 1983, when helicopter gunships destroyed both of them. He hopes someday to rebuild on the old site. During the winter he crisscrosses the Caribbean. In the spring, he heads south to lay up *Iolaire* in Grenada, south of the hurricane belt. In July and August, he can usually be found in Glandore, Ireland, on the family Dragon, *Gypsy*, either skippering her or trimming sheets for his sons.

Preface

When I first bought *Iolaire* in 1957, I found on board what was then the only straight cruising guide to the Lesser Antilles. This was a mimeographed publication produced by the Coast Guard Auxiliary and edited by a Lieutenant Commander Buzby. Carleton Mitchell's *Islands to Windward*, published in 1948, was generally regarded as a good cruising yarn rather than as a cruising guide, but it did have some basic cruising information in the back of the book. Unfortunately, by the time I started sailing outside the Virgin Islands in 1959, *Islands to Windward* was out of print. In 1960, *The Virgin Islands* by George Teeple Eggleston was published, the result of a one-month cruise aboard Eunice Boardman's 55-foot ketch *Renegade*.

In 1961, Percy Chubb III, after a cruise through the Lesser Antilles, produced a small, privately printed *Guide to the Windward and Leeward Islands of the Eastern Caribbean*. In 1964, Linton Rigg authored *The Alluring Antilles*, a combination guide and cruising adventure of a half-year sail from Puerto Rico to Trinidad aboard the 45-foot ketch *Island Belle*.

These seemed to suffice for the small amount of Caribbean cruising done in those days, but starting in the early sixties the charter-boat business suddenly began to expand, and many new boats arrived. It was Frank Burke of Island Yachts who inspired my entry into cruising-guide writing. Figuring that too many of the charter parties were missing the best spots in the Virgins because their skippers had not been in the Islands long enough to get to know them intimately, he asked me to write a cruising guide to the Virgin Islands. This was done, and he had it privately printed. I received the magnificent sum of $100—which to me happened to be a veritable fortune in those days.

This small volume later formed the basis of the Virgin Islands section of my *Cruising Guide to the Lesser Antilles*, published in 1966, after I showed it to Phelps Platt of Dodd, Mead, who encouraged me to expand it to cover the whole island chain. This was followed two years later by Tom Kelly and Jack van Ost's *Yachtman's Guide to the Virgin Islands*, and then by Al Forbes's excellent *Cruising Guide to the Virgin Islands*, notable in that, unlike many guide authors, he had sailed the area for many years before he wrote his.

In 1970, following eight years of cruising the Grenadines, I produced *A Yachting Guide to the Grenadines*, after which, in 1973, came Julius M. Wilensky's *Yachtsman's Guide to the Windward Islands*, which covered largely the same territory as mine. Also in 1973, Gordon C. Ayer produced an interesting small guide covering an island group which had never been detailed before—namely, the Passage Islands.

If, in all this, one guide is found to read surprisingly like another, I ask only that you refer back to my original works to see who said what first. If nothing else, it's a matter of pride.

In *Cruising Guide to the Eastern Caribbean* I have tried to include all the information I have gleaned in nearly twenty-nine years of cruising these islands. I have drawn not only from my own experiences, but, as you can see from the accompanying Acknowledgments, also from the experiences of old friends who are, in addition, good sailors. Thus I feel I have described probably every cove in the Eastern Caribbean where one could possibly think of anchoring.

If you find one I may have missed, please let me know. I boldly asserted in my 1966 guide that the book would never become dated because rocks don't move. Little did I realize how eagerly island governments would actually start moving them, along with creating new islands, making islands into peninsulas, building low bridges, and so forth, as the development of the Eastern Caribbean boomed. Further, any guide is destined to go out of date simply because the idyllic uninhabited spot of one year becomes a thriving hotel and cabaña settlement the next. Indeed, one of my readers lately took me to task because he was using my original guide and expected to anchor off an island described therein as uninhabited. As he rounded between Pinese and Mopion, he was greeted by a brand-new hotel ablaze with celebration, and counted no fewer than forty-five boats moored in the lee of Petit St. Vincent! Please . . . don't blame me.

It is impossible for anyone to say he knows the Eastern Caribbean perfectly; after twenty-nine years I was still discovering new little anchorages. But the time came to look to new fields.

At various times, Venezuelan yachtsmen have extolled the virtues of Venezuela and the offshore islands. I originally went to Venezuela to give a slide lecture to a yacht club and to take part in a race. I then took *Iolaire* to eastern Venezuela for six weeks and later visited western Venezuela on *Boomerang*. There followed a month's cruise in 1978 and a two-week cruise in 1979. Certainly, I have not seen enough to write definitive cruising directions to Venezuela, Aruba, Bonaire, and Curaçao, and this section is not covered as well as are the Lesser Antilles.

However, with the aid of Venezuelan yachtsmen Rolly Edmonds, Dr. Camejo of *Caribaña*, Pedro Gluecksman of *Bayola*, and Otto Castillo, port captain of Sinclair Oil, and yachtsmen from the Eastern Caribbean, including Paul "Pog" Squire, Gordon Stout of *Shango*, Hank Strauss of *Doki*, Richard and Barbara Weinman of *Narania*, Augie Holland of *Taurus*, and Mike Jarrold of *Lily Maid*, I think we have among us put together an acceptable and fairly complete guide to the Venezuelan coast, its offshore islands, Aruba, Bonaire, and Curaçao. Any additions and corrections offered by cruising yachtsmen will be greatly appreciated. Send information to D. M. Street, Jr., c/o Mr. David Payne, Cayzer Steel Bowater, 32/38 Duke's Place, London EC3 7LX, England.

During the summer of 1985, *Iolaire* visited and explored the Azores, the Madeiran Archipelago, the Canaries, and the Cape Verde Islands. The information gained will be included in Volume I of *Street's Cruising Guide to the Eastern Caribbean*—under a new title, *Street's Trans-Atlantic Crossing Guide and Introduction to the Eastern Caribbean*. Now I feel my exploring days are over—the "old Tiger" has retired—and it is time that one of the young "Tigers" (daughter Dory or one of her three brothers, Donald, Richard, or Mark) take over *Iolaire* and explore new fields.

D.M.S.

Foreword

The Lesser Antilles stretch southward from St. Thomas to Grenada in a great crescent 500 miles long, offering the yachtsman a cruising ground of unequaled variety. Some of the islands are flat, dry, and windswept, their shores girded by coral reefs and their land barely arable. Others are reefless, jagged peaks jutting abruptly up from the sea, where they block the ever-present trades and gather rain clouds the year round; water cascades in gullies down their sides and their slopes are well cultivated. The character of their peoples likewise varies—from the charming and unspoiled although desperately poor Dominican, to the comparatively well-to-do and worldly wise Frenchmen of Martinique.

Unless you have a whole season at your disposal, it is foolhardy to attempt all the islands in a single cruise. Not only will you not make it, but you will fail to enjoy the slow, natural, and relaxed pace of life in these tropical islands. The first measure of a successful cruise is how soon your carefully worked out timetable gets thrown away.

Rule number 1 in the Antilles is: Don't make any plan more than a day in advance since you will frequently—in fact constantly—alter your intentions to suit the pace and attractions of the locale.

Rule number 2: Each night before turning in, read the sailing directions covering your passage to the next area, and study the detailed description of your intended anchorage. In some cases this will seriously affect the next day's plans—particularly the hour of departure. Remember, for instance, that when you're on the east coast of Martinique, Guadeloupe, Antigua, and Grenada, you must be in the anchorage by 1400 hours. Otherwise the sun is in the west, directly in your line of vision, making it impossible to see any reefs until it is too late.

Rule number 3: Do not enter a strange harbor at night if at all possible.

Rule number 4: No chart can be absolutely accurate. In the Caribbean, learning how to read the water is as important as knowing how to read a chart. Eyeball navigation is the key to safe and satisfying sailing in the Islands.

Whether Puerto Rico to the north or Trinidad and Tobago to the south should be considered part of the Lesser Antilles is a question for the gazetteers to squabble over. For the purposes of this book, we welcome all three into the fellowship of proximity. Taken as such, the Antilles conveniently break up into a number of areas suitable for two- or three-week cruises. The start and end point of a cruise will be governed by your own tastes and the availability of air transportation. The air services into San Juan and Trinidad are excellent, for example; but neither of these places is a particularly good spot to begin a cruise. San Juan is dead to leeward of the rest of the chain—and who wants to start out with a hard slog into the wind against a strong current? Trinidad is not much better, unless you're going to Venezuela.

But air transportation throughout the area has been improving over the years. Direct international flights now also arrive at Antigua, St. Lucia, Martinique, Guadeloupe, Barbados, Grenada, and Maiquetía, the airport for Caracas. Favorite starting points for cruises are St. Thomas, Tortola, Grenada, and Barcelona/Puerto la Cruz in the El Morro area of Venezuela.

To get to most of these places, you must often rely on secondary, local airlines with shuttle services. These vary from being fairly good from San Juan to St. Thomas and Tortola and the Venezuelan airlines, to downright disastrous with LIAT. LIAT's aircraft, pilots, and maintenance personnel are first class, but the office staff has developed the art of losing baggage and double-booking reservations to an exact science. There are various take-offs as to what LIAT actually means—some people claim that LIAT is an abbreviation for "Leave Islands Any Time," while others insist that LIAT

really stands for "Luggage In Another Terminal."
Still, it's all part of the adventure of a Caribbean
cruise.

Which starting point you choose will say something of your tastes in cruising. If you prefer gunkholing and short jaunts between many little islands
only a few miles apart, if you like snorkeling and
little in the way of civilization, then it is the Virgins
or the Grenadines for you. But you'd best hurry
down because real-estate developers and other
sailors are fast filling them up.

For those of you who want to give boat and crew
a good tuning up for offshore racing, set out from
St. Thomas up through the Virgins, then work
your way across the Anegada Passage to St. Martin
or Anguilla, and finish with a final leg up to Antigua.
In doing so, you will gain a fair sampling of island
diversity and of French, Dutch, and English colonial temperaments. The Anegada Passage is a nice,
hard drive to windward, which should uncover any
weak points in rig or crew.

Those interested exclusively in the pursuits of
diving, treasure hunting, or snorkeling should steer
for the low-lying islands of Anguilla, Barbuda,
Anegada, Los Roques, and Las Aves. The reefs in
these areas are vast and inexhaustible. Fortune
hunters still flock to these islands, where innumerable off-lying wrecks date back hundreds of years,
some presumably undiscovered. Consult the source
books—but remember, these islands are low, flat,
encircled by reefs, and hard to spot. The charts
are based on surveys done mainly in the middle of
the last century. Coral grows, and hurricanes have
moved through the area a number of times; earthquakes have shaken the islands, and sand bars have
moved. In short, you must be extremely careful.
Do not let your boat become the next curiosity for
inquisitive divers!

Saba and Statia (Sint Eustatius) are two attractive islands that are too seldom visited. Their
anchorages are exceptionally bad, but when the
conditions are right, they certainly are worth a go.
Their close neighbors, St. Kitts and Nevis, are of
historical interest, figuring as they do in the lives
of Alexander Hamilton, Admirals Nelson and Rodney, and Generals Shirley and Frazer. St. Kitts is
well worth a visit to see the beautiful restoration
of the old fortress of Brimstone Hill. A number of
the old plantation great houses have been restored
and opened up as hotels and restaurants. Renting
a car to tour St. Kitts is a good scheme.

If you like longer sails, the bright lights of
civilization, and a variety of languages and customs, the middle islands from Antigua to St. Lucia

should keep you happy. The French islands of
Guadeloupe and Martinique afford the finest cui-
sine in the Antilles. The local merchants offer an
excellent selection of cheeses and meats from
Europe and the best wines available outside France.
The tourist shops are a woman's delight, and the
perfumes are at about half the Stateside price.
Martinique offers a fabulous collection of bikinis,
but the prices have gone up so much in France
that the savings for an American are no longer
substantial. Rough rule of thumb: The smaller the
bikini, the more expensive it is.

The string arrived: its size—minuscule; its price—
astronomical. One solution frequently used by the
always-economical French women was to buy only
half the string at half the price. Others felt that
even that was too expensive and sailed *au naturel*—not really showing off, just economizing!

The universal pastime of watching members of
the opposite sex is alive and well in Martinique,
and the visiting seafarer soon gets into the spirit of
things. This pastime can be enjoyed in many ways,
but the two most popular methods are either stroll-
ing around the streets of Fort-de-France or rowing
around in Anse Mitan (which today is likely to have
forty or fifty boats in it) and pretending to admire
the boats while admiring the crews. An added
bonus here is that at Anse Mitan, going topless
seems to be *de rigueur*.

The women in Fort-de-France may not be the
prettiest in the Caribbean, but they are far and
away the most stylish. And the men, sitting at the
sidewalk cafés sipping their coffee or *punch vieux*,
cut figures worthy of the *boulevardiers* of Paris.
But newcomers, take note: The punch will make a
strong man weak-kneed and the coffee tastes not
unlike battery acid.

The French and their chicory-laced coffee have
distressed visiting foreigners for many decades. A
story is told of Count von Bismarck touring France
after the Franco-Prussian War. He was ending a
fine meal in a country inn and called for the maître
d'hôtel and offered to buy all his chicory at 10
percent over the market price. The maître d' agreed
and sold him what he claimed to be all he had.
Again the count offered to buy any remaining
chicory, this time at 50 percent over the market
price; the maître d' produced a second quantity of
the plant. For a third time the count offered to
buy any that remained—at *twice* the market price—
and the maître d' surrendered a small amount,
assuring him that this was indeed all that remained.
Satisfied at last, the count concluded, "Very well,
now you may prepare me a cup of coffee!"

H.M.S. *Diamond Rock*, off the south coast of Martinique, is the basis for many stories in folklore, most of them inaccurate. The true story of Diamond Rock is contained in *Her Majesty's Sloop of War Diamond Rock*, by Stuart and Eggleston.

Dominica is for the adventurous. A ride into the mountains by Jeep and horseback will take you to the last settlement of the Carib peoples. Here the natives fashion the distinctive Carib canoes that are also seen in Guadeloupe, Martinique, and St. Lucia. With nothing but a flour sack for a sail and a paddle as a rudder, the islanders set out in these boats against the wind to fish in the open Atlantic. Not an easy way to earn a living. Because of various unpleasant incidents in the early eighties, Portsmouth in Dominica came to be avoided by many yachtsmen; but I hope that Mrs. Charles, head of the country's new government, will straighten out the difficulties and make Portsmouth once again a high-point of Caribbean cruising.

St. Lucia provides some superb anchorages at Pigeon Island, Marigot, and Vieux Fort, and the truly unbelievable one beneath the Pitons at Soufrière. The volcano and sulfur baths are an impressive spectacle, and it is well worth the expense to explore the island by car or Jeep, an adventure vividly recounted by George Eggleston in *Orchids in a Calabash Tree*.

St. Vincent, just north of the Grenadines, is a high, lush island richly and diversely cultivated. The island has an intriguing history, highlighted by the almost continual warfare among French, English, and Caribs that lasted from 1762 until 1796, when the Caribs were expelled to Central America.

Bequia is the home of the fisherman and whaler, an island where any sailor can explore, relax, and "gam" for days on end. The harbor is beautiful; life is relaxed.

After cruising the entire Caribbean and getting to know all the islands intimately, many experienced yachtsmen declare Grenada to be the "loveliest of islands." The highlands produce enough rain to allow the farmers to grow a large quantity of fresh fruit and vegetables, but the south coast is dry enough to allow the yachtsman to live and work on his boat. The island also has a dozen different harbors, providing at least sixty separate anchorages. Most of these harbors are only short, one- or two-hour sails from each other.

Grenada, with its excellent harbor at St. George's, was once the yachting capital of the Southern Caribbean. It suffered badly at the hands of its politicians for many years, and is only now beginning to recover, since the U.S. liberation of 1983 gave capitalism another chance there. I'm sure the "Spice Island" will soon be able to provide the necessary yachting facilities to match its beautiful natural offerings.

Barbados is relatively remote and seldom visited by yachts except those that are coming downwind from Europe. If your plane stops there en route to another island, arrange for a layover of a day or two. It is undoubtedly the best-run island in the entire Caribbean. Everything is clean and neat (by West Indian standards); the people are charming and speak in the most wonderful accent. They are solicitous and helpful to visitors. The old carenage in Bridgetown should not be missed, nor should the screw-lift dock.

It is a shame that Tobago is seldom visited by yachtsmen. It is dead to windward of Trinidad, and from Grenada it is 90 miles hard on the port tack. Even if you manage to lay the rhumb line from Grenada, it will be a long slog, hard on the wind. Current and sea will drive you off to the west. It is fairly inaccessible except from Barbados, from which it is an easy reach southwestward.

The American and British Virgin Islands have been laboriously described in the various tourist guides, but whatever the evaluation of shoreside life, a sailor can pass a very pleasant month cruising this area.

Throughout the Caribbean, the character of the various island peoples is apt to vary broadly within a relatively small area. Even among formerly British Islands, each has its own peculiar flavor, its own outlook and accent. (In fact, natives are known to complain that they can't understand the English spoken on neighboring islands.) For the most part, the people are quiet and law-abiding. The racially inspired violence that periodically has troubled St. Croix and St. Thomas has been far less a problem in the islands farther south.

As the years go by, the Eastern Caribbean becomes more crowded; hence, yachtsmen are beginning to head west to Venezuela. In the fifties and sixties, cruising in Venezuela was looked on as a dangerous occupation—not because of unfriendliness to yachtsmen, but because Castro was smuggling guerrillas ashore in small fishing boats. The Guardia Nacional and the navy were frequently guilty of shooting first and asking questions later, with the result that a number of boats were ventilated by Venezuelan government agencies. All this is now a thing of the past; although you may have to fill out a lot of forms and papers, everyone is extremely friendly and, to the best of my knowledge, there have been no nasty incidents involving yachts in Venezuela for many years.

Venezuela is, of course, totally different from the rest of the Eastern Caribbean. The people and language are Spanish. The off-lying islands provide some of the finest diving in the Eastern Caribbean, have not been fished out, and are generally uninhabited.

Yachting is only just beginning to make itself felt in Venezuela, and if you put your mind to it, with the exception of the large marinas in the areas of El Morro, Caracas, Tucacas, and Carenero, you can cruise about to your heart's content and see no other yachts except during weekends.

One cruising technique used by some yachts is to arrive at the marina on Friday night as the Venezuelans are all departing and berths are available, stay for the weekend, sightseeing, etc., on Saturday, have a night out on the town Saturday night, have a late sleep Sunday morning, and depart Sunday afternoon prior to the arrival of the returning Venezuelan yachts.

Unfortunately, the great welcome that the Venezuelan private clubs used to give visiting yachtsmen has cooled. As more and more sailors go to Venezuela to escape the hurricane season, the behavior of some has been such that the door has been slammed shut against the rest of us in most private Venezuelan clubs. If you know a Venezuelan yachtsman, write to him ahead of time and he can probably get the door opened specifically for you.

Los Roques, an area of 355 square miles, is almost as large as the American and British Virgin Islands with at least 50 percent of it unsurveyed. This does not mean that it is an area you cannot sail. Venezuelan and a few American yachtsmen (like Gordon Stout) have crisscrossed and spent as long as a week cruising this wonderful place. This is an area that a bare-boat organization should expand into. The boats could be based at Los Roques. Air communication to Maiquetía (Caracas's airport) is excellent from all over the world. It is only a thirty-minute shuttle flight from Los Roques, thus putting the charterer on board his boat in a very short time. Supplies could be shuttled back and forth from La Guaira via the ever-present small diesel-powered Venezuelan fishing boats.

The bare boats would probably have to be specially designed with a very shallow draft. The Hereschoff Meadow Lark draws only 18 inches with the leeboards up; coupled with a Freedom 40

rig, it would be ideal. It will be interesting to see what develops here in years to come.

Venezuela is an area of contrasts. The easternmost tip of the Peninsula of Paria rises 5,000 feet in the air with vertical slopes spilling into the Caribbean on one side and into the Gulf of Paria on the other. From the Gulf of Paria one can visit the mouth of the Orinoco River and Angel Falls, take trips into the jungle, and see unbelievable wildlife directly from the boat.

The north coast of Venezuela, as one progresses westward, begins with heavy jungle which tapers out to brush and ends up finally in Laguna de Obispos. In the Gulf of Cariaco one finds this fantastic harbor—the scenery ashore is like a lunar landscape. It gives the impression that it cannot have rained there in the past twenty years!

As one continues westward, the mountains of Venezuela are always close to the coastline and always barren. The cities are exploding rather than simply growing. Side by side are sophisticated new marinas and small fishing villages. Offshore are low, deserted reefs and uninhabited islands. After Puerto Cabello, most cruisers jump out to Bonaire, Aruba, and Curaçao.

Bonaire is low, flat, and sparsely populated. Its shores rise so steeply from the sea bottom that it is practically impossible to anchor in its lee. The anchorage problem has been solved by the new marina, which has slips and a 100-ton syncrolift dock; adequate supplies—fresh, frozen, and canned—are available. The people are very friendly. Bonaire has some of the best diving in the world, with excellent support facilities right at hand.

If you want to connect up with the outside world, go to Curaçao, with its excellent air communications and first-class hotels. Curaçao, too, has all kinds of supplies and excellent harbors.

Boats going westward usually skip Aruba, but it is a popular place for boats fighting their way eastward from Panama and the San Blas islands. This trip is a long slog to windward, and in years gone by yachts frequently stopped at Cartagena Santa Marta, or anchored behind Cabo de la Vela. However, because of drug trafficking, no yacht these days should even think of approaching the Colombian coast, much less anchoring offshore. Thus, even Aruba, basically a low, flat island covered with oil refineries, looks like heaven after a week or so of slamming into the heavy trade winds and westerly current.

We hope that with the aid of these books you will enjoy the Islands and Venezuelan coast as much as I have for some two decades. Anyone contemplating a cruise aboard a charter boat is well advised to read the supplementary chapters, which will give you much background information. They not only will explain to you why perhaps the charter skipper looks tired (he has spent the last two days fixing his generator under sail while he deadheads to pick you up), but you will have a better idea of what to expect upon your arrival in the Islands. A host of important tips and facts that are not included in the average tourist or charter-boat broker's brochure will, I trust, be found in this book. And needless to say, anyone planning to bring his boat to the Islands should read the whole book carefully with pencil in hand to make notes on what is applicable.

It should be noted that much basic information for the Eastern Caribbean is found in Volume I of *Street's Cruising Guide to the Eastern Caribbean*. That book serves as a companion volume to whatever other volume you are using. Volume I also gives you an overall picture of the Islands and allows you to better choose what area you plan to sail; it also has a very important chapter on Wind, Weather, and Tide.

One caution in particular: In May, June, and July, the Caribbean is usually twelve to eighteen inches lower than it is in the winter. Thus, at the time of a low-water spring tide in those months, the water is a full three feet lower than it is at high-water spring tide in the winter. Although the Imray-Iolaire charts' soundings are based on the lowest-level datum, not all charts or local knowledge take the difference into account. If you have any doubt about your situation, take soundings before you venture into questionable waters.

To repeat, "Sailing Directions" is probably the most important chapter, one that should be read and studied. It should be consulted regularly before finalizing the day's plans. While the navigational features and anchorages of individual islands are described in the chapter concerned with that island, the routes *between* the islands are described in the sailing directions—so be sure to consult them each day.

As an addendum to this, some advice to readers who operate bare-boat charter fleets: Study the book carefully, make your judgments, and mark on the sketch charts of each boat's copy the anchorages you want your charters to avoid.

Finally, be cautious. Practically every place in the Eastern Caribbean where a yacht can anchor has been described or at least mentioned, but not all are easy to enter. Many of these anchorages can be used only in good weather and perfect visibility. Besides, some boats are handier than others, and some sailors are better than others. Thus you must evaluate each anchorage for yourself before entering. The time of day, the weather, your abilities, the weatherliness of your boat—all influence the final decision.

Fair sailing to all.

D.M.S.

Acknowledgments

Yachtsmen who cruise the Caribbean should be thankful to Phelps Platt of Dodd, Mead, who saw my original draft of what was then going to be a privately printed guide to the Virgin Islands and liked it enough to encourage me to write a complete guide to the other islands. Yachtsmen should also thank Bernard Goldhirsch of United Marine Publishers, founder of *Sail* magazine, who did the 1974 updated and expanded cruising guide.

Thanks are now due to Eric Swenson of W. W. Norton and Company, who not only agreed to publish a completely updated guide, but also agreed that it should be expanded to include Venezuela, its off-lying islands, and Aruba, Bonaire, and Curaçao, plus tremendously enlarged sections on "Getting There" and "Leaving." The guide is now so big that we have produced it in five volumes.

I must also thank the many yachtsmen who have helped me with valuable information. Augie Holland (the only person I know who cruises in a genuine Block Island Cow Horn), Ross Norgrove of *White Squall II*, and Carl Powell of *Terciel* all deserve a special vote of thanks for helping me update the Virgin Islands section. Jon Repke of Power Products, a refrigeration expert, electrician, mechanic, sailor, and pilot, solved many of the mysteries of St. Martin/St. Barthélemy/Anguilla by spending the better part of a day flying me through this area. Carl Kaushold supplied an excellent chart and information on Salt River. Ray Smith of Grenada was most helpful in his suggestions on tides and weather patterns in the Caribbean, and in compiling the list of radio stations and radio beacons. His brother, Ron, solved the mystery of the whereabouts of Tara Island, on the south coast of Grenada, which is improperly marked on the chart. Carl Amour of the Anchorage Hotel solved the great mystery of the rocks off Scotts Head, Dominica. Dr. Jack Sheppard of *Arieto*, the late Dick Doran of *Laughing Sally*, and Carlos Lavendero of several boats made possible the inclusion of the Puerto Rican and Passage Islands informa-

tion. Gordon Stout of *Shango* and Peter Lee of *Virginia Reel* made possible the inclusion of Tobago. Jerry Bergoff of *Solar Barque* and Sylver Brin of St. Barthélemy were most helpful in clearing up some of the mysteries of the eastern end of St. Barthélemy.

Pieter van Storn, formerly of Island Waterworld, and Malcolm Maidwell and Peter Spronk, of Caribbean Catamaran Centre, were most helpful in the Sint Maarten area. Hans Hoff, from the 90-foot ketch *Fandango*, is one of the few people who has won a bet from me on anchorages. The standing bet is I will buy a drink for anyone who can find a good, safe anchorage with 6 feet of water in it that has not been mentioned in the cruising guide. I expect to be nabbed once in a while by a small boat, but not by the skipper of a 90-foot ketch! Hans found an anchorage inside the reef on the north coast of Anguilla. Where the chart showed nothing but solid reef, Hans managed to find himself inside the reef with 40 feet of water!

John Clegg, formerly of *Flica II*, Dave Price, formerly of *Lincoln*, and Gordon Stout of *Shango* have continually popped up with wonderful odd bits of information that they have gleaned on their cruises from one end of the Lesser Antilles to the other.

Numerous other skippers have, over the years, given me a tremendous amount of help. They include, in the Antigua area, Desmond Nicholson, of V. E. B. Nicholson and Sons, English Harbour, and Jol Byerley, skipper of *Morning Tide* (and former charter skipper on *Ron of Argyll*, *Mirage*, *Étoile de Mer*, and *Lord Jim*), to name but two. For finer points on the exploration of the east coast of Antigua, I am deeply indebted to David Simmonds of the little cruising/racing sloop *Bacco*; David is also head of Antigua Slipways and the senior marine surveyor in the Eastern Caribbean. Thanks should also go to Simon Cooper and David Corrigan, both of whom unfortunately have left the Islands; Morris Nicholson of *Eluthera;* Simon

Bridger of *Circe* and other boats; Peter Haycraft and George Foster of Tortola, both of them harbor pilots and yachtsmen; Martin Mathias of the sportsfisherman *Bihari;* Bert Kilbride, diver extraordinaire of Saba Rock, Virgin Islands; and the Trinidadians Doug and the late Hugh ("Daddy") Myer of *Rosemary V* and *Huey II.* I want also to thank Arthur Spence of *Dwyka,* Marcy Crowe of *Xantippe,* Andy Copeland of various boats, Mike Smith of *Phryna,* Ken McKenzie of *Ti,* Dave Ferninding of *Whisper,* Chris Bowman of *Water Pearl of Bequia,* and the others whose names I may have forgotten. It is only with the help of experienced yachtsmen like these that a book of this type can be written.

A special vote of thanks must go to Morgan B. MacDonald III, my nephew, who did the sketch-chart drawings for the 1974 edition of the *Guide;* I'm pleased that many of them are still in this edition.

Jim Mitchell did a superb job on the topographical views of the Islands.

Thanks must go especially to the late Tom Wilson of Imray, Laurie, Norie and Wilson, who immediately embraced the idea of Imray-Iolaire charts when I presented it to him, and pushed hard to get the series out as fast as possible. His son "Willie" Wilson is carrying on Tom's work. And the Wilson family graciously allowed me to use sections of the Imray-Iolaire charts as harbor charts in this volume.

Alan Wilkenson, Imray's draftsman, has done a splendid job of drawing up the charts.

Admiral Sir David Haslam, retired head of the British Hydrographic Office, and his successor, Rear Admiral R. O. Morris, have been most helpful in supplying information and giving permission for material from the British Admiralty charts to be incorporated in this book. These appropriations have been made with the approval of the controller of Her Majesty's Stationery Office and the Hydrographer of the Navy.

Jim Young of Dive Tobago provided reams of information on Bucco Reef at the southwest corner of Tobago, on Tyrell Bay at the northeast corner, and on many coves in between. The Tobago sketch charts in this book could not have been done without his help.

Molly Watson, her son Eddie, and all the members of the Trinidad Yachting Association have done a great deal to help get out the word on Trinidad.

I want to thank Patricia Street, my sister Elizabeth Vanderbilt, her husband, Peter, and their son Jay for their help in rechecking many facts.

Finally, a special round of thanks:

Maria McCarthy of Union Hall, County Cork, Ireland, labored long and hard during the summer of 1978, typing up corrections and inserts on the previous edition of this volume.

Audrey Semple spent the winter of 1978–1979 doing a magnificent job of cutting, gluing, correcting, typing, and fitting it all back together again.

Geraldine Hickey, my secretary during the winter of 1979–1980, did similar work under times of trying circumstance.

Aileen Calnan of Glandore, County Cork, not only worked with me in Ireland but also came aboard *Iolaire* in the winter of 1983, then continued in 1984–1985 and is still with us as typist-secretary-crew, sometime babysitter, and sometime cook.

Special thanks should go to Harvey Loomis, who for eight years has labored hard as editor of these guides. He not only is a good literary editor but is also an excellent sailor. As such he has been a tremendous help in rewriting the sailing and piloting directions to make them clear to the reader. Both I, the author, and you, the reader, owe Harvey Loomis a vote of thanks.

The help of these devoted friends of the Street family and of *Iolaire* has been invaluable to the production of this book.

                                                        D. M. S.

Charts

I used to carry on board *Iolaire* about 200 U.S., British, French, Dutch, and a few Spanish charts—all of which were out of date; that is, although they were new charts, the various government offices had not accurately corrected and updated them. The British Admiralty will correct charts of a foreign area only if the government concerned officially notifies the BA. Much worse, U.S. charts are corrected *only* when the whole plate is corrected; if you buy a new chart of Puerto Rico and it is a twelve-year-old edition, no corrections have been made on that chart since the date of the edition twelve years before!

Furthermore, BA and U.S. charts are often on the wrong scale for inshore navigation by a yacht. The charts covering Grenada, the Grenadines, and St. Vincent are 1/72,000, while the famous old Virgin Islands chart is 1/100,000, which is even worse; one needs a magnifying glass to find small anchorages and coves. In addition, it cuts Virgin Gorda in half. Several of the U.S. and British charts break up the St. Vincent and Grenadines area in odd splits not conducive to use by the average yachtsman. The U.S. chart of the Grenadines has an excellent blow-up insert for the Tobago Cays, but it does not have tidal reference points. The British chart does have this valuable information. Furthermore, the U.S. and Admiralty charts are based on surveys made in the 1890s. The latest NOAA and Admiralty charts have new deepwater information but retain the old, inshore errors.

As a result of all these difficulties, I signed a contract with Imray, Laurie, Norie and Wilson, usually known simply as Imray, which traces its ancestry back to 1670, to do updated and accurate charts specifically tailored to the needs of the yachtsman. Our information has been gathered from U.S. NOS and DMA charts, British Admiralty charts, French and Dutch charts, plus unpublished U.S. and British Admiralty surveys, topographical maps, and aerial photography, backed up by the information I have gathered in nearly thirty years of exploring the Eastern Caribbean. Information also has been supplied to me by other experienced yachtsmen. Although it may be that I know the Eastern Caribbean as a whole better than any other yachtsman, there are individuals who know individual islands and areas much better than I do. These yachtsmen have been tremendously helpful in supplying me with their information.

Our charts come in one standard size, 25 inches by 35½ inches, and three colors: blue denotes deep water, white denotes water 5 fathoms or less; and yellow 1 fathom or less. Detailed harbor charts are inserted in the margins of the general charts. Useful ranges (transits) are shown to guide the mariner clear of dangers. Various overlapping coverages and often contradictory information found in the various French, U.S., Dutch, and British Admiralty charts have been eliminated.

Imray-Iolaire charts are kept up-to-date through careful attention to British Notice to Mariners, my own observations, and those sent by readers of these guides and users of the charts. Important corrections are done by hand at Imray prior to shipment; all corrections are logged in on the master sheet so that even minor corrections are included in new editions. Seldom do we go more than six months between printings of a chart. (The most popular Imray-Iolaire charts—those of the U.S. and British Virgin Islands, and Anguilla, St. Barthélemy, St. Martin, and Antigua—are available on waterproof paper.)

As of this writing, forty-seven Imray-Iolaire charts cover the entire Eastern Caribbean, except for Tobago and the area south of Isla Margarita in Venezuela. The Tobago chart will be along in due course. The other will not be done until we can obtain surveys showing what the Venezuelan government has done in this area in recent years. The new U.S. DMA chart of the area is inaccurate and should be used with extreme caution.

The Imray-Iolaire charts have become the

accepted standard; in the Southern Caribbean the U.S. Coast Guard, as well as the St. Vincent and Grenadian Coast Guards, use Imray-Iolaire charts rather than government charts. Very few chart agents in the Eastern Caribbean continue to stock the government charts.

In short, I strongly recommend that yachtsmen use the Imray-Iolaire charts instead of British Admiralty or U.S. government charts.

Most of the harbor charts in this volume have been taken from the relevant Imray-Iolaire charts. The few sketch charts included here are just that, sketches. They are as accurate as I can make them, but they are not official publications, and should be used only in conjunction with *reliable* navigational charts, with common sense, and with eyeball navigation.

Sailors should bear in mind that the Caribbean is roughly twelve to eighteen inches lower in May, June, and July than it is the rest of the year. Imray-Iolaire chart soundings are based on this low, low datum. Other charts may not be.

No chart can be absolutely accurate, but I feel that the Imray-Iolaire charts are the most accurate charts available. They can be kept that way only if experienced yachtsmen continue to feed information and corrections to us to correct the small errors that may still exist or to update charts where the topography has been changed by hurricanes, earthquakes, or dredging.

Please send information regarding chart corrections to: D. M. Street, Jr., c/o Mr. David Payne, Cayzer Steel Bowater, 32/38 Duke's Place, London EC3 7LX, England.

D.M.S.

U.S. Chart Number Conversion Table

Old (C&GS)	New (NOAA)
901	25671
902	25677
903	25668
904	25650
905	25641
909	25687
913	25654
914	25653
915	25655
917	25663
918	25661
921	25667
922	25666
924	25659
926	25685
927	25683
928	25681
929	25679
931	25673
932	25675
933	25649
935	25645
937	25644
938	25647

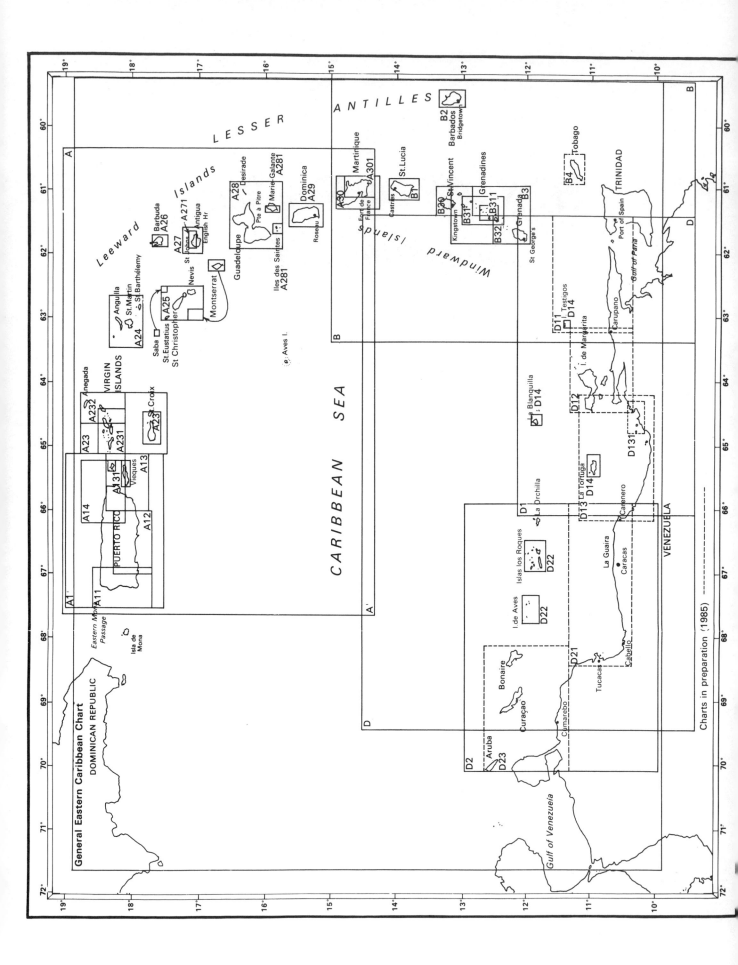

General Eastern Caribbean Chart

DOMINICAN REPUBLIC

Eastern Mona Passage

Isla de Mona

PUERTO RICO

VIRGIN ISLANDS

Anegada

St.Croix

Vieques

Anguilla
St.Martin
St Barthélemy

Saba
St Eustatius
St Christopher

Nevis

Montserrat

Barbuda

Antigua
English Hr

Desirade

Guadeloupe
Pte à Pitre

Marie-Galante

Iles des Saintes

Dominica
Roseau

LESSER ANTILLES

Leeward Islands

Windward Islands

Martinique
Fort de France

St.Lucia
Castries

St.Vincent
Kingstown

Grenadines

Grenada
St George's

Barbados
Bridgetown

Tobago

TRINIDAD
Port of Spain

Gulf of Paria

Aves I.

CARIBBEAN SEA

I. Testigos

I. de Margarita

Carupano

I. Blanquilla

La Orchilla

La Tortuga

Carenero

Islas los Roques

I. de Aves

La Guaira
Caracas

VENEZUELA

Cabello

Tucacas

Cumarebo

Bonaire

Curaçao

Aruba

Gulf of Venezuela

A11
A1
A14
A12
A13
A131
A23
A231
A232
A25
A24
A26
A27
A271
A28
A281
A29
A281
A30
A301
A3

B1
B2
B4
B30
B31
B311
B32
B3

D1
D2
D11
D12
D13
D14
D131
D21
D22
D23

Charts in preparation (1985) ---------

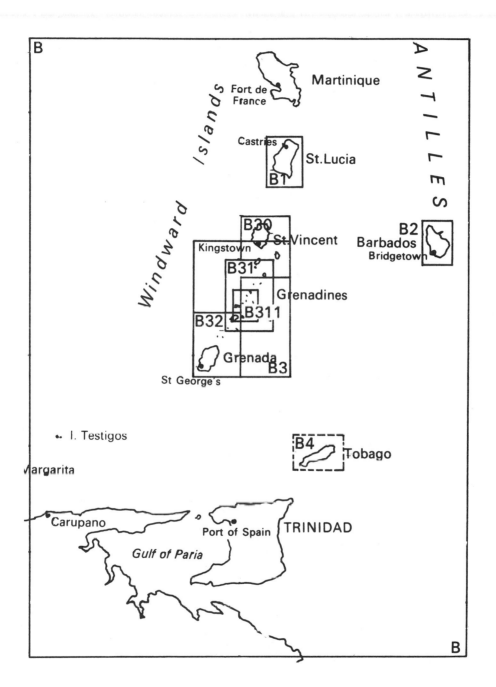

B

A N T I L L E S

Martinique
Fort de
France

Windward *Islands*

Castries
St.Lucia
B1

B30
St.Vincent
Kingstown

B2
Barbados
Bridgetown

B31
Grenadines

B32 B311

Grenada
B3
St George's

I. Testigos

B4 Tobago

Margarita

Carupano

Port of Spain TRINIDAD

Gulf of Paria

B

Street's Cruising Guide to the Eastern Caribbean, Volume III— Martinique to Trinidad

[The Islands] are accessible in every part, and covered with a vast variety of lofty trees, which, it appears to me, never lose their foliage, as we found them fair and verdant as in May in Spain. Some were covered with blossoms, some with fruit, and others in different stages, according to their nature. The nightingale and a thousand other sorts of birds were singing in the month of November wherever I went. There are palm-trees in these countries, of six or eight sorts, which are surprising to see, on account of their diversity from ours, but indeed, this is the case with respect to the other trees, as well as the fruits and weeds. Beautiful forests of pines are likewise found, and fields of vast extent. Here is also honey, and fruits of a thousand sorts, and bird of every variety. The lands contain mines of metals, and inhabitants without number. . . . [Their] harbors are of such excellence, that their description would not gain belief, and the like may be said of the abundance of large and fine rivers, the most of which abound in gold.

—Christopher Columbus, on his return
to Spain from the Caribbean, 1494

1

Sailing Directions

Introduction

In the Eastern Caribbean during the winter months, the wind will vary from east-southeast to east-northeast, occasionally going all the way around to north. The current sets generally west at a knot or more. Thus the greatest problem encountered by the yachtsman new to the area is that of allowing his boat to sag below the rhumb-line course. At the end of the day he suddenly realizes that the anchorage is well to windward—a hard slog against wind and tide. My advice to avoid this situation is to keep a hand-bearing compass handy and take continual bearings; if you can't see the island ahead, take stern bearings.

This problem is complicated in the Grenadines by variable currents that can at times veer strongly to windward. Since the currents will almost always be on the beam, they will rapidly push you off course if you sail strictly by the compass. Hence the reason for ranges; stay on them and you will stay out of trouble.

It is also important to read the sailing and pilot directions for the area concerned the night before, in order to plan the next day's run, and to calculate your departure in time to guarantee arrival at the next anchorage while the sun is still high.

Proceeding South

MARTINIQUE TO ST. LUCIA

From the east coast of Martinique, you can pass to windward or leeward of St. Lucia, an easy reach either way. From Fort-de-France on the west coast, it is still not too rough a sail to Castries. Do not be discouraged if, when you clear Cap Salomon, you are almost hard on the wind. Usually the wind hooks around the south end of the islands, coming in south of east, backing to the east as one sails offshore and to the northeast as Castries is approached. Thus as you leave Martinique, especially in the region of Pointe Diamant, do not fight your way up on to the rhumb-line course; frequently there is a tide-against-wind situation that can make it very rough. Better to ease sheets and alter course to south or even slightly west of south until you can clear off Diamond Rock. Then start to work your way up to the rhumb line, but don't work too hard to lay a course to Castries Harbor. As you approach St. Lucia the wind tends to back and lift you; if you are below the rhumb line you'll be able to work your way back up to it. Being hard on the wind the last six or eight miles is not all that bad, since you're under the lee of St. Lucia and in calm water.

ST. LUCIA TO ST. VINCENT

In proceeding south to St. Vincent, remember that there is usually wind on the lee side of St. Lucia from 1000 until about 1700, but it is likely to be calm the rest of the time. And it is a long sail down to Kingstown, the entry port of St. Vincent, or to Bequia. Thus, plan your departure so as to make sure you are clear of the Pitons by 1700 or you're likely to have to spend the night under the Pitons— a scenic but not swift trip.

Most yachtsmen sail from the Pitons to the west coast of St. Vincent on course 205 magnetic, which normally gives a very easy reach. However, they usually run out of wind in the lee of St. Vincent, and then from the southwest corner of St. Vincent have either a hard slog against the wind and current up into Kingstown Harbor or a fairly close fetch across to Bequia and then a beat up into Admiralty Bay.

I prefer passing to windward of St. Vincent, setting a course from the Pitons of 190 magnetic with adjustments for leeway and current. In most conditions it is an easy reach; at worst, a close fetch. Sail down the windward coast of St. Vincent on an easy reach, enjoying the beautiful scenery. If it really pipes up, stay well offshore, as a heavy Atlantic swell will crest in 18 feet and break in 12. When you get to the southeast corner of St. Vincent, run dead downwind and anchor in Kingstown Harbor. Or, usually better, broad reach across Bequia Channel and enter at Bequia, an easier process than entering at Kingstown.

ST. VINCENT TO PETIT ST. VINCENT

Departing St. Vincent from Kingstown Harbor, Young Island anchorage, or the lagoon presents no difficulties. It is almost always a reach to Admiralty Bay. On the other hand, if you want to go to windward and east of Bequia—"over the top," as the locals say—you must hold high in the event of a lee-going (ebb) tide. Once around, you can stand southeast to Baliceaux or south to Mustique. The only danger here is Montezuma Shoal.

Leaving Admiralty Bay under sail is a good test of helmsmanship, since you will be running dead before the wind. Once past West Cay, stand south leaving Canouan to either side. Windward of Canouan, beware of the reefs that extend well offshore. These carry seven-tenths of a mile windward of Friendship Hill. There is one danger to look out for between the southeast corner of the reefs off Canouan and Baline Rock. The course leads directly across the breaking rock southwest of Channel Rock. The best route is to pass Channel Rock close

Range 1.	Peak of Petit Martinique bearing 161-341 magnetic leads between Pinese and Mopion.
Range 2.	North sides of Baradal and Petit Bateau in line with south side of flat land on Mayreau 099-279 magnetic leads through boat pass.
Range 3.	Glossy Hill, Canouan Island, in line with eastern tip of Mayreau 216-036 magnetic passes Grand de Coi to the east.
Range 4.	Catholic Island between Red Island and Union Island 201-021 magnetic leads west of Grand de Coi and also into entrance Windward Side, Carriacou.
Range 5.	Petit Tobago one finger open from Fota 011-191 magnetic leads between Pinese and Mopion, between Palm Island and to the west of the reef at the north end of Saline Bay, Mayreau. If more than half a finger's width of Petit St. Vincent shows to the east of Palm Island, bear off, or you will fail to clear the dangers at the north end of Saline Bay.
Range 6.	Taffia Hill in line with Channel Rocks 035-215 magnetic leads east of Break Rock.
Range 7.	Northwest side of Channel Rock open slightly from the summit of Friendship Hill, Canouan Island, 058-238 magnetic leads west of Break Rock.
Range 8.	Petit Tabac in line with Jamesby 306-126 magnetic leads into Worlds End Reef anchorage.
Range 9.	Middle hill on Palm Island under High North Carriacou, 042-222 magnetic leads through south entrance to Tobago Cays.
Range 10.	SE point of Petit Rameau in line with NW point of Petit Bateau 070-250 magnetic leads into Tobago Cays.
Range 11.	South Peak of Mayreau bearing 125-305 magnetic clears Worlds End Reef to the south.
Range 12.	Peak of Petit Martinique bearing 046-226 magnetic clears Worlds End Reef to the east.
Range 13.	The cliff on the northwest end of Saline Bay, Mayreau, in line with midpoint of dock. To locate wreck of the *Paruna*, proceed along this range until intersection with Range 14.
Range 14.	Peak on Petit Martinique between easternmost two hills of Palm Island 004-184 magnetic leads over wreck.
Range 15.	Sail Rock three fingers open from northwest corner of Petit St. Vincent 070-250 magnetic. To enter Windward Side, Carriacou, follow down this range until intersection with Range 16.
Range 16.	Fota closing with southwest corner of Petit Martinique 123-303 magnetic. From where this range meets Range 15 the channel through the reef may be eyeballed.
Range 17.	Westernmost hill on Mayreau over low land of Palm Island clears the 1.5 fathom spot off Petit Tobago to the west 026-206 magnetic.
Range 18.	Hill on Frigate in line with the 290-foot hill and radio mast on Union Island. The hill is between the Pinnacle (741 feet) and Mount Taboi (999 feet) leads clear inside shoal spot (4 feet) inside Jack a Dan, 025-205 magnetic to Hillsborough, Carriacou.

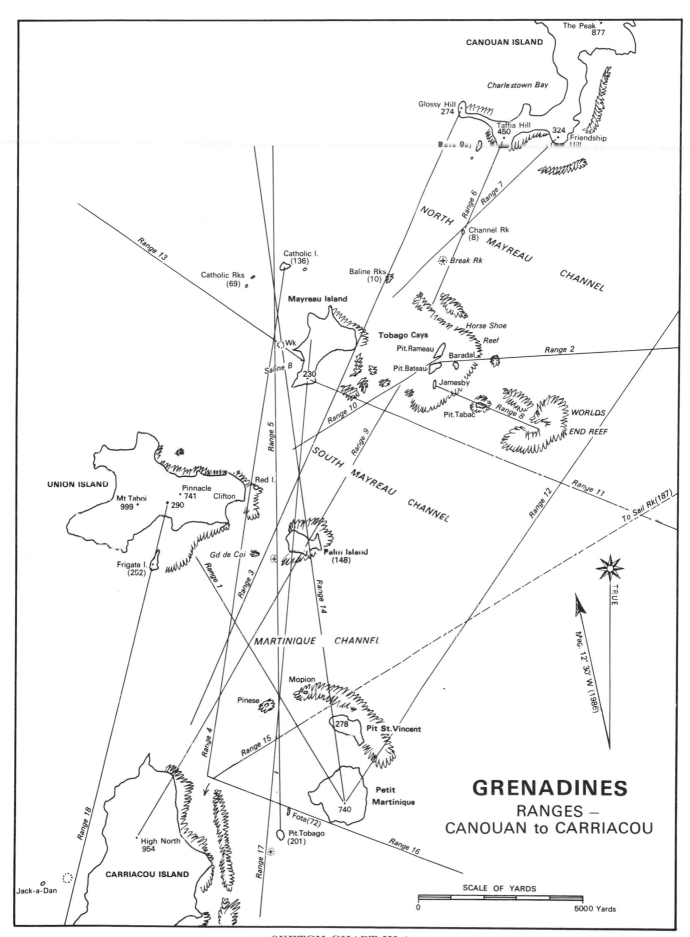

GRENADINES
RANGES –
CANOUAN to CARRIACOU

SKETCH CHART III-A

aboard to the southeast and run to the west until Channel Rock opens slightly from Friendship Hill, Canouan (Sketch Chart III-A, Range 7). Turn to the southwest and maintain this range, 238 magnetic, until close by Baline Rocks.

Passing to leeward of Canouan, there are no dangers between it and the Tobago Cays. Steer course 204 magnetic, making allowance for the current and passing between Baline Rock and the reef northwest of the Tobago Cays. The sailing directions within the Tobago Cays are given in another chapter, and I will not repeat them here. Basically, eyeball navigation will be required to get you clear of the inner reef; then sail southeastward until the middle hill of Palm Island lines up with High North, Carriacou (Sketch Chart III-A, Range 9). This range will guide you south between the windward and leeward reefs of the Tobago Cays. If your plan is to pass to windward of Palm Island, go east until the peak of Petit Martinique bears 190 magnetic. Sail that course until south of Palm Island, then sail southwest magnetic until you reach range 1, with the peak of Petit Martinique bearing 161 magnetic. If you maintain this range, you will come right between the two sand islands off Petit St. Vincent. But remember to follow the range rather than the compass course, since the currents will be tending to throw you off one way or the other.

If you are proceeding from the south entrance of the Tobago Cays to the west of Palm Island, a course of 239 magnetic—and an allowance for current—will take you between the reefs of Union and Palm islands. There are no reliable ranges, and a good deal of precautionary eyeballing will be necessary. Also, keep a sharp look out for Grand de Coi, which must be avoided. There is a new buoy (which may not be in place) west of Grand de Coi (for a short history of classic groundings, see page 112). It can be passed to the westward by staying west until Catholic Island aligns itself between Union and Red islands (Sketch Chart III-A, Range 4) and following this range on south. To pass eastward of Grand de Coi: Once the reefs of Palm Island are cleared to port, head up until Glass Hill joins the eastern end of Mayreau Island (Sketch Chart III-A, Range 3). This range should be maintained, keeping clear of the shoal at the southeast corner of Palm. And if your destination is Petit St. Vincent, hold this range until the peak of Petit Martinique bears 161 magnetic. Follow 161 midway between Pinese and Mopion. Once you have passed beyond the reefs, you may alter course to Petit St. Vincent.

SOUTH AND WEST FROM PETIT ST. VINCENT

From Petit St. Vincent to the windward side of Carriacou, head west until Sail Rock is three fingers off the northern end of Petit St. Vincent. Continue heading 248 magnetic (Sketch Chart III-A, Range 15) until Fota is overlapped by the southwestern corner of Petit Martinique (Sketch Chart III-A, Range 16). At this point you will be inside the reef. From here on south along the coast, use eyeball navigation. A skillful reef pilot in a boat drawing no more than 7 feet with a man aloft could continue south all the way through Watering Bay into Grand Bay.

A less taxing course from Petit St. Vincent is to sail southwest until the westernmost hill of Mayreau lines up with the western side of Palm Island (Sketch Chart III-A, Range 17). Turn south along this range, which will carry you safely to the west of the 1½-fathom spot southwest of Petit Tobago. Once past this danger point, the course should be altered to clear the reef off the eastern point of Carriacou, after which a course approximately southwest may be steered, passing to either side of Île de Ronde and Grenada.

The west coast of Carriacou is far less formidable. From Petit St. Vincent to Rapid Point is a straight-line course with no hazards. Around Rapid Point it is an easy reach down the coast of Carriacou with no dangers until Jack a Dan, at which time you should hook up with Range 18 (Sketch Chart III-A), defined by the peak on Frigate Island placed under the first peak west of the easternmost peak of Union Island. This will carry you clear inside the shoal spot between Jack a Dan and the mainland of Carriacou.

CARRIACOU TO GRENADA

From Hermitage Point at the southwest corner of Tyrell Bay to Diamond Rock (Kick 'Em Jenny) and David Point, Grenada, it is 228 magnetic without taking account of current. This is normally a very broad reach or a dead run. If the wind is in the north, it may be a good idea before you leave the lee of Carriacou to rig your main boom foreguy to starboard and set your jib on the pole to windward. This will save you a lot of rolling and slatting on the way down.

Once round David Point, the wind tends to hook around the island, often putting you dead before the wind most of the way to Black Bay, Grenada, where it will tend to come more abeam. If your destination is St. George's, the course from Molinière Point is 178 magnetic, hugging the shore. If you are bypassing St. George's and heading directly to the south coast of Grenada, a course of 214 magnetic from Molinière Point will clear Long Point Shoal.

Work your way up the south coast of Grenada, continually tacking inshore to stay out of the westward flowing current and the sea. Consult the chart and use careful eyeball navigation.

GRENADA TO TRINIDAD

The sail from Grenada to Trinidad is usually an easy beam reach. The only difficulty is an occasionally strong current along with some tide rips that will set up between the two islands. The normal procedure for most yachts making the passage is to leave Grenada at about 1800, steer 170 magnetic (or 165, if your boat makes a lot of leeway) until you spot the Chacachacare light, and alter your course accordingly. This is a very powerful light, which can be seen as far as 25 miles away on a clear night. Do not head right for it, as it marks the westernmost *boca* (mouth) and the current will be pulling you in that direction anyway. Most boats favor entering the Gulf of Paria through the eastern *boca* in order to save a lot of windward effort. This should put you in Port of Spain early in the morning.

ALTERNATE ROUTES

Although the distance from St. Thomas to, say, Antigua is only about 200 miles, the course is practically dead against the wind all the way. There are plenty of islands in between that afford the opportunity to lay over, rest, and sightsee, but the windward legs will be pure hell nonetheless. In a small boat of 30 or 35 feet, your progress against heavy trades may be reduced to nothing.

Bear in mind that there are other ways to reach the middle or southern islands. Depending on the time at your disposal, you can sail from the Virgins direct to Grenada, St. Lucia, or Martinique, and from any one of these islands you can work your way north in easy stages off the wind to Antigua. The strategy is to define the southern reach of your cruise and to proceed north from there. If you are chartering a bare boat and are willing to pay the deadhead fee, you should consider picking up the boat on one of these southern islands. Otherwise, sail the passage yourself. With a break in the weather, you can lay a straight course from St.

Thomas Harbor to Martinique (143 magnetic), making it in two and a half or three days. This is not a great deal of time to give up if you are planning a cruise of two or three weeks. The disadvantages are that you will be close-hauled the entire way, and if you have just arrived by air from the States, setting out on a long sail direct from St. Thomas allows no time for the crew to get its sea legs or to build up a tan against the sun. Therefore, a preferable course would be to work your way east from St. Thomas through the Virgins for a few days. This will give you the time to shake down the crew, pick up some precious easting and a tan in sheltered waters, and then to take off through Necker Island Passage for Grenada. The course is 170 magnetic; the distance, 420 miles—an easy reach. Even if the wind veers to east-southeast, you will still be under slightly eased sheets and going like mad. If it is east to east-northeast, as is usual, you can make the trip in three days. Let me repeat that if you have the time to invest in this passage, I can recommend no better way of positioning yourself for a cruise of the southern Islands. You will have reached the southernmost of the Antilles without having strained to windward and with no serious windward work before you.

The course from St. Thomas Harbor to Grenada direct is 163 magnetic, 423 miles. You will have to hold one point high on the course for the first 50 miles in order to clear the eastern end of St. Croix, but once clear, the sheets can be eased for a nice easy reach to Grenada. The chances of the wind's swinging so far south as to put you hard on the wind are relatively slim. If the wind should really pipe up, its direction will back and give you a real sleighride. A heavy blow won't faze a small boat, as it will be aft of abeam. For the remainder of the passage there are two things to watch out for:

First, don't run up on Aves Island, which will be right on your track.

Aves Island is low and hard to find; it is a turtle nesting area and the scene of enough disasters and near disasters to fill a book. It has also been mischarted by almost everyone. According to the latest British Admiralty information, it is located at 15°42'10" N. latitude and 63°37' W. longitude. This may not be where it is on your chart, because it has moved three or possibly four times during my thirty years in the Caribbean!

Now the Venezuelan government (which, amazingly, owns Aves Island) has established a well-lit military base on the island. Still no navigation lights have been set up, but if you are in the area and see something that looks like a cruise ship hove-to, it's probably Aves Island. Give it a wide berth.

Second, take sights to assure that you are not falling off to leeward. It would be an awful waste of time to beat the last 50 miles or so to Grenada. The current runs to the west through here as fast as 3 knots. Against a 3-knot current in the same direction as the wind, it would require 6 knots through the water to hold your own tacking in 120°.

Proceeding North

TRINIDAD TO GRENADA

It is best to depart Trinidad in time to arrive at Point Saline, Grenada, by dawn. More than one boat has grounded on Long Point Shoal tacking up from Point Saline to St. George's. Most yachts can hold a course of 015 from the easternmost *boca* to Grenada. Soon after the lights on the hills of Grenada are picked up, airport lights will appear. If entering at L'Anse aux Épines, keep these high lights on the starboard bow but don't approach the coast till dawn or you may come to a sudden stop on the Porpoises. A better course is to head for Point Saline and round close aboard. Hug the coast and short-tack up the beach, passing close to Quarantine Point. This way you will avoid Long Point Shoal, which is most difficult to spot at night. There is no difficulty entering St. George's Harbor at night: anchor in the northeast corner, and proceed at dawn to GYS to clear.

GRENADA SOUTH COAST TO ST. GEORGE'S HARBOR

Do not leave harbors like Bacaye or Calivigny until the sun is high, because in the early morning the path of the sunlight is directly in line with the exit course. Once clear of the harbors on the south coast of Grenada, it is best to head directly for Glover Island, keeping an eye open for Porpoise Rocks (Grampuses); pass close south of Porpoise Rocks and then head for Point Saline. As I said earlier, reefs do extend well offshore between Calivigny Island and Prickly Point. Check bearings and ranges carefully as described above.

If you head directly for Point Saline, you will discover that the wind shifts to the south at Hardy Bay and you end up dead downwind, whereas if you stay offshore, as the wind shifts you may head northwest for Point Saline and still be on a reach. Once Point Saline has been rounded, favor the shore. Stay close in to avoid the sea and to take advantage of better wind shifts than could be found offshore. When approaching Long Point, be sure to favor the Morne Rouge beach area, and stay inshore to avoid Long Point Shoal. If under power, motor directly from Point Saline to Long Point, leaving Long Point 100 yards off the starboard side, and proceed directly to St. George's Harbor or Grand Anse Bay clear of all dangers.

GRENADA TO CARRIACOU

When proceeding north from St. George's, plans must be made to arrive at Carriacou early in the day and in no event later than 1700. This necessitates a very early departure from St. George's. Many boats motor-sail all the way up the coast to David Point and then set sail for Carriacou. If you choose to sail the coast, it is best done close inshore. Every time you get a mile offshore on starboard tack, you should tack back in.

There is little or no wind on the lee coast of Grenada until after 0800 and it dies drastically after 1700. Grenada's highest point is almost 2,800 feet, and the main line of mountains approximately 2,000 feet. Do not make the mistake of standing offshore to find more wind—nine times out of ten you won't find any. *Stay in close.*

When you reach David Point (locally known as Tangle Angle, because of the way the current sweeps around it and causes tide rips), it is again important to tack to the eastward. In fact, you should tack to the east as far as Sauteurs and frequently to Levera Island before setting out for Carriacou. The current runs as much as 2½ knots (normally 1–1½) to the west through this passage. (Remember that many boats make as much as 15° leeway when on the wind.)

Occasionally, with the wind in the southeast, it is possible to lay the course from David Point to Carriacou, but this is very much the exception. Most Grenada–Carriacou races have proved that it is worth tacking to Sauteurs, even with a windward-going tide. In any event, be careful of the shoal spots between Levera Island and the town of Levera, as they can break in heavy weather. Proceed east until you can lay Îlet de Ronde, and then set out. Pass between the Sisters and Îlet de Ronde and stand north on starboard tack until smooth water is reached in the lee of Carriacou.

The best time to arrive at David Point is when the tides have just begun to run to windward. This will give you four hours of either slack water or weather-going tide, enough to reach Tyrell Bay before the tide changes.

As you approach Carriacou's southwest point,

you should note the tide. If you wish to go to Saline Island or One Tree Rock on the south coast of Carriacou, do so only if the tide is running to windward; otherwise it is almost impossible to get up to Saline Island unless you have a very powerful engine. It should also be noted that it is best not to tack east after Diamond Island (Kick 'Em Jenny), as this will put you into the worst of the current. Instead, stand north into the lee of Carriacou; good progress can then be made on port tack in smooth water.

ST. GEORGE'S TO CARRIACOU VIA THE SOUTH AND EAST COASTS OF GRENADA

When proceeding from St. George's to the south coast of Grenada, be careful of the shoals extending from the Islander Hotel over to the Silver Sands Hotel (Range C, Sketch Chart III-36).

Long Point Shoal off Long Point (locally referred to as Quarantine Point) is most dangerous. The northeast corner of the dock transit shed in line with Government House will clear Long Point Shoal to the northwest (Range B, Sketch Chart III-37). Government House may be easily identified, as it is a large, dark-colored house, with large verandas on both first and second stories, situated on the ridge northeast of town. It is the only house on the ridge with two flagpoles, one east and one west of the house.

The other route commonly used by yachts is to head from St. George's Harbor to Long Point, leaving Long Point to port 100 yards off. When Long Point Shoal comes abeam, head for Point Saline, which course will clear Long Point Shoal to the southeast; or use Range A, Sketch Chart III-37, course 062-242 magnetic. There is deep water along this entire shore, and you may sail 200 yards off with no danger and in smooth water. If it is blowing more than 10 knots, tie in a reef before rounding Point Saline.

When rounding Point Saline, give it a 200-yard berth, because when they built the airport they blew up and carted off the hill; most of it was used for fill for the airport but much fell into the sea. No survey has been done of the area since the hill was removed.

Upon rounding, unless you draw more than 10 feet the best procedure is to stay close inshore. This will keep you out of the swell and current. Each time you make a long tack offshore, the current and sea will set you to leeward.

Between Point Saline and Prickly Point, there are few difficulties as long as a lookout is kept during starboard tacks inshore. If beating to wind-ward under sail, short-tack along the shore as close as possible, as it will keep you out of the swell and foul current, and will usually give you port-tack lifts; watch for shoals on starboard tack. From Prickly Point eastward, this coast has numerous reefs and sandbanks. All are clearly visible as long as the sun is fairly high.

It was generally thought that there was a good 2 fathoms of water everywhere between Glovers Island and the mainland. Deep-draft boats have happily sailed between the two without a thought. However, there is at least one 7-foot spot. We discovered it in *Iolaire* while racing along the south coast. We were on a direct line between the Porpoises and Point Saline, absolutely upright doing about 8 knots and with the point that forms the west side of Hardy Bay bearing about northwest. We felt a tremendous crash as we bounced off the top of a rock. Subsequently I have gone back and looked for the rock and have been unable to find it—it must be just a small pinnacle rising up off the bottom.

If you sail down the lee side of Grenada and continue around Point Saline and eastward to Prickly Bay, it means that at the end of your trip you'll have a good hard slog to windward. For this reason many people heading for the south coast would rather pass to windward of Grenada; then you have a glorious beam reach along the weather side of Grenada; you can east sheets around the southeast corner and run dead downwind for half an hour, then jibe over and reach into Prickly Bay. Once again, keep a careful eye on the depth of the water if the sea is running high. Breaking crests can demolish a boat in short order. This happened to Mike Forshaw's *Tawana*, which took a breaking crest on board and sank almost instantly. Luckily the dinghy had been tied on the cabin top with rotten old line, and minutes after the boat sank the dinghy popped to the surface. The crew righted the dinghy, bailed it out, and drifted ashore in it.

When running along the south coast of Grenada downwind, you should be careful about the reefs spreading south from Hog Island and Mount Hartman Bay. A good plan is to clear the south end of Calivigny Point by a half mile or more and continue on a course of west 270 magnetic until Prickly Point bears 300. Then you have to sail inside the Porpoises, which are exposed rocks southwest of Prickly Point with deep water all around *except* for a rock with only 6 feet over it, 40 yards north of the Porpoises.

When proceeding eastward along the south coast of Grenada under power, stay close to shore and keep an eye out for the various shoals. Remember, of course, that you should subtract at least 3 feet from any depths quoted on the charts, and frequently as much as a fathom. Eastward beyond Fort Jeudy Point, there are a number of shoal spots well offshore: off Westerhall Point, Marquis Point, and Menere Point.

During the winter, if the wind is out of the east or northeast, it is unwise to beat up the east coast of Grenada. It can get very rough, with seas breaking fairly far offshore. On the southeast coast there is also roughly a 1- to 2-knot current dead on the nose.

However, if you elect to proceed up the east coast, note how far offshore the shoals extend north of Bacolet Point. Bear in mind that the current will be setting you onshore. Once Telescope Point is reached, a course should be set for Anthony Rock, which will take you clear of the shoals. The current between Telescope Point and Green Island sets very strongly to the south, so strong that the old sailing directions warn vessels about passing and getting south of the entrance of Grenville. The old square-riggers were not too good to windward. Thus, if by mistake they sailed past Grenville, they were advised to continue south, around Point Saline, up the west coast of Grenada, and try again. It seems a long distance to go a few miles, but in years gone by the sailors had plenty of patience, especially in adverse conditions.

Be very careful not to get involved with the 3-fathom spot between Anthony Rock and Sandy Island, as in heavy winter weather the ground swell breaks continually on this spot. The eastern side of Sandy Island kept directly in line with the west peak of Caille Island (Range E, Sketch Chart III-44) will pass clear to windward of this breaking shoal spot.

There is deep water between Sandy Island and Green Island, between Green Island and Levera Island, and between Levera Island and Bedford Point, but the Levera Island side of the channel should be favored for the deepest water. From the northeast corner of Grenada, it is usually an easy sail to Carriacou.

CARRIACOU NORTHWARD

The usual course is to pass along the west side of Carriacou, stopping at Tyrell Bay. When leaving this harbor, pass north of the middle ground, hug the coast, and make allowance for the rocks, which extend about 200 yards offshore from Lookout Point (the point south of Cistern Point). Under power or sail, the best course from Cistern Point

to Hillsborough Bay is between Mabouya Island and Sandy Island, being careful to avoid the reef on the southwestern tip of Sandy Island. Other than that, there are no dangers in this area unless you have a vessel drawing 12 feet. Beating to windward through this gap is good fun, as there is no sea and usually plenty of wind.

Between Cistern Point and Hillsborough, deep-draft boats can easily run aground. The old schooner range is still a safe one. Put Cistern under the stern and the hospital building at the top of the mountain on the bow and proceed straight to the anchorage. Once past Sandy Island, the course can be shifted slightly toward the Hillsborough jetty. North of Hillsborough there is one danger, between Jack a Dan and the mainland. This is a ¾-fathom spot with quite a few dents in it. It can be passed inside by placing the hill on Frigate Island directly in line with the 290-foot hill on Union Island, which is the hill just west of the highest and easternmost peak on Union (Range 18, Sketch Chart III-A, course 023 magnetic). Be sure to stay on this range, as this shoal is particularly hard to spot.

Under power, you may steer direct from Rapid Point to the dock of Petit St. Vincent and clear all dangers. Under sail, it will be a dead beat to windward. On port tack, beware of the shoal off Little Carenage Bay and the shoal on the north end of Watering Bay. On the starboard tack, watch out for Pinese and Mopion, the two sand islands northwest of Petit St. Vincent. (Pinese may not be visible; it has recently been reported as being underwater.) There is ample water between these two islands but eyeballing is called for, as they both are continually growing and shifting.

Grand de Coi is now marked by a buoy west of the reef. For discussions on the buoy and its problems, see Chapter 7.

To head north from Petit St. Vincent, pass midway between the two cays and continue on course until Fota and the east side of Petit Tobago are one finger open (Range 5, Sketch Chart III-A, course 010 magnetic). This will take you east of Grand de Coi and east of the detached reef off Palm Island. Care must be exerted here, as the current will be at a right angle to your course and will tend to sweep you leeward. Thus a continual check must be made that you are still on range. A good lookout must be kept, or you may come to a sudden stop before you realize you're too close.

An alternate route clear of Grand de Coi is provided by Range 5 on Sketch Chart III-A, course 033 magnetic. This is Glass Hill (Glossy Hill) on

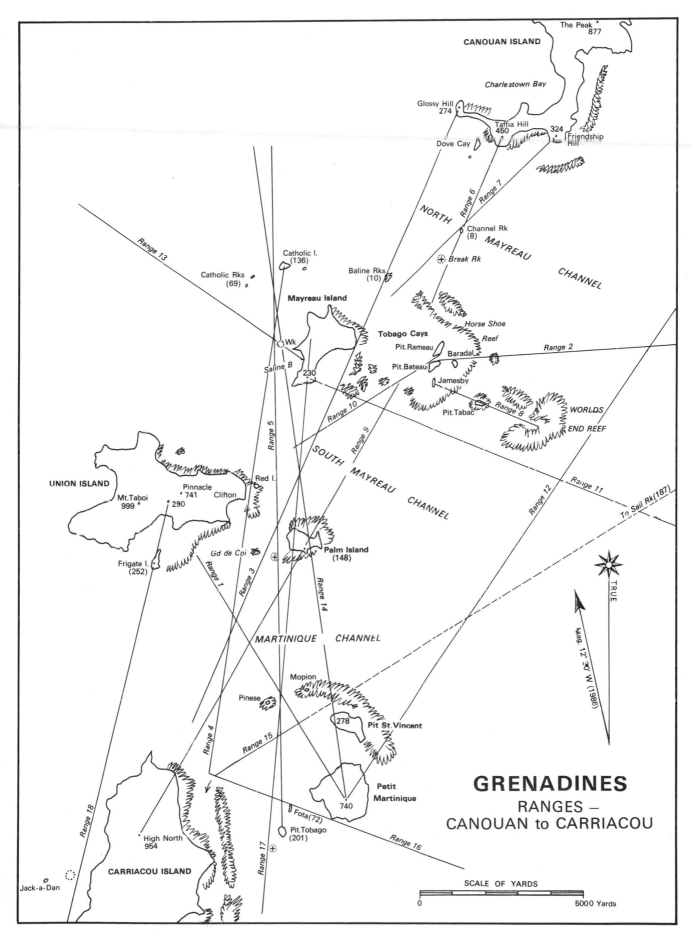

GRENADINES
RANGES —
CANOUAN to CARRIACOU

SKETCH CHART III-A

CANOUAN ISLAND

The Peak
877

Charlestown Bay

Glossy Hill
274

Taffia Hill
450

324

Friendship Hill

Dove Cay

Range 6

Range 7

NORTH

MAYREAU

CHANNEL

Channel Rk
(8)

Break Rk

Range 13

Catholic I.
(136)

Catholic Rks
(69)

Baline Rks
(10)

Mayreau Island

Horse Shoe

Reef

Tobago Cays

Pit.Rameau

Baradal

Range 2

Wk

Pit.Bateau

Saline B

230

Jamesby

Range 10

Range 9

Pit.Tabac

Range 8

WORLDS

END REEF

SOUTH

MAYREAU

CHANNEL

Red I.

UNION ISLAND

Mt.Taboi
999

Pinnacle
741

Clifton

290

Range 5

Range 11

Range 12

To Sail Rk(187)

Gd de Coi

Palm Island
(148)

Frigate I.
(252)

Range 1

Range 3

Range 14

MARTINIQUE   CHANNEL

TRUE

Mag. 12° 30′ W (1986)

Mopion

Pinese

278

Pit St.Vincent

Range 4

Range 15

**Petit
Martinique**

740

Range 18

Fota(72)

Pit.Tobago
(201)

Range 16

High North
954

Range 17

CARRIACOU ISLAND

Jack-a-Dan

SCALE OF YARDS

0

5000 Yards

the western point of Canouan in line with the eastern end of Mayreau Island. Glass Hill will appear as a detached island west of Taffia Hill, as it is connected to Canouan by only a low sand split.

Beating to windward from Rapid Point to the region of Union Island, you will want to avoid Grand de Coi. Catholic Island placed between Union Island and Red Island passes clear to west of Grand de Coi (Range 4, Sketch Chart III-A, course 018–198 magnetic). North of Grand de Coi, you will have to tack to the east to clear the reefs to windward of Union Island.

North beyond Palm and Union islands is about the most dangerous area of the Grenadines. A reef at the north end of Saline Bay has damaged many yachts proceeding north along the lee coast of Mayreau. To clear the end of this reef, put Fota one finger open from the east side of Little Tobago (Range 5, Sketch Chart III-A, course 010–190). As you approach Grand Coi Point at the north end of Saline Bay, Mayreau, check to see if any of Petit St. Vincent is showing east of Palm. If Petit St. Vincent is at all visible, bear off to the west or you will come to a sudden stop on the reef off Grand Coi Point (profile insert, Sketch Chart III-1). With this reef behind you, there are no other dangers standing north from Mayreau to Canouan.

APPROACHES TO THE TOBAGO CAYS

When approaching the Tobago Cays from the west, if you are coming in under power, no problem—just head for the buoy northwest of Baline Rocks and pick up the newly installed range. The range is 139 magnetic. This leads directly to the anchorage in the slot. If, however, you are beating to windward under sail and cannot lay in the range, be careful of the 9-foot spot approximately 800 yards southwest of Baline Rocks—really a case of eyeball navigation.

If you are coming from Petit St. Vincent, sail west until the peak of Petit Martinique bears 160 magnetic over the stern, come to course 340 magnetic, eyeball your way between Pinese and Mopion—once clear of these two islands come hard on the wind until the eastern peak of Petit St. Vincent bears 190 magnetic. Stay east of this line of bearing until Union Island Airport bears due west magnetic. Then bear off until the middle hill on Palm Island lines up with High North on Carriacou (Range 9, Sketch Chart III-A, course 040 magnetic). Stay hard on this range until you have passed between the eastern and western reefs. The western one may be spotted by a small sand

island. However, these sand islands are prone to disappear at irregular intervals.

If you are coming from between Palm and Union Islands and heading for the southern entrance of the Tobago Cays, you must fight your way up to windward, until, again, the middle hill on Palm lines up with High North on Carriacou (Range 9, Sketch Chart III-A). Follow this bearing into the cays.

Or if the range to the south is obscured, a second range on the northwest corner of Petit Bateau just touching the southeast corner of Petit Rameau 063–243° also leads into the south entrance of the Tobago Cays.

TOBAGO CAYS TO CANOUAN

From the north end of the Tobago Cays to the western end of Canouan, there are no dangers at all. Glass Hill is easily laid from Baline Rocks. If you are bound for the windward side of Canouan and are tacking below Channel Rock, I urge setting out in slack water or a fair tide. Great care must be taken to avoid the submerged rock one-half mile southwest of Channel Rock. This rock is covered and breaks in a swell. Friendship Hill touching the northwest side of Channel Rock passes clear to the west of the breaking rock (Range 2, Sketch Chart III-A, course 050 magnetic). Channel Rock in line with Taffia Hill passes the breaking rock clear to windward (Range 1, Sketch Chart III-A, course 030).

CANOUAN TO BEQUIA

This trip should be made at slack water or when the tide is running to windward. The distance is 15 miles, and should the tide be running its full limit of 2 knots to the west, a vessel making 5 knots through the water would have to steer 045 magnetic, as opposed to the 028 rhumb line. Unless the wind were southeast, this would put you very close on the wind. During the winter, with the wind toward the north and a leeward running tide, you stand very little chance of laying West Cay, leaving you a tough beat into Admiralty Bay. Against a foul tide be sure to hold high on the course, passing close aboard to leeward of Pigeon Island. There are no dangers on the course to Bequia. If you depart during a weather tide, the only difficulty will be a strong tide rip off the north end of Canouan. Once Pigeon Island is reached, Quatre and Petit Nevis serve to break the swell, giving a glorious sail the rest of the way in with plenty of wind and smooth water.

Once you have rounded West Cay, you may turn on the iron genoa and head for the anchorage at Elizabeth Town with no dangers in the way, or you can put the sport book into sailing and beat up into the harbor, but be very careful of the shoals on its south side.

BEQUIA TO ST. VINCENT

Bequia Channel has the well-deserved reputation of being exceedingly rough at times. This brief eight-mile passage has done in any number of small boats and dinghies over the years. The water is smoothest during a leeward tide. A windward tide will offset your leeway, but it will also manage to churn up a nasty, steep sea. I have seen the waves making up into almost boxlike shapes—6 feet high and 6 feet between each crest—a great place to lose a dinghy under tow.

From Admiralty Bay, round up close aboard Fort Point, watching out for Wash Rock 100 yards off Devils Table. Play the wind shifts close to the Bequia shore and keep inshore until you feel you can comfortably lay Young Island. If this does not seem logical, let me note that the 45-foot gaff-rigged schooner *Stella Maris* twice beat *Iolaire*—a 45-foot Marconi-rigged yawl—between Bequia and Young Island in just this way, tacking northeast along the Bequia shore before setting out.

Young Island is easily identified by a high peak just south of it on Duvernette Island, which looks like a loaf of French bread put on end. Kingstown will also be readily visible to leeward.

ST. VINCENT TO ST. LUCIA

There are two routes to St. Lucia from the south coast of St. Vincent. The more usual is to proceed up the west coast in easy stages, stopping off at Wallilabu. The lee of St. Vincent is frequently becalmed, so you may be forced to stoke up the engine. Hold high the course across St. Vincent Passage, as the current sets strongly northwest; at the southwestern corner of St. Lucia it becomes even more severe. If you fall four or five miles offshore when Beaumont Point comes abeam, you're going to have a rough beat inshore.

It is extremely important that you stay east of the rhumb line between the lee side of St. Vincent and Beaumont Point (the rhumb-line course is 015 magnetic). To be certain you are staying to wind-ward of this course, continually take back bearings to make sure you are not sliding off to leeward. Frequently St. Lucia will not be visible from St. Vincent, thus the necessity of stern bearings. This is where a good hand-bearing compass is worth its weight in gold.

When you get discouraged about the sea conditions, remember that Vieux Fort, out to windward, tends to break the sea. Once you are halfway across, the seas should ease up. The last quarter of the trip will be in comparatively smooth water, with the seas hooking around the south coast of St. Lucia and coming much more on the beam. Similarly, the wind frequently hooks around the south end of St. Lucia, lifting you to windward and enabling you to ease sheets as the coast of St. Lucia is approached. This effect is generally only felt to windward of the rhumb line; to leeward of the rhumb line you will not be getting the lift and will have to fight your way up to the Pitons against wind and current.

The sail from St. Vincent to St. Lucia used to be a long one, because you had to go all the way to Castries to clear. It was illegal to stop anywhere in St. Vincent along the way. Finally, in 1985, the St. Vincent government did something I've been urging in print for fifteen years: They made Soufrière a preclearance station. This shortens the run by 12 miles. You still can't stop first in the Pitons, though—preclear in Soufrière, then backtrack to the Pitons.

The other way to St. Lucia is to take off south-eastward from Young Island or Blue Lagoon until you are off soundings. When the swell eases up, tack and head directly for Vieux Fort, a distance of about 45 miles. This is a course for able boats to windward and should be undertaken when the tide is running eastward. This is an excellent sail when the wind is in the east or south of east, and less than excellent if it veers northeast.

ST. VINCENT TO MARTINIQUE

Castries to Fort-de-France is one of the finest sails in the Caribbean. The first five miles are sheltered by Pigeon Island on the northeast corner of St. Lucia—smooth water and plenty of wind. On leaving Castries, it is best to come hard on the wind till north of Pigeon Island, and then to bear off direct for Diamond Rock (Rocher du Diamant). The course is 005 magnetic, usually a splendid close reach across 18 miles of open water. The wind swings further aft under the southeast corner of Martinique. Quite likely you will become briefly becalmed under Cap Salomon, but a good breeze resumes once you enter the bay of Fort-de-France. If you are making this trip at night, watch out for the unlit Fond Blanc buoy on the northeast corner of Banc du Gros Îlet; it is dead on a line between Cap Salomon and Fort-de-France.

MARTINIQUE TO DOMINICA OR GUADELOUPE

I prefer to head south, gunk holing around Martinique's east coast, before taking off from Tartanne, clearing Caravelle Peninsula, and laying a course for Scotts Head, Dominica, 45 miles away on a broad reach. If you wish to bypass Dominica, steer 010 magnetic for the light on Îles de la Petite Terre southeast of Guadeloupe, a magnificent reach all the way.

If you decide to sail up the west coast of Martinique, don't set out before 1000, as there is no wind before this time. With any luck you will pick up a light breeze along the coast before clearing the lee of the island and setting out for Scotts Head.

NOTES

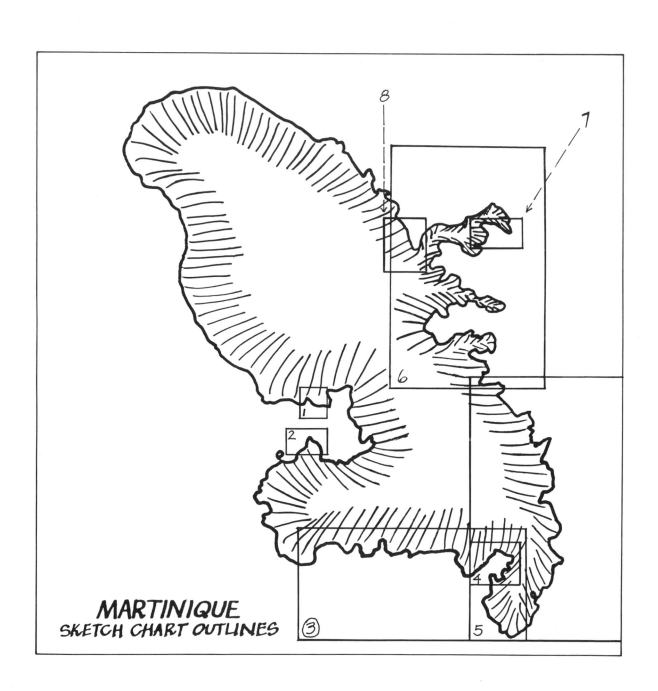

MARTINIQUE
SKETCH CHART OUTLINES

2

Martinique

III, A, B, A-30, A-301

Martinique is one of the largest and most populous islands in the Eastern Caribbean, with 425 square miles and 340,000 people. The spoken languages are two strains of French, one fairly pure and the other an indecipherable patois. The natives, who are in fact French citizens, regard themselves as Frenchmen rather than West Indians, and this is reflected everywhere. Fort-de-France is a sort of Paris of the New World. Its women are beautiful and well dressed, and the sidewalk cafés are always filled with an assortment of types sipping their *punch vieux* and admiring the passing scenery. The restaurants are of a very high quality, and the local boutiques offer many of the latest fashions.

Martinique is high and lush. Mountains tower over vast fields of cane and banana. Country roads vary from beautiful four-lane highways to grotesque contours of rubble and mud. The good beaches are on the east coast for the most part and difficult to reach, except by boat.

In the last twenty years, tourism has arrived in wholesale fashion. As late as 1965, it was considered a noteworthy event to have ten yachts moored off the Savanne. In December 1973, I counted eighty-six; in February 1985, there were almost 100 boats anchored off the Savanne and another 100 in Anse Mitan, and all 120 berths in the Marina du Bout were filled. Monsieur Le Breton, head of Customs and Immigration for yachts, reports that during January and February of 1985, fifty to sixty boats cleared every day. It's a far cry from the days when there were so few yachts and things were so informal that the recommended method of entering a yacht in Martinique was to write out one's crew list and hand it to the first gendarme you saw, who would probably lose it.

Customs and Immigration is open seven days a week from 0800 to 1200, and 1500 to 1700. With your ship's papers and passports visit the office at the head of the water and fuel dock at the western end of the anchorage; you will be greeted by Monsieur Le Breton (affectionately known to his yachting friends as 007), who will handle your entrance and clearance with tremendous enthusiasm and cheerfulness and no charge at all. (Other Islands should take note of the swift, efficient, and free Customs and Immigration service granted in Martinique.)

The amount of paperwork the French require is substantial, but they do supply pens, paper, carbon paper, and a running commentary as to why the French Islands are far superior to the former British colonies.

You may enter at Saint Pierre, Fort-de-France, Marin on the south coast, or La Trinité on the north coast (if you can find the Customs officer). However, you can leave only by clearing out of Fort-de-France. Your boat does not actually have to be in Fort-de-France: if you are on the east coast you can grab a bus, taxi, or car from the boat to town, fill out the Customs and Immigration papers, and return to the boat. Similarly, when entering, it is perfectly acceptable to anchor in Anse Mitan, hop in the ferry, go over to Fort-de-France to enter, and then come back via ferry—at least it was in February 1985.

Flight service in and out of Martinique is excellent, with direct flights from Paris and the States, plus inter-island service to the Eastern Caribbean.

Cruise ships plow in and out all winter long. I have seen as many as three enter Fort-de-France on a single day. Hotels and guest houses are to be found throughout the island. Most of the new ones are expensive, geared to the needs of the modern tourist. Some of the old-fashioned ones are not only less expensive, but much more fun, and have better food. There are many fine small restaurants on the island that do not appear in the travel brochures. On a French island, one should never worry about the outside appearance of a restaurant. Simply arrive around 1230 and observe the clientele. If it is predominantly French-speaking Martinicans (or Martiniquais), sit down and enjoy a meal. Like the Frenchman, the Martinican demands good food and value for money spent.

A stop at the tourist office is well worthwhile, as there you can pick up a brochure covering the vast majority of hotels and restaurants in Martinique. Cross check with the locals, who will be able to recommend which ones are best at the moment.

Out in the countryside there are a number of restored estates that serve as restaurants, guest houses, and hotels. It is a long ride from town, but Plantation Leyritz on the northeast side of the island in the foothills of Pelée has an extremely good reputation. Various others are also worth visiting.

The yachtsman who doesn't want to travel for his dinner or sightseeing should remember that the restaurant on top of the yacht club has excellent reviews—and is only a dinghy ride away.

Martinique is a prime spot to stock up on foods of all kinds. The various self-styled "supermarkets" carry an excellent selection of imported meats, cheese, and poultry. *A word of caution about French poultry:* It is frequently sold plucked and frozen but not cleaned. Be sure to gut it as soon as it thaws. (Buying chicken in Martinique is something of a risk anyway. The last time we purchased chicken in Martinique, my excellent mate and cook Alston Blackett prepared it in his normal superb fashion. After dinner we decided that Alston had made a bad error: after cooking the chicken for hours he should have thrown it overboard and served us the roasting pan, which would have been easier to chew than the chicken. We concluded it had flown all the way from France.)

The yachting industry has increased so much in recent years that some of the stores offer free delivery to the yacht landing; check with Yacht Services Martinique (YSM), the small office at the head of the dock, for further information.

The supermarket on the road parallel to the waterfront is good, has a friendly staff, and will deliver to the dinghy dock on request.

For years Philippe Vatier has supplied yachts with wine, champagne, and liquor. His choice of wine is superb, varying from cheap to the finest of the fine. We have always ordered from the bottom (cheap) end of his list and we have never had a bad bottle. He has moved his warehouse from underneath Ship Shop to the main port, but the chap who runs Martinique Yacht Services at the head of the fuel dock is his agent and will take orders and payment and arrange delivery. Place your order when you arrive and they will arrange delivery just before you leave; you must present your clearance papers before they will deliver the booze.

YSM also stocks the Street guides and, I hope, Imray-Iolaire charts.

When it comes to stocking the boat with food, you will find an enormous selection from which to choose. But I can recommend the second street in from the waterfront, Rue Ernest Déprog, where among other stores you'll find a greengrocer and some wholesale food shops where you can buy sacks of onions, potatoes, and so on.

A stop on any Eastern Caribbean island is not complete without a visit to the local market, and Martinique's covered market, its roof supported by ornate cast-iron pillars, was by far the best and most picturesque market in the entire Eastern Caribbean.

When I arrived in Fort-de-France in March 1986, I was shocked to find just an empty lot where the market used to be. My disappointment was replaced by joy, though, when I discovered it had not been demolished but had been disassembled to be repaired, restored, and rebuilt. If the restoration of the market is as good as the restoration of the cathedral (be sure to visit the cathedral), the market will turn out to be magnificent. The market, now totally open-air, has been temporarily moved to the east bank of the River Madame, near the river's mouth.

The easiest way to get to and from the market is via dinghy. Land at the small fueling station and tie your dinghy alongside the dock, using a couple of fenders. The secondary market, which is also the fish and meat market (plus an ice house, where block ice can be bought), is further up the river and has a larger and more convenient dinghy landing. There are also a couple of small supermarkets across the street. From the upper market you can load everything directly into the dinghy.

A word of warning: The River Madame is also the local sewer. Don't fall in; I don't know which would be worse—to drown in the river or to be rescued from it. If you have a leaky dinghy, be sure you are wearing sea boots or your toenails will dissolve in the bilge water.

Don't go to the market too early; the French don't really get going until 0830.

I cannot think of a better way to wind up a morning of shopping than to sit down at the open-air bar at the Impératrice or on the balcony of the Gallia, order a cold beer, and watch the fantastic scenery passing by. One can debate as to whether or not the women of Martinique are the most beautiful in the Eastern Caribbean, but they are certainly the best dressed and have the most fantastic carriage. The local boutiques offer the latest fashions, but at a price that is so high I think the extremely chic Martinique women must make their own clothes.

For marine supplies visit the Ship Shop on Rue Joseph Compère; around the corner, on Rue François, you will find SCIM, which has some marine supplies and plenty of fishing gear. Unfortunately, if you want marine paint you may have to hop in your dinghy and go all the way around to the eastern side of the Baie du Carénage, where you'll also find the Ship Shop's fifty-ton travel lift. They run a good operation that is building up an excellent reputation (although I would be very leery of lifting a heavy boat on that travel lift), and when the franc is soft on the dollar, the Ship Shop's hauling facility offers excellent value. It has the advantage of being right on the edge of the main dry dock. Thus all the shops that service the dry dock can also service a yacht in the Ship Shop facility.

You are allowed to do your own work there or hire outside labor; men are available to do excellent repairs on fiberglass, and there are facilities for spray painting, sand blasting, marine painting, engine repair, welding, electrical repair, inflatable repair, and life-raft servicing. Practically anything you want done can be done in Martinique if you find the right person.

Since I obviously cannot list all the facilities available in Martinique, the best thing to do is to find someone who knows Martinique well and who speaks French and English; hire him as an interpreter and set out to solve your problems. Miquel at Yacht Services Martinique (telephone: 57-78-60) is excellent, and yachtsman Hank Strauss highly recommends Fok Chak Lindsay, who can be found around the Ship Shop hauling facility or called at 732-360.

Large yachts, of course, can haul in the big main dry dock, but that is practical only for yachts of more than 90 to 100 feet. One word of caution regarding the main dry dock: Hauling there during hurricane season is tricky, for if a hurricane comes anywhere near the area, the dock gate gets removed, and the dock is flooded. If you happen to have a few planks out, or some plates off the bottom of a steel boat, that's tough; you are sunk in the dry dock. This has happened more than once in years gone by.

Martinique now boasts four sail makers. Fidol has been holding fort for well over twenty years at Pont de Redonte, voie No. 2, telephone: 4227. Helenon (telephone: 97200) is in 34 Boulevard Allegre, the road on the east side of the River Madame. At Anse Mitane, sail makers can be found at the Bakoua Marina; they do quick repairs right there at the marina; they make sails and do major repairs at their main loft on the east side of the road from the Hôtel Bakoua to Anse Mitane; and West Indies Sail (Quai West PB 704, telephone: 63-04-80) is found on the west side of the main dry dock.

For paint, Camic is the main supplier. They have a small in-town office at Immeuble Somarec, Point Simon, Fort-De-France 97026 (telephone: 71-52-42). This is a five-minute walk from the dinghy landing. Their main office is on the west side of the main dry dock. They stock paint and fiberglass, and also sell, repair, service, and certify life rafts and rubber dinghies.

Freshwater showers in Martinique have always been hard to find. Showers are available at Club de Voile on Point Simon (introduce yourself to the manager as a member of another club and you should get guest privileges) and also at the restaurant on the fueling pier. None of these showers are all that clean. If you don't mind a public shower, try the open-air arrangements free to all at the eastern end of the Savanne beach. (Actually, showers in Martinique are usually a blast of water from a pipe, since all the shower heads seem to have disappeared.)

At Anse Mitan, there are open-air showers by the pool at the Hôtel Méridien. At the small marina under the Hôtel Bakoua people sometimes hold the hose over their heads and have a clean, airy, but rather public wash.

The French take a two-hour lunch, so the shopping hours are slightly different from those on the English Islands: 0800–1200 and 1430–1730, with a large number of small shops also opening at 1600 and closing at 1800.

Overseas telephone calls are difficult. Using the phones in the main post office is a slow, costly, and frustrating experience. Pay phones ("taxi phones") are excellent in that you can call anywhere in the world once you ascertain the code. First, though, you have to find a phone that works, then have handy a stack of five-franc coins. Finally, you have to find the right code: the 1984 French code book, for instance, listed the British Islands code as 45; it is actually 49. So, the best deal in phoning we found was at the Hôtel Méridien, in Anse Mitan, whose operators are fast, efficient, and extremely friendly and speak English. Telexes can be sent from the Ship Shop, from the main post office, and by anyone you find who has a telex and who is in a friendly mood.

Public transport around Martinique is excellent. Some routes are covered by buses, others by public taxi—*taxi pays* or *taxi collective*. Just go to the taxi parking area by the fueling pier, look for a *taxi collective* with the destination you want painted on its side, and hop in; the ride is fast and cheap. When taking a *taxi collective* to a distant part of the island, though, be sure to note when the last one returns in the evening; if you miss it you could face a very expensive regular taxi ride.

Depending on the dollar-franc exchange, you may find renting a car in Martinique to be relatively inexpensive. You can spend a few interesting days exploring the island this way. A word of warning if you go swimming in any of the rivers: Flash floods sometimes rush down the river gorges, sweeping all before them; woe betide anyone in the water at the time. Friends of ours who are good swimmers very nearly lost their lives in one of these flash floods.

Among the sights to see in Martinique are the *gommier* races. The Carib canoes are about 30 feet long and carry a massive cat ketch rig. Spiritsails are set loose-footed on both masts, with the main overlapping the mizzen like a genoa jib. A crew of five men hang over the weather side on hiking poles (the sliding seat and the trapeze are nothing new to the West Indians).

According to experts, there are three types of boat referred to generically as *gommiers*. The original canoes were carved out of single logs; nowadays the bottom is a single log, with frames and planks added to provide the necessary freeboard. Basically there is no keel, but they feature a long ram bow. Apparently the original cat rig had one small sail forward—the long ram bow acted like a centerboard to keep the bow from blowing off to leeward.

A later version, called a *yole*, looks similar but is built up with a proper keel, frames, and planks. The newest addition to the fleet is the *petit yole* class, started in 1984. These are approximately 18 feet long (instead of 25 to 30 feet), carry the same rig, and are sailed in the same way—but by kids,

usually the sons of the men racing the big boats. The hope is to get the kids hooked on the sport early so they will keep it going in the future. (I am told there are also rowing races in *gommiers*.)

All these canoes are commercially sponsored and are raced with tremendous enthusiasm and skill, and they provide a real spectacle—if one can figure out the racing schedule. The schedule seems to be a military secret, but basically there are about twenty races a year, twelve of them occurring in July, August, and early September. I have been told that if you check with the Office du Tourism, Borge Postal 520, Fort-de-France, you might be able to get a copy of the schedule.

I have never seen a race in Martinique, although I have spent the better part of twenty-five years chasing them; fate was always against me. But I did finally see the *gommier* races on Irish television, of all things. I happened to be in the Marine Hotel at Glandore, County Cork, having a pint of Guinness, and what should come on the "telly" but an excellent fifteen-minute color program featuring the *gommier* races in Martinique. The races are extremely exciting, closely fought with cash prizes to the winners, masses of people following from the shore and on the water—definitely worth watching one way or another.

Small-boat sailing in general is popular in the bay of Fort-de-France, which is ideal for it, as it is large enough to give plenty of room for exploring; the land to the east breaks any sea but is low enough so that it does not block the wind. Windsurfing is extremely popular and there are at least two schools where beginners may learn—one at the Hôtel Méridien and another on the open beach at Anse Mitane.

Martinique is one of the best-charted islands in the Caribbean. The American National Ocean Survey publishes four charts of Martinique (NOAA 25084, 25085, 25086, and 25087). The British have two (BA 371 and 494). The French, on the other hand, publish ten, all of which not only are fairly well up-to-date, but are also the best and most modern charts in the entire Lesser Antilles. This resulted from the fact that during World War II the French Antilles sided with Vichy France, and an aircraft carrier, numerous destroyers, and a cruiser loaded with all the gold from the Bank of France took refuge in Fort-de-France harbor. The U.S. Navy blockaded these ships from the time of the fall of France in 1940 until the Free French took over in mid-1944. The officers of the blockaded fleet had nothing to do, so they set to work recharting the islands of Martinique and Guadeloupe, and did a superb job.

From all these charts—French, British, and American—and from my own observations, I have developed two Imray-Iolaire charts, A-30 and A-301, which cover Martinique at a scale useful for yachtsmen.

These two Imray-Iolaire charts are all you will need for normal cruising on the south and east coasts of Martinique. If you really want to poke in and out of the reefs, though, I advise you to buy the *Cruising Guide to Martinique*, by Philippe Lachesnez-Heude and Jérôme Nouel. Philippe is a *Bekee*, a descendant of the first settlers of 1640, and a yachtsman who has spent his life sailing the coasts of Martinique. Jérôme is a French yachts-

man who has spent ten years exploring the island.

Incidentally, make sure you have on board the latest Imray-Iolaire charts, because the French are continually adding new buoys, lights, and ranges. They are also in the process of switching *from the European buoyage system (green-right-returning) to the North American system (red-right-return-ing)*.

Baie de Fort-de-France

FORT-DE-FRANCE HARBOR
(II A-30, A-301; Sketch Chart III-1)

Baie de Fort-de-France is commodious, contain-

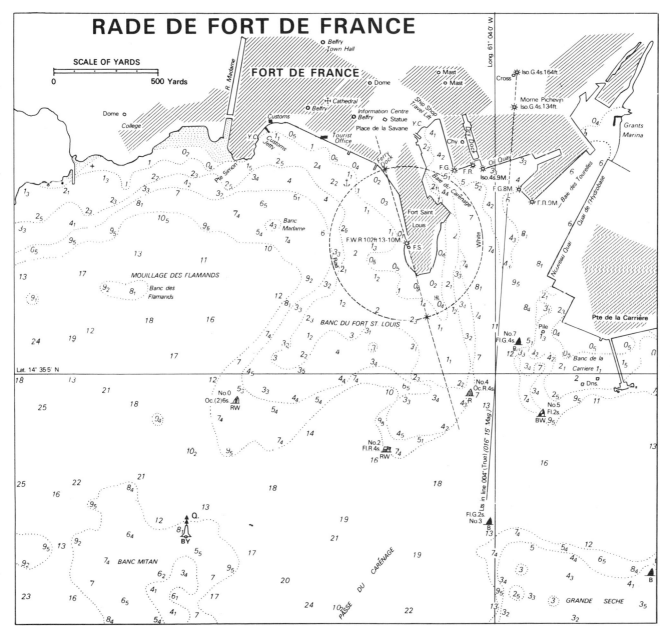

SKETCH CHART III-1   Rade de Fort-de-France

ing many anchorages and coves that will provide shelter in all weathers. If one of these becomes rough under certain conditions, you only have to move a short distance to a more favorable spot.

When entering the harbor at night, the course from Cap Salomon to the anchorage at the Savanne leads almost directly across the position of a large unlit buoy in the middle of the harbor. Keep a good lookout for it, because it is big enough to do substantial damage to your boat.

The principal yacht anchorage is off the town at the Anchorage des Flamands. Anchor southwest of the covered pier, due west of the north end of Fort St. Louis. Feel your way in with the lead and anchor at a convenient depth. The bottom shoals very gradually. If you are passing the night, keep an eye on your outboard. Some islanders find them exceedingly adaptable to their fishing canoes. The anchorage is satisfactory in normal weather; when the wind swings around to south or southwest, it is time to move along. When this happens, I would advise crossing the harbor to Anse Mitan.

The advantage of anchoring off the Savanne is that it is only a short dinghy ride ashore. You can tie up to the fueling pier, where fresh water and ice are also available. You can also take the dinghy up the River Madame to the market for fresh fruit and vegetables; a supermarket is across the street, an ice house is alongside the fish market—everything is in one place. This way, you can load the dinghy and avoid the traffic jams at the other supermarkets.

BAIE DU CARENAGE

(II 1, A, B, A-30; Sketch Chart III-1)

East of Fort St. Louis, this is the home of a yacht club—a good shelter if you are willing to put up with the heat, the dirt, the odor, and the noise. The yacht club has a well-stocked bar, shower rooms, and fresh water. Boats drawing 6½ feet can moor stern-to for short periods. The smell is so atrocious that I can't imagine anyone's staying more than an hour or so. On the east side of the bay are the steamer docks and the main dry dock.

BAIE DES TOURELLES

(1, A, B, A-30; Sketch Chart III-1)

East of the steamer dock, Baie des Tourelles has a first-rate yacht yard that was run for many years by M. Jean Grant. Some charts of this area do not show that deep water now carries all the way up the mouth of the river just east of the yard. Favor the eastern shore.

Unfortunately, Monsieur Grant, a wonderful man whose yard had much to do in keeping *Iolaire* going in my early years of owning her, is no longer with us. Gabriel, who worked with M. Grant for fifty-five years (yes, for fifty-five years—he started working at age ten), has now retired but still lives at the yard.

Draft at the yard is limited to 6 feet, but at full high-water springs they were able to get *Iolaire's* 7′3″ on the cradle. If you own a wooden boat, be aware that many of the old shipwrights who worked on *Iolaire* twenty-odd years ago are still there today.

There is a vast supermarket at Monoprix, within walking distance from Grant's; thus you can take your dinghy to Grant's, walk to the supermarket, do your shopping, get a taxi ride back, load stores into the dinghy, and be off. Alternately, take *taxi collective* Famentir from town, do your shopping, and take the taxi back to the dinghy landing.

ANSE MITAN

(II 1, A, B, A-30; Sketch Chart III-2)

The chart lists it as Anse de Cocotiers; Anse Mitan, the local name, is more commonly used. This is an indisputably fine anchorage and understandably popular with the French. It has one of the few decent beaches in the area within easy access of the town—a three-mile reach coming and going.

A word of warning to those sailing from the anchorage off the Savanne: Do not head directly for Anse Mitan or else you will come to a resounding halt against the shoal that extends southwest from Fort St. Louis. Instead, keep west of the line bearing 210 magnetic from the Savanne pier. When the large flashing buoy approaches the port beam, head for the Hôtel Bakoua at the northern end of the anse.

Another hazard to be reckoned with on the way to Anse Mitan is a shoal with coral heads about 500 yards due west of the hill on the north end of the beach where the Hôtel Bakoua is. You can avoid it by laying a course from the shoal off Fort St. Louis direct to Pointe du Bout and thereafter hugging the shore south to the Anse Mitan anchorage.

So many boats have hit this reef, which lies right on the line from the Anse Mitan anchorage to that at Fort-de-France off the Savanne, that the locals call it Cay de Cauillos, or Idiots Reef. In March of 1985 the reef was marked by a small yellow buoy. It may still be so marked—but don't count on it.

On the weekend, Anse Mitan is inundated by

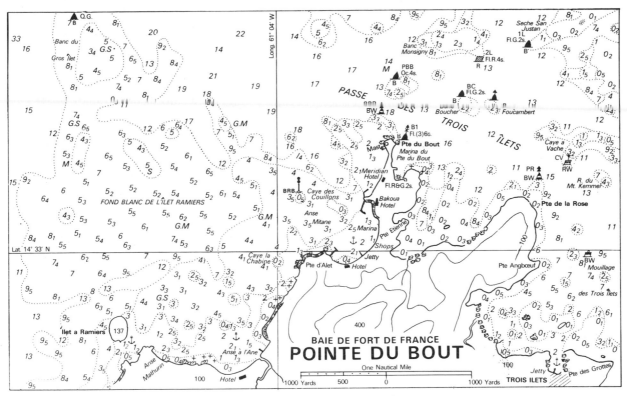

SKETCH CHART III-2   Pointe du Bout

the French from Fort-de-France. They love to tear around the bay at full throttle in their little hot-rod outboards. Swimmers take heed: If you want to get ashore, row.

Anse Mitan remains a good refuge from the crowded, dirty anchorage of the Savanne, with excellent ferry service both to the dock at Anse Mitan and to the Marina Pointe du Bout, from which it is only a short walk through the hotel to the anchorage on the beach.

Excellent meals are available at Anse Mitan. The Méridien and the Bakoua are first-class international hotels, sometimes with lavish entertainment. Elsewhere on the beach are too many restaurants to be listed here. A great occupation if you are staying at Anse Mitan for a week or so is to have lunch at a different restaurant each day and dinner at a different restaurant each evening; all are good—some are just better than others.

Happily, we discovered in 1985 that all supplies are available in the Anse Mitan area; there is a supermarket over in Marina Pointe du Bout, a bank (closed on Mondays but open on Saturday mornings), restaurants, a small marine store on the road that leads to the Hôtel Méridien, and a newsagent. Down in the middle of Anse Mitan, by

the windsurfer Pedalo establishment, an excellent patisserie sells fresh bread, sticky buns, and croissants at 0700 in the morning. Up the small road next to the *patisserie,* on the left-hand side, is an excellent greengrocer; further up you'll find a superb butcher and a nice little supermarket. One thing not available at Anse Mitan is block ice, but cube ice can be bought from the hotels or from the marina at the Bakoua, run by Charlotte Honnart. Here you can find water, fuel, bread, pastries, and books (including the Street guides and Imray-Iolaire charts).

You can get back and forth between Anse Mitan and Fort-de-France by two ferries: the Méridien-Bakoua ferry, which comes in to Marina Pointe du Bout, a big, fast catamaran that leaves town on the half hour and leaves the marina on the hour; and the smaller and more erratic Anse Mitan–Anse l'Âne ferry. This ferry leaves Anse Mitan sometime between a quarter and half past the hour, goes to Anse l'Âne and then back to Fort-de-France, whence it leaves on the hour.

About the only thing that seems to be lacking in Anse Mitan is a post office; the nearest one is at Trois Îlets. A bus goes from Anse Mitan to Trois Îlets on the half hour and returns on the hour.

TROIS ÎLETS

(II I,A-30; Sketch Chart II-2)

In the southwest corner of Baie de Fort-de-France, Trois Îlets is an out-of-the-way spot, difficult to reach by car and seldom visited by yachts. The anchorage (due north of town) is mud bottom and is frequently used as a hurricane hole. The holding is not too good, but if you drag there is only soft bottom to end up on.

When sailing to Trois Îlets from Fort-de-France, be careful of the numerous shoals that litter the eastern side of the bay. They are all buoyed and there is plenty of water between them.

A better idea is to anchor at Anse Mitan and take the bus to Trois Îlets. It's worth an afternoon's visit. La Pagerie, the museum of Josephine Bonaparte, is there, as well as a botanical garden. It's a nice, old-fashioned Martiniquais town with tiled roofs and boasts a number of small restaurants as well as the post office.

COHE-DU-LAMENTIN

(II A-30; French 5916)

In the northeasternmost corner of Fort-de-France harbor, this area offers the Port Cohe Marina, an excellent hurricane shelter. Draft in the channel is limited to six feet, though, and once there you are in the middle of nowhere, as the airport is two km away on a rough road.

I've never been there, and will rely on the directions supplied by Lachesnez-Heude/Nouel: "Steer 100 degrees from the red-and-white buoy marked CAR situated in the middle of Cohe-du-Lamentin, proceed toward the entrance of the small channel, which is hard to see from a distance but identifiable once you draw near a grounded barge, which must be left to port." In theory, at least, the rest of the channel is marked by gas lights.

Leaving Anse Mitan for Fort-de-France, hug the shore until past the Bakoua, and then head for the buoy marking the end of the shoal off Fort St. Louis. If you are bound for Pointe des Nègres, again stay inshore until the Bakoua is abeam, as otherwise you may clip the 5-foot spot that lies on the line between Anse Mitan and Pointe des Nègres.

MARINA POINTE DU BOUT

(II 1, A, B-30; Sketch Chart III-2)

East of Pointe du Bout there is a marina, perfectly sheltered, with ten feet and possibly a little more water inside. It is entered from the north through a buoyed channel that, while narrow, is wide enough to accommodate the big, powered catamaran that runs the ferry service from the Savanne to Marina Pointe du Bout.

The marina provides a place to lay alongside, with showers, water, and electricity for the yachtsman who wishes to spend some time in Martinique but does not want to lie in the crowded and filthy waters of some of the anchorages. The marina is also completely landlocked, and would provide an excellent hurricane hole as well as a place to leave a boat in Martinique if you had to be away during the hurricane season.

Do not try to enter the marina without first anchoring at Anse Mitan or in the lee of Pointe du Bout and walking over to see if there are mooring slips available (there's barely room to turn around); every time I have looked at the marine it has been jam-packed, and people tell me there is a waiting list to obtain docking space.

I don't know anyone who has explored the eastern side of the Baie de Fort-de-France in a yacht, but if I were to do it, I would certainly have the detailed French harbor chart No. 5916 on hand.

In general, remember that Baie de Fort-de-France can be a veritable death trap if a hurricane passes over the island, or even if one passes north of it. This would build up a large westerly swell, which makes all normal anchorages completely untenable. Some boats try to hide in Cohe-du-Lamentin; but this is also a commercial anchorage and is likely to be loaded with freighters. If the marina is not filled, smaller boats can get up the creek to that haven, as described above. Trois Îlets, also mentioned above, is well-sheltered but a poor holding. The carenage east of Fort Royal would be disaster, as a strong surge pours back and forth through there, making it impossible to anchor or get secure to the dock.

If a hurricane looms, my advice is to get out of Baie de Fort-de-France and go to Cul-de-Sac du Marin; or, if you have time, get around to the east coast of Martinique and duck into one of the many excellent hurricane holes there.

ANSE À L'ÂNE

(II A-301; Sketch Chart III-2)

As you leave Anse Mitan and head for Cap Salomon and the mouth of Baie de Fort-de-France, you come to Anse à L'Âne. It is a real sleeper—

one of the more attractive anchorages in the area—and until recently was seldom used by yachtsmen.

It is quieter, with nowhere near so many people as Anse Mitan. Yet it has an attractive hotel at its western end and a number of restaurants along the beach. The easternmost one is a drinking man's delight: a classic *petit punch* for four francs; three dollars' worth would send almost anyone down in flames.

Another attraction of Anse à L'Âne is a hand-powered, carved wood carousel equipped with an amazing set of bearings: one shove spins it three full revolutions. Think how fast it could get going at fiesta time with a bunch of well-lubricated celebrants spinning it around!

Ashore at Anse à L'Âne it is only a short walk to a small grocery store and an interesting shell museum. The ferry dock is a good place to tie up the dinghy, but be sure to use the southwest side, since the ferry comes along its northeast face.

When sailing from Anse Mitan to Anse à L'Âne, pass outside the shoal due west of Pointe d'Alet. Then watch out for the four-foot spot out from the center of Anse à L'Âne beach. Both of these hazards had marks on them in 1985; don't count on their still being there. Incidentally, the reefs west of Pointe d'Alet provide excellent snorkeling.

A somewhat erratic ferry connects Anse à L'Âne with Anse Mitan, as described above; you can also make the trip by a perfectly pleasant dinghy ride in sheltered water.

In normal trade-wind weather, Anse à L'Âne is a well-protected anchorage. If the wind backs to the north, or a ground swell starts coming in from the northwest, it will definitely become uncomfortable (as will Anse Mitan)—but probably not dangerous, since the beach is flat. (Remember that you can tell when a beach is dangerous in northwest ground-swell conditions: It is always very steep-to, with soft sand.)

The rule of thumb for comparing the Savanne anchorage with those of Anse Mitan and Anse à L'Âne is the same as that for comparison between Basse Terre, St. Kitts, and Charleston, Nevis. If the anchorage is calm in the Savanne, it is likely to be choppy on the other side of the harbor; similarly, if the wind goes into the southeast, when Anse Mitan and Anse à L'Âne are sheltered, the Savanne will be rough.

If you have an exploratory urge, a lot of fun can be had with a dinghy or outboard in the various rivers and canals that radiate from the harbor of Fort-de-France. Many of them extend quite far inland to towns east of the harbor.

ÎLET À RAMIERS
(II 1, A, B, A-30; Sketch Chart III-2)

This is the little island at the southwest corner of Fort-de-France Harbor. The preferred anchorage is in the channel between the island and the mainland. Anchor in 10 feet of water over a white-sand bottom. Drop the hook when the dock on the island bears due north. This channel shoals to 6 feet east of Ramiers. Here, too, the swimming is excellent.

Unfortunately you are not allowed ashore, as the wonderful old fort that we used to explore in years gone by is now forbidden to visitors. When it was first closed we decided that at least it must be a secret missile site. It turns out that all the secrecy is merely to conceal a private club for the French military!

ANSE NOIRE AND ANSE DUFOUR
(II A-30)

These two small coves, which I have only looked at, are notable for the fact that although they are side by side, one has a white-sand beach, the other a black-sand beach.

In the winter, the ground swell would make them uncomfortable or even untenable. In periods when there isn't a ground swell, or in the summer, either of these bays could make a quiet, secluded anchorage.

At Anse Dufour, you'll find a white-sand cove, a fishing village, a small shop, a restaurant, and an excuse for a road leading up the valley. If you anchor too close inshore, the fishermen may ask you to move so that they can shoot their nets.

At Anse Noire, you will find, besides the black beach, the Coconut Grove, a thatched roof restaurant with its own lobster tank. It's apparently a nice little place to visit.

For a chart of these two coves and more specific directions, consult the Lachesnez-Heude/Nouel *Cruising Guide to Martinique.*

Southwest Coast
GRANDE ANSE D'ARLETS
(II 1, A, B, A-30; Sketch Chart III-3)

This is the first cove south of Cap Salomon and one of two good anchorages on the southwest coast. The bottom is white sand and good holding, with 2 fathoms in the southeast corner of the harbor. A slight roll is not too bothersome. The swimming is excellent.

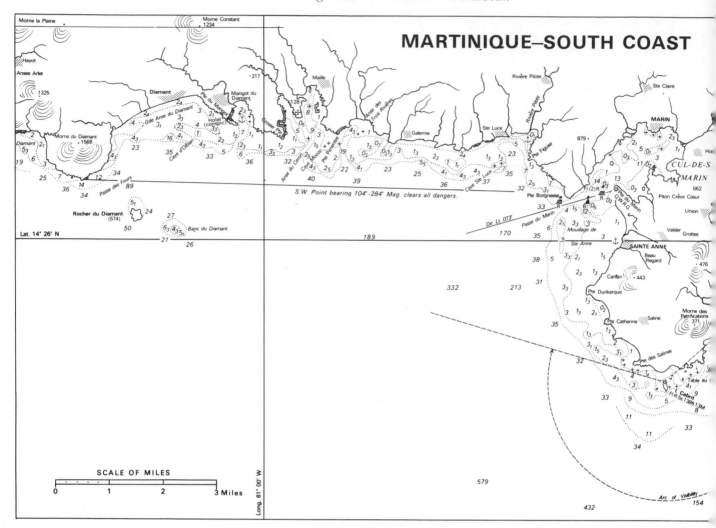

SKETCH CHART III-3 Martinique—South Coast

What you want to do, ideally, is feel your way in to the extreme southeast corner and anchor in 2 fathoms, being sure to get your hook onto the edge of the shelf, since the bottom drops off steeply. But the fisherman shoot their nets here, as in Anse Dufour, and there has been friction between them and yachtsmen in the past. So it's wise not to get too close inshore. Stay about 200 yards off and you should be okay.

There is no real town at Grande Anse d'Arlets, only a fishing village with a variety of canoes, nets stretched out to dry, dogs, cats, goats, roosters, and bare-bottomed urchins running to and fro. As is usual in any small French village, there is a restaurant and bar.

At the north and south ends of the beach are some beautiful small cottages owned by wealthy citizens of Martinique, who come here in the summer to beat the heat of Fort-de-France. The cove is likely to be crowded with local yachtsmen on Saturdays and Sundays.

PETITE ANSE D'ARLETS

(II 1, A, B, A-30; Sketch Chart III-3)

This is the next cove south of Grande Anse and not as sheltered, but it has the advantage of a good restaurant and ferry communication to Fort-de-France. Anchor off the town, but be careful of the coral bank at the northern end of the harbor; here, too, the bottom drops off steeply. The anchorage in the northeast corner usually avoids the swell. If you want to get away from town, a little cove to the south, Anse Chaudière, provides privacy, good snorkeling, and, in settled weather, a good anchorage in 2 fathoms. It's within dinghy distance of town. Avoid the sunken wreck south of the town dock.

The well-to-do citizens who come here from Fort-de-France used to travel by boat to avoid the kidney-busting roads. Now the roads are so improved that they commute by car. Still, the town has apparently kept its quaint character. Philippe Lachesnez calls this one of the best-preserved of the old Martinique towns.

PETITE ANSE DU DIAMANT
(II 1, A, B, B-30)

A small white-sand beach but not very good anchorage. I do not advise stopping here.

The most spectacular sight on the south coast of Martinique is the Rocher du Diamant or, as the British prefer, H.M.S. Diamond Rock—so called because in 1781 Admiral Hood somehow managed to establish a gun battery at the top of the mountain. The guns swept the channel between Diamond Rock and the mainland, closing it to all coastal traffic. Against the best efforts of the French, the British succeeded in holding out for some eighteen months. When they finally surrendered, the French arranged for their immediate exchange as prisoners, as it was felt that men so brave and resourceful should not be left to rot away in prison. How wars have changed!

How the French have changed! They have lost their sense of humor. Some years ago their navy was sending a squadron to Martinique to celebrate a national holiday. Two young Englishmen decided to have some fun. The night before the squadron's arrival, they scaled the cliffs of Diamond Rock and hung a huge white ensign, the symbol of the British Navy. In the morning as the French squadron sailed past H.M.S. Diamond Rock, the white ensign was clearly visible on the south face. The French admiral was apoplectic; he ordered a helicopter to lower a man on the rock to destroy the flag. The French complained through diplomatic channels, and before the dust settled, it had become something of an international incident.

For those who are interested in the history of the rock and its British occupation, the fighting, and the French recapture, there are two fine books: *Her Majesty's Sloop of War Diamond Rock*, by Stuart and Eggleston, is an extremely readable account of the affair. Dudley Pope turns the historical event into an excellent novel in *Ramage's Diamond*.

South Coast

This coast offers few really good anchorages until you get to its eastern end, and with the excellent harbor of Ste. Anne beckoning from there, it would be my inclination to skip right on by the rest. Nevertheless, there are a number of small stopping places (which I haven't been in), and if you're a good reef pilot, have a small boat, and are into gunkholing, then these out-of-the-way spots might be a lot of fun.

A general warning, though: The water along this south coast is not so clear as it usually is in the Caribbean. Furthermore, the shoal water extends as much as a mile offshore in some places. (Cay Ste. Luce, for instance, which breaks only in heavy weather, is a full half-mile offshore.) To complicate matters, a strong westerly current works along the coast.

So although getting inshore on the shelf will get you out of the current, the water will be choppier as the swell comes up on the shelf, and will also be much harder to read. Basically, a safe policy is to tack offshore as soon as you see bottom. And keep a lookout in the bow and a chart on deck at all times.

Back bearings on the southwest tip of Martinique are a useful guide. If your bearing on the point under Diamond Rock is 285° or more, you should be in deep water. If the bearing gets less than 285°, watch out for shoal water. A good hand-bearing compass is a big help here.

The distance from Petite Anse d'Arlets on the southwest coast to Ste. Anne is only 13 miles, but it is best to allow the better part of the sailing day for the trip because of head winds and the strong westerly set. As you get closer inshore, the wind will get variable; play the lifts and headers for all they're worth and you'll save some time. *Do not try to push on beyond Ste. Anne after 1100*, because you will be unable to reach the east coast harbors before the light fails.

MARIGOT DU DIAMANT
(II 1, A, B, A-30, A-301; Sketch Chart III-3)

This is a proper little harbor, location of the Diamond Rock Hotel. Be careful of the reefs that extend out from Pointe du Marigot. A small dock under the hotel in the southwest corner offers fuel and water alongside. Do not go north of the buoys in the center of the harbor, since it shoals rapidly here. A good anchorage, in clear water, and sheltered in all winds except those from the south.

To the east of Marigot du Diamant, anchorage of sorts can be found at Anse du Céron (two little coves for the brave and careful), at Anse des Trois Rivières, at Ste. Luce, and at Rivière Pilote. All are shown on Imray-Iolaire chart A-301, and on Sketch Chart III-3, but for these nooks and crannies, I highly recommend that you carry the *Cruising Guide to Martinique* by Lachesnez-Heude and Nouel; it has greater detail and a better scale.

Cul-du-Sac du Marin is a large harbor with numerous coves, many of which provide perfect hurricane holes. In fact, practically anywhere in the harbor provides good hurricane shelter if you have really good ground tackle.

When approaching the harbor, check the chart and the buoys, which by the time you read this *should be* "red right returning," i.e., green buoys on the port hand, red buoys on the starboard hand. Leave the buoy off Pointe Borgnesse to port, stay north of the next buoy, which marks a 4-foot spot, and south of the next marking a 3-foot spot; which many boats have hit despite its being noted on the chart. A bearing of 088 magnetic on Pointe du Marin will lead you clear of all dangers.

Club Med has an establishment on Pointe du Marin. Visitors are not welcome ashore unless they are members of the club—an attitude that will be made clear to you in no uncertain terms.

West of Club Med is not a good anchorage because the bottom drops off steeply down to 60 feet. You can find an anchorage near a white-sand beach on the shelf north of Pointe du Marin. Here you'll not only be sheltered from winds in all directions, but you'll also have excellent scenery ashore—the northern Club Med beach seems to be the one preferred by those who like to swim and sunbathe *au naturel.*

As you go on into the harbor, be careful. Most but not all of the shoals are buoyed. Eyeball navigation is the rule. There are too many coves to enumerate here. My advice is to anchor right inside the harbor off Club Med, get in your dinghy, spend an hour or so exploring Cul-du-Sac du Marin, then pick an anchorage that suits your taste. Some of the off-lying cays have good anchorages and there will be good snorkeling around the edge of the reefs. Other anchorages are tucked up inside mangrove coves and provide excellent fishing and birdwatching (of the feathered variety). The land east of Cul-du-sac du Marin is low—thus the trades are unobstructed, making the area cool and relatively bug free.

In the northeast corner of the harbor is Club Nautic, which seemed closed the two times I visited it. But I am told it is possible to get alongside the end of the dock to take on water; this could be important if you're going around to the east coast because there's not much chance to get water there.

Looking at the number of boats stacked around Club Nautic, I imagine it would be a very active place over the weekend. That would be a good time to visit the club and find out more about Cul-du-Sac du Marin and the east coast.

If you're a serious oarsman, it might also be fun to find out who owns the lovely scull I came across there. She was of light clinker construction, had outriggers, a sliding seat, and a passenger seat—the only craft of its kind I've ever seen in all my years in the Caribbean.

The town of Marin has a Customs office, and the Customs officer has a job that I would love to have: He works on Wednesdays from 9 to 12 only. However, it's not much help to enter Customs in Marin, as you still have to do Immigration in Fort-de-France; so the best thing to do is to hop in a *taxi collective,* go to Fort-de-France, and take care of your paperwork there.

The town of Marin is not one of my favorites, as I almost died of thirst before I could find a bar. Nor are there many markets—but it does have four banks, whereas the neighboring town of Ste. Anne has none.

Cul-de-Sac du Marin is a good safe anchorage, an excellent hurricane hole, and a good place to practice small-boat sailing and windsurfing.

MOUILLAGE DE STE. ANNE
(II 1, A, B, A-30, A-301; Sketch Chart 4)

This is one of the most attractive anchorages in the whole area. An excellent shelter in normal trade-wind weather, the entrance is simple and straightforward. Anchor west of town in 2 fathoms, feeling your way in; the bottom shoals gradually. Once there, you have easy access to the town of Ste. Anne.

This is basically a resort town, so the stores seem to be open seven days a week until late in the evening. A fish market, a small vegetable market, two or three unsuper supermarkets, a source of block ice, and a post office supply all the basic necessities—everything except a bank.

On the beach is the Filet Blue, with its glass dance floor. Underneath the floor are the lobsters you can have for lunch or dinner. Also along the beach are various small typical French seaside snack shops.

In town, the Hôtel Dunette has a pleasant bar and restaurant overlooking the harbor. A short

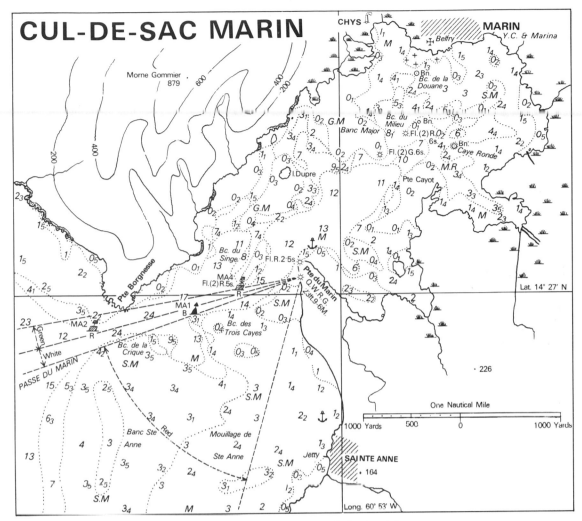

SKETCH CHART III-4   Cul de Sac Marin

walk south takes you to the restaurant Au Mahogany, which has been serving delicious meals to locals and visitors for a couple of decades.

In the next bay south is the Hôtel Caritan, a most hospitable place with boutique, restaurant, swimming pool, nightly music, and a helpful and efficient telephone operator. There is a pleasant, small beach south of the hotel.

The anchorage in Mouillage de Ste. Anne extends over a mile and a half of very pleasant territory and is never too crowded with yachts.

East Coast

This coastline is thoroughly charted by French 384, 385, 389, and 390; and II A-30 and A-301. The east coast should be explored only by an experienced yachtsman sailing a good, weatherly boat, a cruising guide in one hand, the appropriate French or Imray-Iolaire chart spread before him, and a man on the pulpit—or, better, on the spreaders. It offers wonderful cruising in an area where you are not likely to encounter many yachts. It may be rough or windy at times, but there are any number of harbors and coves that are completely sheltered and calm as a mill pond. At François, Robert, and Trinité, food and supplies can be bought. Lobster is plentiful and inexpensive. *Sudon*, the Caribbean cherrystone clam, can be found in the shoal water.

In planning a trip up the east coast, bear in mind that this is a lee shore with a strong current setting on it. Until you go through Passe du Vauclin, there will be no protection from off-lying reefs. Once you get behind the reefs, they will dampen the

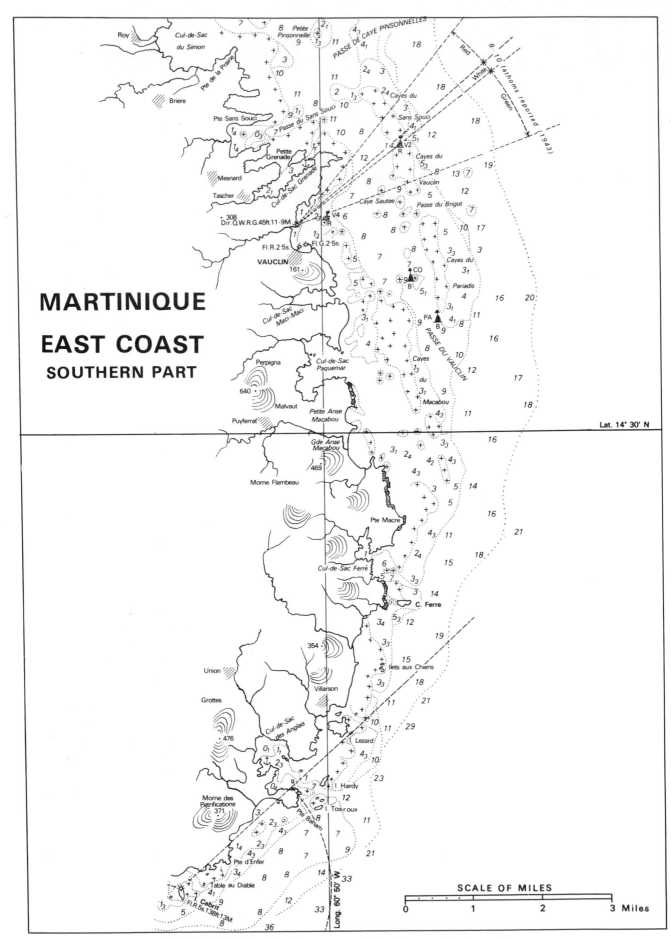

MARTINIQUE

EAST COAST

SOUTHERN PART

SKETCH CHART III-5   Martinique—East Coast—Southern Part

swell to give you a great sail. But you must stay on your toes as you thread through the reefs; looking back, it will not seem as bad as you anticipated.

Imray-Iolaire chart A-301 has all the information you need for normal cruising on this coast. Once again, though, if you're in a shoal-draft boat and have the time to explore every nook and cranny of the coast, I advise you have the Lachesnez-Heude/Nouel guide aboard. It is based on the authors' own experience and is not plagiarized from other guides.

I first cruised this coast in *Iolaire* in 1964, and believe she was one of the very first nonlocal yachts to do so. One other foreigner I know of to have cruised here in the early days is John Guthrie, who visited Cul-de-Sac des Anglais several times in his engineless Brixham trawler, *Pas de Loup*. But how he beat to windward out of that place in a Brixham trawler is beyond me. To tack one of those boats, you put the helm down, lash it, throw off the jib and jib-topsail sheets, leave the staysail sheeted, and go below and grab a cup of coffee; when you get back on deck, the staysail is aback, she has started to fall off on the other tack, and you are in time to unlash the helm and sheet in your headsails!

The French have always been very conscientious in establishing good buoyage systems, and Martinique's east coast is no exception. In fact, it's being expanded and improved so often that even the French charts are often out of date. The Imray-Iolaire charts are hand corrected to conform to the latest Notice to Mariners, but they, too, are sometimes not *au courant* with the latest developments. So be on your guard.

This coast makes a wonderful cruising ground, but it should be approached only in good light. Many leading lights guide local fishermen as they return home at night through the reefs, but no yachtsman should try it after dark on his own.

Furthermore, I'd strongly advise against running dead downwind through any passes to get behind the reef. Better to approach from north or south and find a range that gets you through a pass on a reach.

If you're coming in from the north, pass to weather of Presqu'île de la Caravelle. Once Pointe Caracoli is abeam, bear off for Îlet de Ramville, or jibe around and head into Cul-de-Sac Tartane. The former course will put you to leeward of Loup Bordelais, the unbuoyed, northernmost shoal of the off-lying reefs. If you're heading south, just stay in blue water and you'll be all set.

In approaching from the south, stay well offshore in deep water until you pick up the buoys at the south end of Passe Sud du Vauclin; then ease sheets and run up behind the reef. In heavy weather, don't even think about trying any of the passes through the reef between Vauclin and the pass east of Cul-de-Sac Frégate. It would be like running a New Jersey inlet in foul weather. On the other hand, once you do get behind the reef at Vauclin, you'll find comfortable sailing.

If you're coming from St. Lucia to explore the east coast, stop at Ste. Anne, check in, spend the night, and go around the next day. It is virtually impossible to get from St. Lucia to Passe Sud du Vauclin by 1200 on the same day; and if you get there any later than that, you will be running dead downwind into harbors with the sun in your eyes—a guaranteed way to get yourself into serious trouble.

When you leave Ste. Anne for the east coast, you've got to get around the corner. In the winter months whens it's blowing hard, this can be a problem. In these conditions, beating around Îlet Cabrit (the southeasternmost part of Martinique) is to be avoided at all costs—the Atlantic swell shortens as it comes in on the island, humps up, and becomes horrendous.

Instead, stand south on a close reach after passing Pointe Dunkerque until you are in good deep water, then come on the wind and sail southeast. Tack north when you think you can clear Cap Ferré by a good bit (Cap Ferré looks like an island from distance). Do not allow yourself to fall down on the coast, as the sea becomes so steep and confused that it makes tacking difficult. Remember, too, that even after you pass Cap Ferré, the coast, and particularly its reefs, tends northeast for another 3 miles.

Once around the corner off Grande Anse Macabou, you can ease sheets and head for Passe Sud du Vauclin, which is well marked. Leave the red buoy to starboard and stand north inside the reef. Put a man in the bow or on the spreaders to help you avoid the various unbuoyed shoals north of the pass.

When it's blowing hard, I recommend that you go right to Cul-de-Sac Frégate and avoid all the harbors south of that—Vauclin, Anse du Sans Souci, Cul-de-Sac Grenade, etc. They are for gunkholing in calm weather.

General warning: When sailing on the east coast of Martinique, you must remember that almost all the entrance channels lead due west. Entrance should therefore be made before 1400; otherwise the sun will be in your eyes and eyeball navigation will be impossible. Similarly, when leaving harbors and heading due east, it is extremely difficult to see the reefs before 1100, as the sun will be in the east and in your eyes.

CUL-DE-SAC DES ANGLAIS
(II 1, A, B, A-30, A-301; Sketch Chart III-5)

Tackling the entrance to Cul-de-Sac des Anglais in bad weather is, once again, like running a dangerous New Jersey inlet; furthermore, there's not much room to round up once you're inside. But in favorable conditions, the entrance is straightforward and the rewards are generous. This is an excellent anchorage, with lots of exploring possibilities.

Enter from the southeast on a course roughly northwest. Watch out for the rocks on the port side as you come in and round up under Îlet Hardy. Proceed as far north toward shoal water as your draft will permit, and anchor.

It is possible to take 7 feet up into Cul-de-Sac des Anglais. Its inner harbor is nothing more than soft mud with mangroves around the sides—good fishing, I suspect, and excellent birdwatching; peace and quiet in the mangrove and an enclosed anchorage. To do this, consult the Lachesnez-Heude/Nouel *Cruising Guide to Martinique* for detailed directions.

The dinghy can be taken northeast to Îlet Lézards, a mile away across reef-sheltered water and white-sand bottom. This area would be superb for windsurfing, as the wind sweeps unobstructed across the reef, while the reef breaks the swell completely.

A distinctive feature of this area is the fishermen who work from long, narrow bamboo rafts that they pole along just as if they were punting on the Thames. They sit on chairs secured to the raft; from three or four hundred yards, though, you can't see the raft, which is almost flush with the water. So all you see are men sitting on chairs in the middle of the sea. It's very startling.

The French chart shows an entrance between Pointe Baham and Îlet à Tois Roux. I am told that there is definitely no passage between these two islands. If you are coming up from the south and trying to sight Cul-de-Sac des Anglais, look for the black cliffs on Tois Roux.

CUL-DE-SAC FERRÉ; CUL-DE-SAC DU PAQUEMAR; CUL-DE-SAC MASSY-MASSY
(II 30, II 301)

These are all summertime anchorages for shoal draft boats. Consult the *Guide to Martinique* for details.

VAUCLIN
(II 1, A, B, A-30, A-301; Sketch Chart III-5)

This is the first town of any size that you will encounter going up the east coast. It is easily spotted from seaward by its church, which has a green roof. The chart shows a white, green, and red sector light that provides a nighttime range through the channel between Cayes du Sans Souci and Cayes du Vauclin. This is strictly for small-boat fishermen returning or for someone who really knows the area. It should not be attempted by yachtsmen under any circumstances; among other things, if you're running downwind with a big swell, steering control would be minimal.

The basin behind two breakwaters at the south end of Baie du Vauclin is strictly a small-boat refuge with 5 feet of water at its outer edge and 3 feet in the main part.

The bay itself is wide and shoal, and provides an anchorage of sorts; but there's no real shelter when the trades are up because the reef is so far to the east that there's room for a sizable chop to build up. There seems to be an anchorage due east of town behind the unnamed islet south of Baril de Beouf. On the beach south of town is a windsurfing school and a campsite; thus as you sail up the coast you will see windsurfers flitting across the flats south of town, a great place to windsurf, with white-sand bottom only 3 feet down.

CUL-DE-SAC GRENADE
(II 1, A, B, A-30, A-301, French 384, 385; Sketch Chart III-5)

Cul-de-Sac Grenade is not very well spoken of by the French, but I found it a delightful spot, a perfect anchorage, and a wonderful place to try out the sailing dinghy or explore with an outboard. In fact, with a dinghy one can stay inside the inner reefs and visit almost all the remaining east coast of Martinique, all the way to Robert, 10 miles to the north. Spotting the break in the reef that leads into Cul-de-Sac Grenade is none too easy unless you have someone high up in the rigging. In the spring of 1973, a Morgan 41 missed the channel entrance, hit a coral head, and sank. (In fact, put a man in the rigging when cruising *anywhere* on the east coast of Martinique.) The outer part of the channel is deep, with seas breaking on the reefs on both sides, giving a definite line of demarcation. Once you spot the break, the course is about southwest by south.

In 1963, I found the channel to have a depth of 9 feet, sounding with a lead line. In the late seventies, a Gallant 53, drawing 7′9″, got in and weathered a hurricane. However, I've heard that the channel has shoaled up in recent years. So I advise sending a dinghy in to sound the channel before you enter. Remember that if there is a swell running into the channel, the safe depth will be reduced to 6 or possibly only 5 feet.

Once you do get in, the place is indeed a perfect hurricane hole. Put anchors to the west, tie your stern to trees, and sit it out safe and sound.

As you pass between Petite Grenade and Pointe du Vauclin, you will notice a low spit of land to port; round up behind the spit of land and anchor. It is a beautiful cove with 20 feet of water right up to shore; you can put out a stern anchor and run your bow line to a tree. There is a beautiful white-sand beach on the point, but it turns out to be a great disillusionment—there are only 6 inches of beautiful white sand over soft, gooey, black mud.

There is a small fishing village at the head of the Cul-de-Sac, where a taxi could probably be obtained or a bus found for a ride to Vauclin.

Baie des Mulets, northwest of Petite Grenade, is a good deserted anchorage. Although there are few soundings shown on the chart, I found fairly regular depths of 8 feet through most of the bay, gradually shoaling when the inner edge of the reef was approached. I had no difficulty finding a break in the reef for the dinghy, allowing me to enter Passe du Sans Souci.

PASSE DU SANS SOUCI
(II 1, A, B, A-30, A-301; Sketch Chart III-5)

This is another good anchorage with plenty of water and no town or village of any sort. Anchor near the mouth of the pass, as the land is low and swampy at the head of the bay, where it would tend to be hot, airless, and bug infested.

GRANDE PASSE DU SIMON
(II 1, A, B, A-30, A-301; Sketch Chart III-5)

This passage is fairly open to the east. It is littered with reefs that are so steep you could round up under just about any one of them and drop your anchor right on it. If no contact with shore were desired, you could comfortably spend the night with the likelihood of a nice cool breeze.

On the south side of Grande Passe du Simon is Pointe de la Prairie, with a reef and shoal water extending quite far to seaward. You can work your way into an anchorage behind this curving reef.

There are also several tight little anchorages behind bits of reef at the west end of Cul-de-Sac du Simon.

CUL-DE-SAC FRÉGATE
(II 1, A, B, A-30, A-301; Sketch Chart III-6)

Easy to spot and easy to enter. On the north side of the entrance is Îlet Thiery, a good landmark. On the island's northeast point is a large white house with a large veranda around the entire house. Also on the east side of Îlet Thiery is a black cliff with a large cave at the water's edge. When entering, sail between the two easily spotted reefs, which are always breaking. But before you ease sheets, make absolutely sure of your bearings: You should be looking down between Îlet Aubert and Îlet Long at a bearing of 260 magnetic. If, coming north, you bear off too soon, you can get tangled up with the 10-foot spot that always breaks in heavy weather. (Some of the gray hairs in my beard were caused by doing just this, many years ago, with the late Sam Lane on board. Fortunately he, an excellent sailor and good helmsman, realized our error and suddenly headed up and tacked without asking for orders.)

Favor the reefs on the north side of the channel; they are more steep-to and more clearly defined than the reefs on the south side. Once your position is definitely established, run on in and anchor in the lee of one of the many islands.

We found the anchorage off the house of M. Hayot the best. Run along the north shore of Îlet Long past the small cove with the fishing boats, give the point to the west of the cove a berth of 100 yards, jibe over, then harden sheets and round up in the next cove. There is a white house with a small marine railway to the east of it. There is plenty of water close to shore, so run in until the eastern point of the cove lines up with the western point of Îlet Thiery. This anchorage is perfect no matter what direction the wind blows, and the holding ground is good. If you would like to be nearer diving water, you may move the lee of Îlet Thiery; be careful of the detached coral heads.

Although the chart shows coral heads and no soundings, a draft of 5 feet may be taken between the western end of Îlet Aubin and the mainland. Go slow, keep your lead line going, and try to make some sense out of the private stakes placed by the locals to mark the shoals. Pass close to the western shore of the island, hold a course of west-northwest; you should spot two stakes that mark the channel. However, be careful and don't rely too much on local marks. There is also a dinghy

MARTINIQUE–EAST COAST
NORTHERN PART

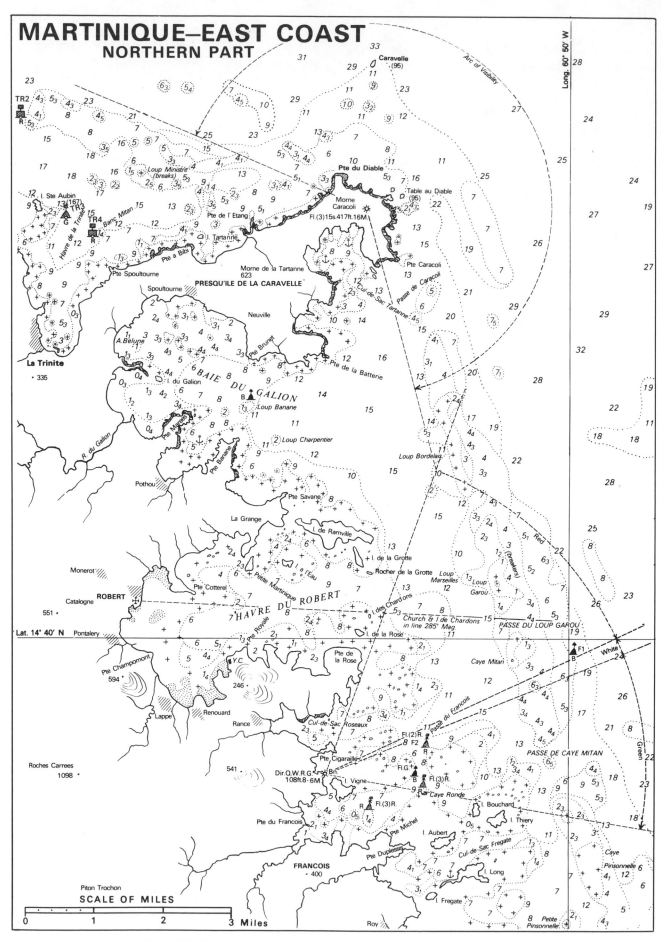

pass around the western end of Îlet Long into Grande Passe du Simon.

FRANÇOIS
(II A-313; Sketch Chart III-6)

A typical middle-sized French town of Martinique, at which full-scale tourism has not yet arrived. The town is especially attractive to the sailor, as there is a drainage canal that leads right to the edge of town, where you can tie up the dinghy among the French fishing boats. Here there is an active fish and vegetable market early in the morning. After making your purchases, walk to town, where you will find various markets that are more than adequate, and an excellent bakery. Buy your supplies, and if they're too heavy, grab a taxi at the main square. Halfway down to the dinghy landing on the north side of the street is a cold storage warehouse where block ice is available. There is also, of course, a post office, a telephone pay booth, and various small bars and restaurants.

This whole area around the towns of François and Robert is especially interesting, as many people live on the various islands and in little coves on the mainland that are not connected to the main roads; as a result, there is a continual flow of canoes to and fro, some rowing, some sailing, and some motoring, almost completely hidden by their great bow waves.

MOUILLAGE DU FRANÇOIS
(II 1, A, B, A-30, A-301; Sketch Chart III-5)

You can enter this excellent anchorage by either Passe du François or the channel between Îlets Thiery and Bouchard and the reefs to the northwest. If you use this southern entrance, be careful of the 7-foot spot north-northeast of Îlet Thiery. (A bearing aligning the eastern end of Thiery with the eastern end of Îlet Long extends right over this shoal.)

The northern pass leads between Petite Caye, which always breaks, and Cay Brigantine, which is now marked by buoys. A line between buoys F2 and F3 bears 033° as you enter; but the center line of the channel is more or less north-south, so it's a reach both ways. Even if the wind is around in the north as you leave, you can stand well to the eastern side of the channel and then easily lay the course out on the starboard tack. When entering, you can be sure you're on the right line if you keep the buoy on Cave Ronde (F4) between the other two.

I would strongly advise against entering François by the eastern passage, Passe de Caye Mitan; it's dead downwind and unmarked.

Once inside the harbor, keep your eyes peeled for the various shoal spots. There are three coves on the south side of Mouillage du François. The first two west of Pointe Michel have picturesque fishing villages on their shores. However, I would not advise spending the night. as I think that they would tend to be hot, airless, and full of bugs. A better anchorage is in the third cove, where they have a yacht club with showers, a restaurant-bar, fuel, water, and what have you. Dockage is available or you can anchor out. On Sundays, Frenchmen from all over the east coast come here for an all-out three-hour banquet. The fact that there are few foreigners means that it must be very good indeed.

From here you can visit François by taxi or by outboard; if you go by outboard, take it easy—you may churn up mud at various points in the canal. And don't capsize: I don't know which would be worse—to drown in a Martinique canal or to be rescued from one. The canal is hard to spot; but if you continue southwestward alongshore from the yacht club, you will have no trouble picking it up.

Behind Îlet Lavigne there is an excellent anchorage with deep water right up to the shore. Swing around the south end of the island, sail north, and round up when the slot between the two hills faces east. You will have absolutely calm water, yet the wind will sweep across the hills guaranteeing a cool and bug-free anchorage. Do not be put off by the muddy water southwest of Îlet Lavigne—it is only a tidal eddy that stirs up the mud. Behind the island the water is clear and clean.

Swimmers can then take the dinghy and visit the outer reef anchorages and have a fine time snorkling and spear fishing, though the latter will probably be unprofitable, as the area is pretty well fished out. With the aid of the sketch chart in the *Guide to Martinique*, a boat drawing 5 feet or less can explore probably a dozen anchorages in Mouillage du François.

CUL-DE-SAC DES ROSEAUX
(II 1, A, B, A-30, A-301; Sketch Chart III-6)

This is just north of François. I have not visited it. However, I did climb to the top of Pointe de la Rose and enjoyed a commanding view of the entire area. The main harbor of Cul-de-Sac des Roseaux is easy of entrance, but of course the shoal water must be reckoned by eyeball. On the north side of the harbor along the south shore of Pointe de la Rose are two coves. The easternmost of these, Anse Coco, has deep water right up to shore, not too much vegitation to gather mosquitoes, and a narrow entrance through the reef; even the entrance channel is sheltered by offshore reefs. In short, a good hurricane hole or, in fact, a good stop at any time. Check the chart carefully, enter only with good light and a man on the bow or in the rigging. The western cove, Anse des Roseaux, is even more sheltered, as it has high hills on three sides and a good hurricane hole, but otherwise is likely to be hot, airless, and bug infested.

A path leads from a small dock up the hill to the road; the climb is well worth it—follow the road westward and you will come to the ruins of an old sugar mill from which you may survey the entire area.

There is another cove to the west of Pointe Chauve Souris, which has plenty of water. It makes a good hurricane hole and a nice spot to visit by dinghy. Don't spend the night. The hills rise vertically on three sides and no air reaches the cove at all. Looking down on it from the hill above the fishing village, I could not see a ripple in the water, although the trades were blowing so hard they almost blew me off the ridge. The western part of Cul-de-Sac des Roseaux is shoal at its head and you would have to anchor quite far offshore. There is little or nothing to attract one ashore.

This area is described in excellent detail and covered by good sketch charts in the *Guide to Martinique*. If the *Guide*'s sketch charts should ever disagree with Imray-Iolaire chart A-301, proceed with extreme caution, but rely more on the *Guide*. Lachesnez-Heude and Nouel have done inshore work on places along this coast that I on *Iolaire*, with a draft of 7′6″ and no engine, could not do justice to.

HAVRE DU ROBERT
(II 1 A, B, A-30, A-301; Sketch Chart III-6)

The largest harbor on the east coast and a sister town to La Trinité, Havre du Robert is beautifully shown on the French detail chart 390. This harbor is wide and easy to enter, with innumerable coves on both sides of the harbor. There is an anchorage at its head near the town of Robert. Robert itself is perched on the edge of a hill. A delightful open-air restaurant is located right next to the dinghy dock. The one difficulty with the restaurant is that they have no menu and they don't speak a word of English; I can vouch for the *sudon* and *langouste*. As usual with French towns, there is plenty of bread, cheese, wine, fresh fruits, vegetables, and seafood.

The east coast of Martinique is so featureless that a stranger may not know exactly where he is. Some of the towns are not visible from the sea. Let me list the key Robert landmarks to look out for: Vauclin—church with a restored roof; Îlet Thiery—a large house on the northeast end with a veranda all around, and the black cliff with caves on its eastern shore; Cay Pinsonnelle—the reef always breaks and a wreck of a sunken steamer is visible at the south end; Loup Garou—a small, bleach-white sand island off the entrance of Robert.

When standing north toward the entrance to Robert, remember that the shoal water east of Pointe de la Rose extends well east of the Pointe. Even after you've passed this shoal, don't bear off until you are north of Îlet des Chardons. Then run down into the harbor, which has so many anchorages that you'll have to choose by throwing a dart at the chart.

The government chart gives ranges for entering Robert, but the ranges are for large vessels standing in from seaward and not for inside the harbor itself.

When running into the harbor, I would not pass much west of Petit Martinique, as the anchorage off the town tends to be choppy and the water is not clear and is not well marked. Just west of Pointe Cotterel is a new fish farm, and the natives do not appreciate having yachts anchor in that area.

The south side of the inner harbor is shoal and muddy. Stay out near the entrance and visit the town by dinghy. The bottom off the town is soft mud, with plenty of grass: all right for an old-fashioned fisherman anchor, but not good for a plow or a Danforth.

Behind Îlet à l'Eau, or northwest of it in the basin, an excellent anchorage is sheltered from the sea but has plenty of wind. I would imagine the snorkeling is good here since it has crystal-clear water.

Another excellent anchorage on the north side of Havre du Robert is behind Petite Martinique. Deep water runs right up to the shore, and you can literally run aground and jump off the low of the boat onto shore. Be careful, though, as the wind curves over the top of the hill and comes back from the west—even though it may be blowing 30 knots from the east on the southern tip of the island. We discovered this to our chagrin while exploring here in April 1985; we ended up aground on a steep-to shore and had an interesting time getting off.

Another anchorage is west of the bluffs. An even better one can be had just west of the buildings on the north end of Ilet Duchamp (Ilet de al Grotte): deep water goes right up to the shore, with sand bottom, good holding, and no swell; it's breezy and bugless besides. The French chart is wrong: There is no passage, except for a dinghy, between Îlet Ramville and Îlet Duchamp (Îlet de la Grotte). But there's good snorkeling, and the area is a good place to teach children to swim—great sand flats with only 1 foot of warm water over them between the two islands. If you wish to visit Rocher de la Grotte, it is best to leave the dinghy at Îlet Duchamp and wade across from the island.

The cove of Îlet Duchamp (Îlet de la Grotte) on the south side of Îlet Ramville is shoal- and reef-encumbered. I would not advise entering it in anything but a dinghy.

The first anchorage on the south side of the harbor is to the west of, and in the lee of, Îlet des Chardons. There is deep water right up to the reefs on both sides, dinghy passages among the reefs, excellent diving, and lobsters galore. Very close to this anchorage is another in the lee of Îlet de la Rose. Deep water carries close to shore on the western side; a long arm of the reef extending out to the north and a solid reef across to Pointe de la Rose give complete protection. Both these anchorages are good and there should be plenty of wind to keep you cool and bug free.

To the west of Pointe de la Rose is Baie de Saintpée; be careful of Banc de la Rose when entering. Best anchorage is under the lee of the reef with the north end of Pointe de la Rose bearing due east. There is plenty of water all the way to the head of the bay, but the head is all mud flat and mangroves. Take a dinghy, tie it to the mangroves, and walk up the hill to the old sugar mill: a wonderful view, a cool breeze, soft grass, and a big spreading shade tree.

The next cove, unnamed, between Pointe du Sable Banc and Pointe Hyacinthe, is completely sheltered and deep. Watch Banc Guillotine when you enter; 4 feet could easily bring you to grief. The pond at the head of the bay is full of mosquitoes; I would advise mooring near the mouth of the cove, where there is a breeze.

East of Pointe Royal is the last noteworthy cove on the south side. It is easily spotted by an old sugar mill with a modern house next to it, a number of old cannons pointing seaward, and three or four boats moored in the cove. There is never a problem with bugs and always a breeze in this perfect shelter. The house is used mainly as a summer residence.

(A word about holiday habits of the Martinican: Like the Frenchman, he takes his vacation in late July and August, deserts the city, and goes to the beach. The west coast of Martinique is hot, muggy, and wet, while the east coast not only is cool and dry but also has the sand beaches. Hence in the summer you will find the east coast heavily populated, but in the winter the various summer residences will be empty. The locals will tell you that it is winter and cold, even though the temperature is in the low eighties all day.)

BAIE DU GALION
(II 1, A, B, A-30, A-301; Sketch Chart III-6)

A large open bay with several anchorages but not much to warrant more than a lunch stop. A reef runs south from the mainland east of Pointe Brunet, giving good shelter from the sea. Moor close to the reef at its northern end as close to shore as you dare. This puts the boat out of the swell, but there is still plenty of wind sweeping across the reef. Another good anchorage is north of Pointe Brunet, off an old farm that is still in operation. There are numerous reefs in the bay; the water is none too clear, so be careful. I circled Îlet du Galion in the dinghy and found nothing of interest except to a mountaineer eager to practice belaying. I did not visit the village of Galion, but I did find an old jetty near the cane cutters' cottages on the western shore of Baie du Galion. The cottages are below the old sugar plantation. A landing can be made at the jetty; a short walk up the hill brings you to the main road, where there is frequent bus service to La Trinité. A taxi may be hired for the ride back; the driver will take you down the hill to your dinghy. If you speak French, it might be possible to get a tour of the sugar estate.

There are other small coves in this bay to be visited; again, consult the *Cruising Guide to Martinique*.

CUL-DE-SAC TARTANE
(II 1, A, B, A-30, A-301; Sketch Charts 6 and 7)

Also referred to as Treasure Cove or Treasure Harbor, reputedly a pirate hideout in days of yore. It is one of the most beautifully sheltered harbors

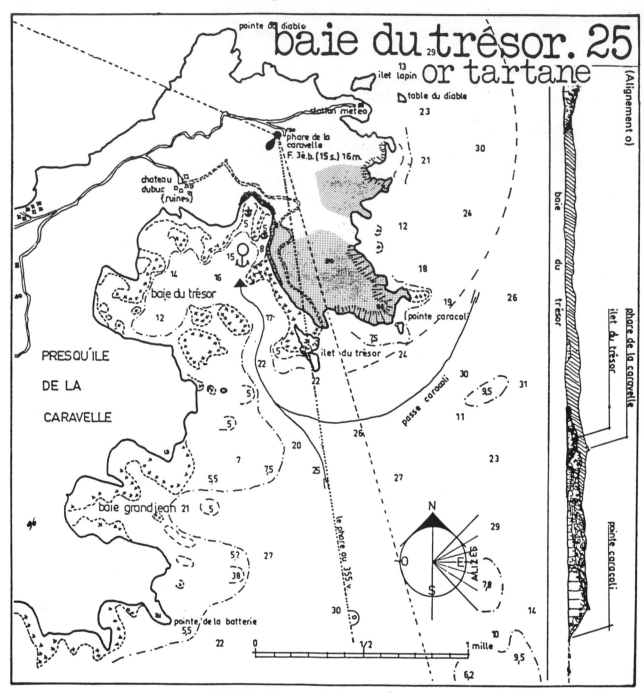

SKETCH CHART III-7   Baie du Tresor

I have ever seen. We were there in September 1964 when a hurricane up north was kicking up a ground swell over 6 feet high along the east coast of Martinique, large enough for the seas to crest in 15 feet of water. Lying in the northeast corner of Cul-de-Sac Tartane, we felt not the slightest motion: it was as smooth as a mill pond, with a pleasant breeze hooking around Pointe Caracoli, and no bugs. The water is either shoal or very deep and

everywhere steep-to. I was able to lay *Iolaire* parallel to the shore so close that you could step from the port side of the boat into 1 foot of water. We put a tackle on the main halyard and heaved her down far enough to paint the waterline. Even so, there was water enough to dive between the sand bank and the boat's bottom and to come up on the other side.

When entering the harbor, it is easy to see the

reefs on both sides, as they always break; once in the pass, head for the lighthouse on the hill, skirting the western edge of the reef that will be in your path and rounding up north of the reef. Shoot across on the back side of the reef, drop your hook off the stern, snub up, and drop a bow anchor once you have actually reached the reef. Be sure to lay your anchor on the reef, or the beach. They are both a near-vertical drop into 50 feet of water. Make sure that your stern anchor is well set; when the wind drops at night, the current running out over the top of the reef will tend to shove you into shoal water.

In April 1985, when we revisited this anchorage, we sailed on in and literally ran the bow up on the beach, jumped ashore with an anchor, dug a hole and buried it, and ran a stern anchor out. Although it was blowing 20 knots outside, we had an absolutely calm anchorage with a nice breeze across the boat.

The whole area is a wildlife preserve and offers the birdwatcher a field day: the great heron, blue heron, turnstone, plover, yellow-legged sandpiper, and other types of birds are here.

There are numerous small fishing boats, all chasing squid, and I can vouch for the lobsters in the area—I caught one while checking the anchor. There are other anchorages in the western side of the bay behind the main reef. Although the northwestern corner of the bay is reef encumbered, it does provide some perfect hurricane moorings. The water is deep between the reefs; it is possible to place the anchors on top of the reefs and run stern lines to trees ashore. With hills on three sides and overlaping reefs at the entrance to the harbor, it would be hard to find a more ideal spot.

For those who like to explore, there are the ruins of an old estate, the Château Dubuc, which is also reputed to have been a pirates' or smugglers' hideout. It is high on a ridge but so overgrown that it is impossible to spot from seaward. It must have been quite a place in its day: it included a reservoir (now a mudhole) and a dam some 30 feet high that must have held a good-sized pond 200 years ago. Old bits and pieces of iron abound, some huge molasses pots known as people pots (what they cooked missionaries in), sugarcane machinery, an old power magazine—a whole morning could be spent rummaging about. To find the old castle, land the dinghy in the cove to the west of the middle point projecting out into the bay where a group of fishermen are always making fish pots or working on their canoes. From there a path leads up the hill to the ruins.

It's easy to see why this might have been a bad guys' paradise in the old days: A lookout posted at the top would be able to see all the way south to Cap de Ferré, and northwest to the northern parts of Martinique. Anyone coming to interfere with smugglers or pirates would have to come by ship, since there was no overland route in those days, and any ship would be spotted almost a full day's sail away (remember that square riggers were not very good to windward). If the lawmen came from the north, the bad guys could scoot south; if the danger was to the south, it was only a short beat out of the harbor, around the corner, and off to the north. A perfect setup.

Above the ruins you will find a road eastward to the Caravelle lighthouse. The lighthouse keepers are most happy to give you a tour. There is also a road west to the towns of Tartane and La Trinité.

North Coast

(III 1, A, B, A-30, A0301; Sketch Chart III-6)

Along the north coast of Presqu'île de la Caravelle there is a small cove east of Pointe de l'Étang, and the fishing village of Tartane. Both are strictly summertime stops for small boats. They are well covered in the *Guide to Martinique*.

Otherwise La Trinité is the only port worth mentioning on Martinique's north coast. It is an excellent harbor when the trades are south of east; in winter, though, the swell from the north makes the anchorage pretty roly. Witness the beautiful white-sand beaches on the south and east sides of the harbor, proof of a good surge.

When sailing from Treasure Cove to La Trinité, stand southeast on the port tack, then tack back to the north and pass between Pointe Caracoli and the 5-fathom spot southeast of the point—it can break in heavy weather. Head northeast, ease sheets, and pass outside Table du Diable. Continue north in the deep water, staying out beyond the 10-fathom shelf, as the Atlantic swell coming into shoal water can really hump up. Once you turn west, there are two choices:

1. Sail west until Îlet Tartane bears 230 magnetic, then run in on this line of bearing until the south end of Îlet St. Aubin bears 285 or you can line up the buoy on Banc Mitan on a bearing of 278. Run west along either of these lines of bearing (don't sail *over* Banc Mitan!) and then pick up the entrance buoys to La Trinité.

2. Alternately, pass north of all the shoals, staying in deep water until the center of the beach at the head of La Trinité harbor bears approximately

195; jibe over and run south on this line of bearing, which will put Loup Ministre on your starboard hand. When you get into the harbor, anchor on the eastern side, off the beaches.

As for going the other way, from La Trinité to Cul-de-Sac Tartane, if it's blowing hard, I wouldn't. If you must, stand well north from La Trinité and do your windward work in deep water. The winter trades roil the sea over the shoals, making it very hairy to tack safely through them. In spring and summer, though, when the wind is south of east, you can easily short-tack up the beach and stay out of the current.

LA TRINITÉ
(II, 1, A, B, A-30, A-301; Sketch Chart III-8)

The town of La Trinité is much the same as the other towns on the east coast of Martinique, only

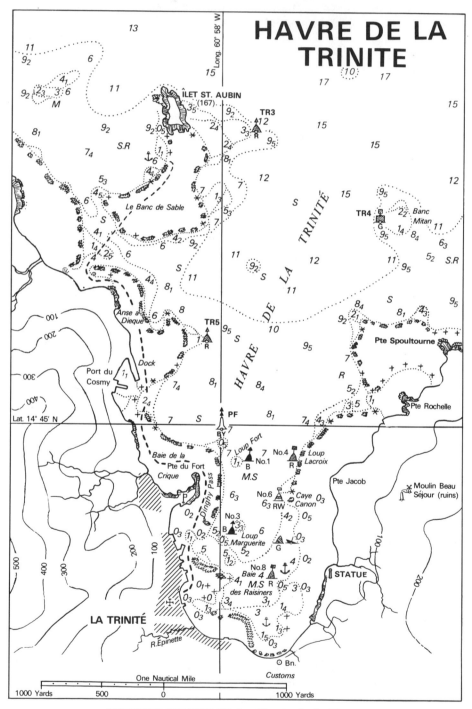

SKETCH CHART III-8   Havre de la Trinité

larger, with good road communication to Fort-de-France. La Trinité is a port of entry for Martinique but only for Customs. It is best to take a *taxi collective* into Fort-de-France to clear, a one-hour ride costing about $3.00 U.S.

The harbor would certainly be more convenient if the dinghy landing facilities were better. There are two small docks. One is by the fish market, and is also near a vegetable market, a supermarket, an ice storage plant with block ice, a couple of small, friendly bar / restaurants, a phone booth, and a nice waterside park. Be sure, though, to throw out a stern anchor to keep the dinghy from beating against the pier. The other dock is 200 yards south; here there is a beach, and if your dinghy is light enough you can slide it up on the beach above the high-water mark.

While at La Trinité, it is worth visiting the Hôtel St. Aubin, a wonderful old turn-of-the century French Victorian hotel, which I admired from afar. I am sure it would provide a perfect setting for a good three-hour French lunch. Call the hotel and arrange for a taxi.

ÎLET ST.-AUBIN
(II, 1, A, B, A-30, A-301; Sketch Chart III-8)

I visited this place for the first time in 1985, and I feel we have discovered an anchorage that is not included in any previous guides. That this is a good anchorage was news even to Philippe Lachesnez, who has spent his lifetime cruising Martinique's waters.

Approach it from the east as you would La Trinité, swing around the north end of St.-Aubin, jibe around the island, head south, eyeball your way right up behind the reef, and anchor in 50 to 60 feet of water, depending on how close to the reef you want to get. If you anchor really close to the reef, I would strongly advise anchoring bow and stern, as I am sure that during the night, when the wind dies down, a change in tide could swing you against the reef.

The swell hooks around Îlet St.-Aubin in a great circle and catches the western corner of the reef, so it's best to anchor about a third of the way down the reef (where the anchor is shown on the latest Imray-Iolaire charts). You will be guaranteed privacy and a calm, bug-free anchorage with a huge area to snorkle and dive. The number of fish-pot markers on the edge of the reef suggests that there must be a fair amount of fish around.

One of the great advantages of this anchorage is that you are only 1½ miles by dinghy from La Trinité; almost the entire trip can be made behind the reef, sheltered by the outer reef. (See the dinghy pass marked on Imray-Iolaire Chart A-30 and Sketch Chart III-8, plan of La Trinité Harbor.)

It is possible to sail south from Îlet St.-Aubin through the pass between the end of the St.-Aubin reef and the reef on the mainland; there is ample water and even room for *Iolaire* to tack in the passage.

West Coast

ST.-PIERRE
(II 1, A, B, A-30)

The town was totally destroyed by the eruption of Montagne Pelée early in this century. A museum commemorating the catastrophe is a spectacular tourist attraction. The anchorage is not good. For the most part it is an open roadstead; the swell usually runs in and the bottom drops off very steeply. Make sure that you are on the shelf before you let go the hook. Many a boat has almost lost its anchor when its depth gauge registered bottom—on the second time around the dial.

The best anchorage is off Pointe Ste.-Marthe, where there is a restaurant right at the water's edge, and a group of *gommiers* pulled up on the beach.

There is good diving on the wrecks of the ships sunk when the volcano blew in 1902—only one ship out of about thirteen or fourteen escaped destruction. The wrecks are plotted in the *Cruising Guide to Martinique*. Lachesnez recommends that you contact the Carib Scuba Club, Hôtel Latitude Carbet; they run regular diving tours to the area, know the wrecks, and are fully equipped to take you diving.

St.-Pierre is a good place to stop if you have had a rough trip from Dominica and arrived late in the day, and want to rest before heading south to Fort-de-France. Conversely, if you have left Fort-de-France at midday or later, then St.-Pierre is a good place to stop for the night prior to an early-morning departure for Dominica.

The weather conditions in Rade de St.-Pierre are variable—sometimes flat calm, sometimes blowing like mad, and other times with hard gusts suddenly dropping down off the mountains. Take care.

POINTE DES NÈGRES
(II 1, A, B, A-30)

This is an excellent shelter in normal weather. The only difficulties are posed by deep water and the lack of swinging room. In the past, arrangements could be made to moor bow and stern to the dock; however, I am informed that this is now a private club of the French military and is closed to visitors.

In conclusion, I would say that Martinique is probably the most underrated island in the Caribbean for the average yachtsman. After having spent three years in the mid-1980s reexploring the Caribbean from Mona Island to Trinidad and Tobago, and having hit every island between, my wife and I have come to the conclusion that Martinique is our favorite. Do not judge the island by the anchorage at Fort-de-France off the Savanne or the pleasant but crowded Anse Mitan. Go explore the other harbors, especially those on the east coast.

The only problem we found with the east coast is drinking water. After leaving the Fort-de-France area, the only place with even a possibility of getting water alongside is Club Nautic in Cul-de-Sac du Marin—and even that's iffy. So take a minimum of eight five-gallon, collapsible water jugs and be prepared to carry your water out in the dinghy.

Otherwise, the east coast is a cruiser's delight. Don't miss it.

NOTES

NOTES

NOTES

NOTES

NOTES

3

St. Lucia

II 1, B, B-1

St. Lucia, a semi-independent British affiliate, lies between Martinique to the north and St. Vincent to the south, and on most days it is visible from both these islands. There are two good harbors and sundry anchorages on its western side. The harbors were the cause of violent clashes between colonial powers in the eighteenth and early nineteenth centuries. Castries, the capital of St. Lucia, was important to the British as a fleet harbor in the eighteenth century and as a coaling station in the nineteenth. It was continually built up and fortified until the early years of the twentieth century. During the 1920s, its importance declined with the passing of coal-burning ships, and the island fell into an economic depression. The activities of World War II and the establishment of a large American base at Vieux Fort revived the economy for a brief period, but soon after the war the air base was closed, and the island returned to third-world oblivion. In the very earliest colonial days the island had grown rich off its sugar; now a second economy based on sugar, bananas, and tourism is established, and St. Lucia is stirring again.

Because of its many hills and mountains, St. Lucia is one of the wet islands. During the wet season, it seems to rain almost continually, tapering off in the dry season to a couple of short squalls per day. Although the island is high, it is not the solid block of Dominica. It is more like a series of ventilated hills, and a breeze is usually to be found along the western coast close inshore.

The tides are so minimal that they are not listed on the tide tables. I found an old British chart that listed the HWF&C as "1 h 36m" (high water full and changed: the average interval between the transit—upper or lower—of the full or new moon and the next high water). The current north and

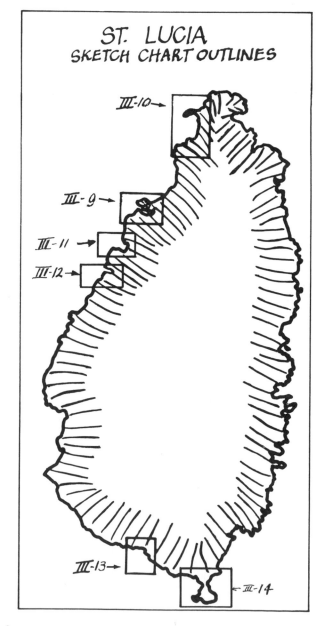

ST. LUCIA
SKETCH CHART OUTLINES

III-10→

III-9→

III-11→

III-12→

III-13→

←III-14

south of the island sets into the Caribbean at a knot or more.

Because of inaccuracies found in both the British and American charts, I recommend using Imray-Iolaire Chart B-1 exclusively.

St. Lucia has a number of good hotels and restaurants, although the island's restaurants open and close with great frequency. It is not a bad idea to ask the various marine operators which restaurants are currently the best.

Air communication into St. Lucia is excellent in that it is served by Island Air, LIAT, and Air Martinique, all of which "island hop" to St. Lucia through Vigie Field, which is right next door to the harbor of Castries. The old American World War II airbase near Vieux Fort is now called Huinora, and its runways have been extended to carry even the biggest jumbo jets. Now St. Lucia receives jets that fly direct from many parts of the world.

There is only one fly in the ointment. When it was decided that the old airbase would be St. Lucia's major airport, the British government financed a beautiful highway from Vieux Fort to Castries to reduce the driving time from three hours on a treacherous road to one hour on an excellent road. As part of the deal, a bus service was to have been installed from the airport direct to Castries, Vigie Field, and the hotels just north of the town at Rodney Bay. However, this has never come to pass. Thus St. Lucia is a very poor transfer point, as one flies in from Europe and then gets stung for a $50 E.C. taxi ride to Castries, to the hotels, or to Vigie Field for transportation to other islands in the Eastern Caribbean.

There is a good open-air market in the town of Castries, as well as three or four stores where frozen foods, canned goods, and so forth are available. The yachtsman will have no problem securing all the normal food supplies.

A visit to Bagshaws, two miles or so out of town, is a must. Here you will find dresses, skirts, and decorative yet practical items for the home made of silkscreened cotton, silk, and linen. There are also lengths of material to be made up by the nimble-fingered, and the visitors are welcomed to the studio to see how it's done. Go by taxi and ask the driver to wait.

A very worthwhile excursion when visiting St. Lucia is a trip on Bob Elliot's *Unicorn*, a brig fully rigged to the royals—she looks like something out of the last century. Needless to say, she has a diesel engine, but given favorable wind conditions, Bob and his excellent crew really sail the boat. Even the most experienced ocean racer will get a

thrill and be extremely interested in the sail handling of the square rigger.

When approaching St. Lucia from the north, there are no dangers lying off the coast. Castries is easily identified during the day by the forts on Vigie Point, and at night by the lights on either side of the harbor entrance. Do not stop at Pigeon Island before entering Castries; wine smuggling is a great occupation here, and the authorities take a dim view of yachts that stop before clearing at Castries. (Or, alternatively, you can clear at Rooney Bay in the lagoon—depth 8 feet. Alert Customs and Immigration by calling on VHF channel 16.) When coming from the south, unless you are heading for Vieux Fort (a port of entry), head directly for the Pitons, which are very easy to spot at a great distance, appearing like two loaves of French bread standing on end on the southwest corner of the island. There is only one hazard. On the lee side of St. Lucia, off Grand Caille Point north of the Pitons, the rocks extend 200–250 yards offshore. They have only a few feet of water and a tide rip over them most of the time. Give them a wide berth.

Castries is the main port of entry to St. Lucia, but as of March 1985, Customs offices were also established on the west coast in Rodney Bay Marina and Marigot Bay (Hurricane Harbour Hotel). Contact them via VHF channel 16 to give advance warning before you enter. Vieux Fort, on the extreme southern tip of St. Lucia, is also a port of entry.

The good news is that you can now also get preclearance at Soufrière. Anchor bow to the beach and clear with the local police sergeant. His clearance will cover you until you get to an official port of entry. This welcome development is a vast improvement over the old days when there was no entry point south of Marigot Bay on the west coast. It meant that anyone coming to St. Lucia from the south who succumbed to the temptation to anchor at the Pitons or Soufrière along the way was illegal and in danger of incurring fines or even jail. (I'd like to think that my sounding off about this situation in earlier guides had something to do with the new rule.)

Beware, though. I hear through the grapevine that Customs *still* takes a dim view of yachts anchoring at the Pitons before clearing. Now, though, Soufrière is just a stone's throw away.

CASTRIES
(II B-1; Sketch Chart III-9)

The harbor is deep, well sheltered, and easy to enter. So easy is the entrance that during World

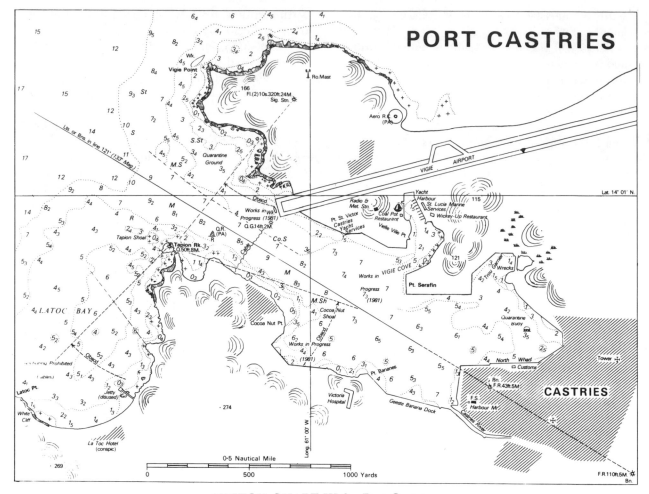

SKETCH CHART III-9   Port Castries

War II a German submarine entered after dark, sank a freighter along the dock, and departed, allegedly leaving an unexploded torpedo embedded in the soft mud under the town.

There is deep water up to fairly close inshore. As of March 1986, dredging and filling were still going on in Castries Harbor on the northern side on the Vielle Ville shoal southeast of Vigie Cove; in addition, a barge sunk off the end of the airport runway, supposedly lit, has not been moved. Exercise caution in this area.

If you must enter at night (I would advise against it) follow the range—two fixed red lights—right into the harbor. The range may seem to cast you very close to the south shore of the harbor, but this is correct and there is nothing to worry about except that the dredge companies are notoriously lax about lighting their equipment. In a contest of yacht against dredge, the dredge will win, Keep an eye out.

To clear Customs, anchor off the north side of

the east-west wall of the steamer dock. You may tie up alongside the dock, but this is not really advisable, as Castries has long had a reputation for having the most unfriendly, and foulest-mouthed, longshoremen in the Lesser Antilles. Their language will blister the paint right off your boat. Better anchor off the dock and row ashore in the dinghy to clear Customs and Immigration, which is right on the dock.

When anchoring here, stay clear of the turning basin; be sure you are positioned east of the white, unlit, quarantine buoy. If you are anchored in the turning basin, the pilot launch will tell you in no uncertain terms to move.

After clearing at Castries, if you're not ready to move on to Rodney Bay, Marigot Bay, or other more scenic spots, it's best you go back to Vigie Cove on the north side of Castries Harbor.

The harbor improvements have made trouble in Vigie Cove. The main harbor has been dredged right to the mouth of the cove, and the east and northeast sides of the cove have been covered with stone riprap. Now the cove, which used to be a semi-hurricane shelter, has become untenable whenever the northwest ground swell comes in. The swell ricochets off the stone riprap and finds its way into the innermost reaches of Vigie Cove.

Furthermore, when you anchor in the mouth of the cove, you find an almost vertical slope, as the bottom drops off suddenly from 10 to 35 feet. If you let out enough scope, your swinging circle (the wind frequently dies during the night and comes in light from the west) is just too large; either use a Bahamian moor or anchor bow and stern. Also be aware that the *Unicorn* and the *Jolly Roger*, both big vessels, do day trips almost every day. Leave them enough room to maneuver.

At Vigie Cove one finds St. Lucia Marine Services, formerly known as Ganter's, where for twenty years Gracie Ganter took care of itinerant yachtsmen and charter skippers. She acted as fairy godmother to us all. Now Gracie is back in England; various people have taken over the operation, but no one seems to have established a first-rate marina. Still, St. Lucia Marine Services is useful for taking on fuel, water, and a fair selection of food supplies from their commissary. They also have showers. Eight feet can be squeezed into the docks.

More yacht facilities are available now at the Castries Yacht Center, newly established on the north side of the harbor, just east of the airport runway. They have a thirty-ton travel lift, and provide hauling and long-term storing facilities. (Box 120, Castries, St. Lucia; telephone: 809-480-9453 or 4253.)

To get bottled gas in Castries, take your bottles to the Texaco depot in town; it's a bit hard to find, as it is in a lumber warehouse about two blocks south of the western end of the commercial docks. Leave the bottles and they will be filled by the following day. (You can also get bottled gas in Rodney Bay, at Stevens Yachts, where Ian Cowan, with his usual efficiency, can fill your bottles while you wait; if a bottle is half full, he'll charge you for only what he puts in it.)

Ice on St. Lucia used to be cheap in 200-pound blocks; now it's available at the cold storage plant only in small ten-pound blocks, or at St. Lucia Marine Services by the bag in cubes.

Laundry services are extremely expensive, and the commercial laundry in town is a dead loss. It is best to find a local laundress—but check the price first. (Or, again, wait till you get to Rodney Bay, where Stevens Yachts has laundry machines.)

Near St. Lucia Marine Services is a small restaurant, the Wicky-Up, that serves drinks and short-order meals.

On the opposite side of the cove, facing St. Lucia Marine Services, is Bob Elliot's Coal Pot restaurant, where one can get superb food and wine in a lovely setting, with entertaining conversation from Bob Elliot, who has been in and out of the islands for more than twenty years. Reservations are usually necessary. The prices are not cheap, but it's worth it if you can afford it. It also has the advantage that you can come and go by dinghy. To sit on the Coal Pot's open porch hearing the water lap under your feet and looking at the moon over the tall masts of *Unicorn* makes for a memorable evening.

Elliot can also put you in touch with his brother-in-law, Mr. O. Alceé, whose Dive St. Lucia operation is on Vielle Ville Point (Box 412, Castries).

PIGEON ISLAND AND RODNEY BAY
(II B-1; Sketch Chart III-10)

An excellent anchorage for yachts. It is illegal to put in to Pigeon Island if you are coming from Martinique. You must clear through Castries, Rodney Bay, or Marigot Bay beforehand. Pigeon is an island in name only, as it has been connected to the mainland by a causeway. This gives full shelter from the sea hooking around the northern corner of the island, and the causeway is low enough that it doesn't block the wind, allowing for a cool and bug-free anchorage in 12 feet of water. The causeway has created a wonderful harbor, although it has spoiled the seclusion of Pigeon Island. The island was formerly a bird sanctuary, but I suspect the influx of cars and day-trippers has driven the birds away.

If you are approaching Pigeon Island from Castries, hug the coast. There are no hazards and you should be able to make it in one tack. Head for the thatched huts on the south side of the island, round up behind the causeway, and anchor about 200 feet offshore. But stay south of the dock on Pigeon Island, since the water shoals to 3 or 4 feet directly off the dock. Do not anchor too close to the east coast of Pigeon Island, as this can be a lee shore; but the causeway and the island of St. Lucia to windward will break any sea, although you may experience a small chop.

If you want a calmer anchorage, work your way up to the northeast of St. Croix Roads. (The American chart is wrong here—use Sketch Chart III-10.) In December 1978, we found an excellent

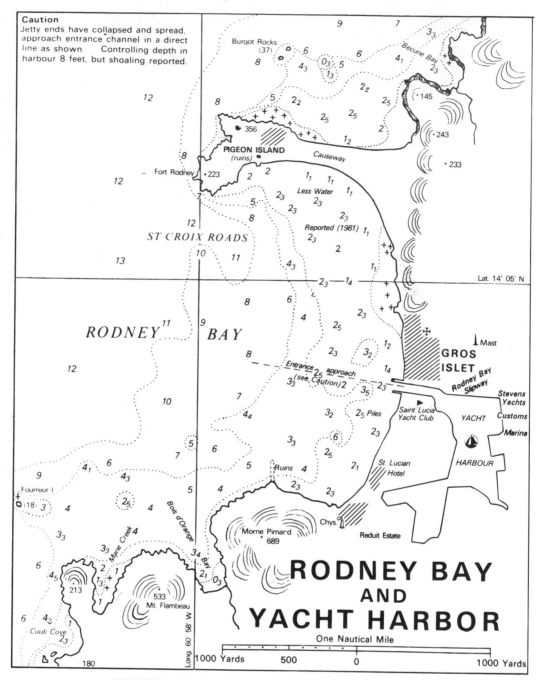

SKETCH CHART III-10   Rodney Bay Yacht Harbor

anchorage in 10 feet of water with the fort on an eastern peak of Pigeon Island bearing 315, a distinctive cliff north of the causeway bearing 035, and the breakwaters forming the entrance to Rodney Bay bearing 155 magnetic. Feel your way in with the fathometer and / or lead line.

Pigeon Island was formerly owned by Mrs. Josette Leigh, better known in yachting circles as Madame Snowball. Her thatched-cottage hotel on the beach vied with Mary Pomeroy's Beachlands on Nevis as

the most famous and hospitable hotel in the Lesser Antilles. Mrs. Leigh sold out some years ago and the hotel is no more. The thatched cottages still stand. Visitors are welcome to tramp about or visit the old ruins. A climb to the top of the watchtower at Fort Rodney is well worthwhile.

These waters may be the only place in the world where fish are still caught with rocks. Two or three mornings a week, about twenty-five dugout canoes assemble off the beach. Nets are strung out at right angles to the shore and the canoes are laden gunwale-deep with rocks gathered from shore. The canoes arrange themselves in a line some few hundred yards off, where the fishermen wait for a school of fish to come along. When the fish are sighted, the natives throw the rocks to drive the fish into the nets, which are then looped together and dragged ashore. This is a wonderful opportunity to take some good photographs, as well as to obtain fresh fish at reasonable prices. The fishermen are friendly and enjoy having strangers help them haul the nets.

South of the village of Gros Islet is the dredged channel to the lagoon of Rodney Bay Harbor, originally referred to as "Rotten Bay" by the charter skippers of the Stevens fleet who arrived in the early stages of the development when nothing much was there. Whoever decided to do the dredging did not do his homework, since it was dredged to a controlling depth of only 8 feet—there are *not* the 12 feet in Rodney Bay indicated in other guidebooks. Ian Cowan, general manager of Stevens Yachts, agrees that the controlling depth must be regarded as 8 feet. Admittedly a couple of the Swan 65 skippers who know and understand the tides can coax a Swan 65 into Rodney Bay Harbor on high-water springs, but that only gives them six days a month when they can get in and out. A day later in leaving means a ten-day delay.

In 1979, dredging was proposed again, and the talk was still going on in 1986. Rodney Bay will never be fully developed until the channel and the basin in the yacht harbor are dredged to 12 feet.

The harbor *does* finally have a full-service marina, though. It has good docks, water, electricity, marine supplies, a restaurant, and a specialty grocery store with goodies from Martinique.

Stevens Yachts has leased space in the marina, with Ian Cowan still in charge. Besides its charter business, Stevens also has a good sail loft, the best laundry facilities on the island, and the previously mentioned propane source. Ian Cowan, a man of many parts, helped me compile the Imray-Iolaire charts. He also stocks them and the Street guides.

Stevens has one of the better communications systems in the lower Caribbean: they stand by during working hours on SSB high-seas frequency 4139.5 from 1100 to 1130 and from 1500 to 1530, VHF channel 16 (address: P.O. Box 928, Castries; telex 333 Steve Yacht).

On the north side of the Rodney Bay yacht harbor the marina runs a fueling pier, hauling facilities with a fifty-ton travel lift, woodworking, fiberglass, paint, machine, and engine and electrical shops with ample storage space to dry-store boats.

You must be very careful when entering the harbor: various storms have dislodged rocks from the breakwaters; if you are off to one side or the other of the channel, you're sure to hit solid rock. Stay absolutely in the center of the channel.

From the gate of the marina there is excellent, cheap bus service to town. Before you get in, though, make sure it is a bus: the buses and taxis look the same, but the bus fare to town is $1 E.C. and the taxi fare is $14 per person. Be careful!

Within Rodney Bay Harbor are numerous restaurants that jut out over the water; an evening's pub crawl can be done by climbing in your dinghy and visiting the various restaurants. Since there seems to be considerable turnover, you'd better get up-to-date local information about what's open.

On the south side of the entrance to the lagoon is the St. Lucia Yacht Club—typical of the West Indian yacht club in that although its sign reads "Members Only," it really means "and visiting yachtsmen." So don't be put off. The club is active on weekends only, but an afternoon with the local yachtsmen is time well spent.

Over Whit Weekend (Whitsunday is a movable liturgical feast), the St. Lucia Yacht Club hosts a three-day version of the fun and games of Antigua Sailing Week's Lay Day festivities. It is also couples with the WIYA match-racing championships. Member clubs send teams, and Stevens Yachts and the Moorings provide the boats for a Congressional cup type match racing series.

GRAND CUL-DE-SAC BAY
(II 1, B, B-1; Sketch Chart III-11)

Two miles south of Castries, this bay is not too attractive. It has become a deep-water oil port, where large tankers—300,000 to 400,000, possibly 500,000, tonners—come to offload their oil into storage tanks, which are then transferred to small tankers, mere 100,000 tonners. Obviously not a yachting anchorage.

MARIGOT HARBOR
(II 1, B, B-1; Sketch Chart III-12)

Four miles south of Castries, this is a narrow, deep harbor. In years gone by, before the construction of the hotel and guest houses, yachts usually sailed right by Marigot without taking notice. Now it has become a popular anchorage. You will notice small cottages along the water's edge on the

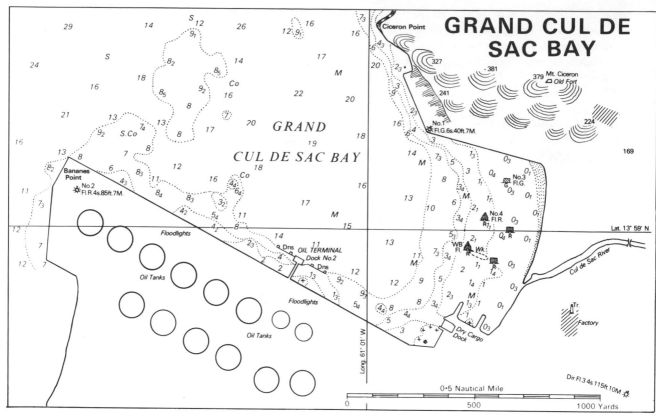

SKETCH CHART III-11   Grand Cul de Sac Bay

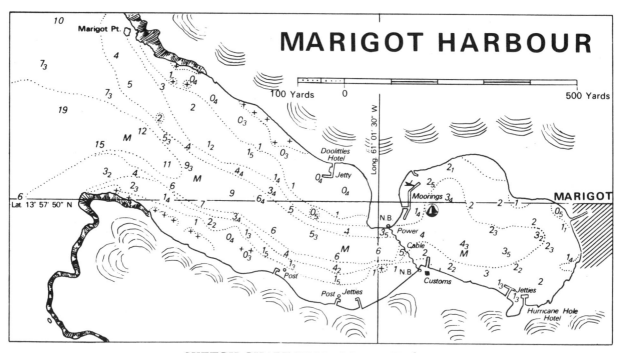

SKETCH CHART III-12   Marigot Harbor

north side of the harbor, and a lot of new houses on the steep hillside forming the south side. Entering is easy: favor the south side of the outer harbor; shoal water extends 200 yards west by north from the southern tip of the palm-covered spit on the north side of the entrance. Shoal water can easily be spotted in this outer section of the harbor.

When entering the inner harbor, stay north of the line of bearing of 090 on the end of the Customs jetty on the south side of the harbor or you may come to a grinding halt (as *Iolaire* once did) on a rock with 6 feet of water over it a hundred yards west of the Customs dock. Otherwise, tacking through the narrow neck to the inner harbor isn't a problem because there is deep water close to shore. In fact, it is perfectly possible to lay a large vessel alongside the end of the palm-covered spit on the north shore and moor to the trees with plenty of water. If you do this, set an anchor out to the southeast to hold her off. The one disadvantage of palm-tree anchorages is mosquitoes. For this reason, I prefer the middle of the inner basin off the new hotel and dock.

On the south side of the harbor at the ferry landing is Customs and Immigration, ably run by Scotty, who, along with M. Le Breton in Fort-de-France in Martinique, is a friend of the yachtsman. Both men are cooperative, humorous, and helpful.

Marigot Harbor is sheltered in all weather, even in a hurricane. In normal weather it is always calm and peaceful. On the south side of the inner harbor is the Hurricane Harbour Hotel, with a bar, a dining room, dancing to steel bands, and a dock with moorings and water available. Water is not plentiful, as it is all catchment water; Marigot Bay has not been connected to the water main. For this reason, showers were not available to yachtsmen—but there is a freshwater pool.

Marigot is now the southern base for the Moorings, the Tortola-based bare-boat charter service, which has taken over Doolittle's hotel cottages and the sandspit on the north side of the island. The hotel is still called Doolittle's (it's where the Rex Harrison movie *Dr. Dolittle* was filmed) and has excellent meals at a reasonable price and also a beach bar, where you can swim between drinks. The only problem is that it has the most hungry "no-see-ems" I have ever encountered. After 30 years in the Caribbean, I am pretty impervious to them, but Doolittle's takes the cake.

Doolittle's has a small launch that shuttles back and forth to the landing stage on the other side of the harbor—the signal for the ferry is three blasts on a car horn. If you are anchored in between and

want to go ashore, the launch will oblige. There is an underwater power cable crossing the bay, running southeastward from the tip of the sandspit, and this is marked with warning signs at either end. Do not anchor on top of it.

While anchored in Marigot Bay, read *Ramage and the Freebooters* by Dudley Pope; part of this novel is set in Marigot Bay.

Between Marigot Harbor and Grand Caille Point there are a number of anchorages that could be used as daytime stops for a swim: L'Anse-La-Raye, off the village of that name; L'Anse Cochon; and L'Anse des Canaries. They might be interesting to investigate, but only under the right conditions. They are definitely not all-weather anchorages. In any case, you should anchor bow and stern. A ground swell would make the anchorages completely untenable. I also wonder about the wisdom of spending a night where you don't know the sentiment of the local populace toward yachtsmen.

Those who like to dive might check over Anse Mamin just north of Grand Caille Point. Here you'll find the Anse Castenette Hôtel, good dinners, and a diving operation run by Nick Troobiscoff. Be sure to moor bow and stern, though, and be ready to move out if the ground swell builds up.

SOUFRIÈRE
(II 1, B, B-1; Sketch Chart III-12)

South of Rachette Point, north of Petit Piton, Soufrière is the second largest town on St. Lucia, and, although it is not a port of entry, you can get preclearance here, as mentioned above.

Anchoring off the town of Soufrière is virtually impossible, as the bottom drops off almost vertically and the dock, as of March 1985, was in a very bad state of disrepair. The only really possible anchorage in Soufrière Harbor is in the northeast corner, off the Hummingbird restaurant. Sail on in, drop a stern anchor, call on VHF channel 16, or sound a horn and Harry, the handyman and general factotum, will grab your bow line and tie it onto a tree. I am told that Joyce at the Hummingbird will provide a memorable meal at a reasonable price. Tucked in here, you are well sheltered by Rachette Point from the northwesterly ground swell. Moored bow and stern, the yacht should be perfectly safe under any normal conditions.

The major attractions of Soufrière are the sulfur baths and volcano. A taxi may be hired to take you to both spots. The baths are reported to be refreshing and invigorating, something just short of a fountain of youth. The volcano is one of few in the world whose crater can be explored without a lot of mountain climbing. It is immensely popular, although some people may say that it is nothing more than a blowhole on a hillside.

ANSE DES PITONS
(II 1, B, B-1; Sketch Chart III-12)

A short way south of Soufrière is by far the most spectacular anchorage in the Lesser Antilles. On either side are the Pitons, towering about 2500 feet in the air. At the head of the bay in the northeast corner is an excellent anchorage, off the Jalousie boathouse, as long as you are able to find bottom. The only way to moor is to sail in close, drop a stern anchor about 50 yards offshore, luff up, and have someone jump off the bow with line to tie to a coconut tree. I have lain within half a boat length of shore and had plenty of water under the keel. Be sure that your stern anchor is well set, as hard gusts (back eddies off North Piton) can blow you down on the rocks to the south of the boathouse. Further, although it seldom happens, the ground swell can sometimes find its way into this northeast corner; if it does, you will have to get out fast before the stern anchor drags and you are high and dry on the beach.

In years gone by, one would usually have the Pitons all to oneself and nothing but the friendliest of locals on shore; inevitably times have changed, and nowadays you'll probably find eight or ten yachts moored bow-in to the palm trees and small urchins demanding money to tie you up to a tree. You'd better pay them, or they're likely to cut you loose at night.

This situation in the Pitons was really getting out of hand in the early 1980s, when Ian Cowan of Stevens and Bruce Cameron of the Moorings, with the aid of some of their St. Lucian friends, launched a massive education campaign to convince the boat boys that they would make more money by being friendly to the yachtsmen than by frightening them off. I am told the drive has borne fruit, and they are much more friendly ashore. Still, I advise you check with Stevens Yachts or the Moorings before visiting the Pitons.

Another hazard is that fishermen will often claim they cannot set their nets because the yachts are in the way—they demand money to compensate them for fish not caught. This is an absolute racket. Net fishing is never done in this northeast corner of the harbor, one reason being that the water is much too deep for net fishing. If you are approached

with this tale, tell the fishermen you are going to call the police on your VHF; this usually scares them off.

Ian Cowan has, in fact, presented the police in Soufrière with a VHF, so you might actually be able to reach the police if you call. I'm not sure it would do much good, though, because getting to Piton from Soufrière by road is none too easy. What these islands need, incidentally, rather than the big 70- to 110-foot patrol boats they are building, is a fleet of 35- to 40-foot police launches built to be fast, maneuverable, and indestructible. Police and Customs launches in the Eastern Caribbean seem to have a life expectancy of about three years, but "it is an ill wind that blows no good." The unreliability of the boats, coupled with the inability of the Customs and police to maintain their boats, does not help the yacht yards in the area.

Ashore you will find some most interesting ruins, and an old coconut plantation that has been bought by Colin Tennant. No one seems to know his plans for the place, but one of his first acts was to buy an elephant in India and hire an elephant handler, or mahout. Both were brought to St. Lucia, and now an elephant happily wanders through the estate munching grass and leaves. It is certainly a much easier life than pushing teak logs through the forests of India or Burma! (A word of warning: Evidently small boys have been teasing the elephant, and as a result the animal is not always friendly. Do not approach the elephant unless the mahout is around.)

If you enjoy exploring the countryside, my friend John Clegg says to take a cab down the Choiseil Road from Soufrière. Go about four miles and take the road to the right. It's not much of a road and the driver will probably protest, but take it just the same. Bounce along for another mile until you reach a group of houses. Although the inhabitants speak no English, for five or ten dollars one or two of them will guide you to Gros Piton. If the weather has been dry, it will be about a two-and-a-half-hour scramble. The route swings around the south of Gros Piton at roughly 600 feet and climbs the west ridge from there. At the top you will find yourself in the thick of a mahogany forest. Climb a tree and take a gander. The view will prove well worth the struggle.

George McLellan, who has also made this trip, recommends contacting Tonka Prosten, who can be found in Soufrière; ask at the Texaco service station in the middle of town. He can rustle up a taxi driver who will take you to the closest approach to Gros Piton, about a mile outside Soufrière; he knows the way up quite well. McLellan advises setting out around 0700 so you get back down to town or the harbor by noon or so, before it gets too hot.

The hike to Petit Piton is another worthy struggle. Again, you will need a guide. The route goes up the col from the anchorage toward Soufrière to about 800 feet, then down again to about 200 feet before winding its way up the northwest ridge. For the most part, the trip is a pretty standard scramble through thorn scrub, with the exception of a 30-foot patch of rock, where some basic climbing technique may be required. The top of the piton is open and breezy. If you clamber down about 150 feet and climb a tree, you can get a good shot of your boat anchored at Jalousie. Allow about six hours for the entire trip up and back. Be damn sure to take some liquid refreshment.

LABORIE
(II 1, B, B-1; Sketch Chart III-13)

Laborie, on the chart but seldom visited, is a most intriguing anchorage. This harbor should be entered only under ideal conditions with the sun high. The man who made the Admiralty chart appears never to have seen the harbor. The reef on the eastern side of the entrance to Laborie Harbor is not as indicated on that chart, but extends at least 150 yards westward from the eastern point.

To enter, bring the houses on the western side of town to bear about 015 magnetic and keep a good lookout to starboard. Once the reef is abeam to starboard, head northeast toward the church, round up, and anchor wherever it is convenient. There are about 9 feet of water in the harbor.

Mike Smith of *Phryna* has warned to keep an eye on the rain clouds before entering Laborie. In heavy rainfall the stream that empties into the harbor spews out so much mud that it is impossible to find one's way in or out. Thus it might be wise to avoid this anchorage during the summer rainy season, or in periods of southeast winds. Phil and Joan Cardon of the Whitby 42-foot ketch *Glissade* report that they have made three visits to Laborie, enjoyed all the visits, found the people extremely friendly, and saw no other yachts. They pointed out, though, that a misprint in my 1974 guide resulted in a wrong range for this entrance. They favor the bearing, mentioned above, of 015 magnetic on the western end of town, which will keep

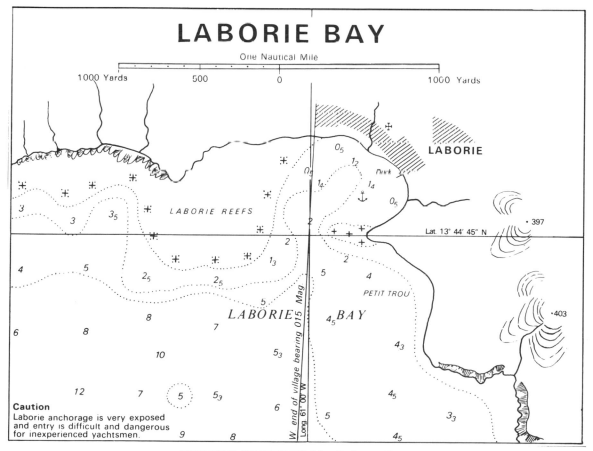

SKETCH CHART III-13   Laborie Bay

you close to the eastern edge of the reef. (It's always better in a channel to touch on the windward rather than the leeward reef.) If you'd rather be dead center in the channel, though, you might prefer a bearing of 020 to 025 magnetic.

VIEUX FORT BAY
(II B-1; Sketch Chart 14)

On the south end of St. Lucia, this is a large banana-loading port as well as a port of entry. Well to the east on the way north, it is difficult to lay from St. Vincent and is seldom visited by yachts. However, if you are disposed to visit Laborie and the Pitons without going to Castries first, you might do well to clear through Vieux Fort. In normal trade-wind weather this is a good anchorage. Use the area southeast of the large pier. (North of the pier is a prohibited zone.) When coming from the south, approach with Cross Hill (the hill north of Battery Point) in line with Morne

Belle Vue, bearing 035 magnetic. Go to the head of the harbor and anchor. Hoist your "Q" flag, go ashore, and find Customs.

There is not too much else ashore at Vieux Fort, but there is excellent reef diving and lobstering thereabouts. If you are the lazy sort, lobsters are cheaper to buy here than elsewhere in the Eastern Caribbean.

One advantage of anchoring southeast of the main steamer dock is that it is out of the swell and is only 500 yards across the spit of land to Point Sable Bay. I am told that the beach of Sable Bay is a full mile long, has pure white sand, and is completely deserted: a well-worthwhile walk for those who really like beaches.

POINT SABLE BAY
(II B-1; Sketch Chart 14)

I have seen Point Sable Bay from sea and from the air, and it intrigues me as an anchorage—but I

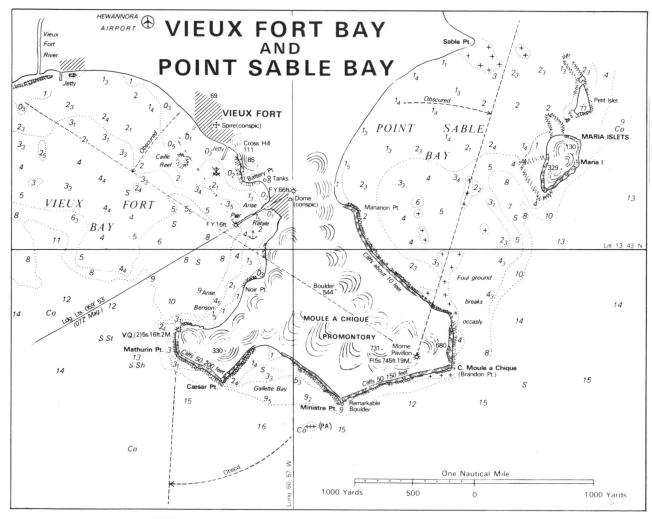

SKETCH CHART III-14   Vieux Fort Bay and Point Sable Bay

haven't tried it yet, nor have I talked to anyone who has. It looks as though a good anchorage would be in the lee of Maria Island, with its northern hill bearing about southeast, tucked in behind the reef. Pure speculation on my part—but it looks like a good spot to get away from it all. Exploration of this anchorage should be done only by experienced sailors under *ideal* conditions.

The eastern shore of St. Lucia has some small coves that are used by the natives for launching canoes, but there is nothing that can be really called a harbor. I know of no yacht that has visited this area.

One last work of warning: *Under no circumstances should one swim in St. Lucia's streams.* There is a parasite in the water that can enter the bloodstream and cause all kinds of trouble. This is the same parasite that plagues the upper reaches of the Nile in the area of the Aswan Dam.

NOTES

NOTES

NOTES

4

St. Vincent

II 1, B, B-3, B-30

St. Vincent is somewhat smaller than St. Lucia, its neighbor to the north. It is a lush, wet island with peaks rising to well over 3,000 feet. Sections of it have been lavishly cultivated, the crops laid in neat green tiers reminiscent of the English countryside. From the sea, the town of Kingstown presents a pleasing aspect, nestled in a hollow with mountains rising around. The island was discovered by Columbus on his third voyage to the New World. Like Dominica, it had been populated by Carib Indians who resisted every attempt to colonize the island. Only when the Caribs became embroiled in their own civil war were the Europeans able to establish a presence on the island. In 1675, a slave ship bound from Africa went down off St. Vincent. Many of the slaves swam ashore and settled, producing through intermarriage the Black Carib of today.

The story of St. Vincent is one of continuous warfare. The Caribs entrenched themselves at the north end of the island while the British settled and fortified the towns of Kingstown and Calliqua. The Caribs were supported against the British by the French, who imported other Caribs as mercenaries from neighboring islands, primarily St. Lucia. These hired Caribs always landed on the northeast and northwest of the island, grouped, and proceeded south overland against the British. It is for this reason that many of the old fortifications on the island, such as those on Duvernette Island, Dorsetshire Hill, Richmond Peak, and Sion Hill, and the earliest ruins at Fort Charlotte, all have their cannons aimed inland.

When the Caribs were finally conquered, around 5,000 of them were placed on the island of Baliceaux and later shipped to British Honduras. How they managed to cram 5,000 people onto an island the size of Baliceaux is very difficult to imagine, and I suspect the loss of life was heavy.

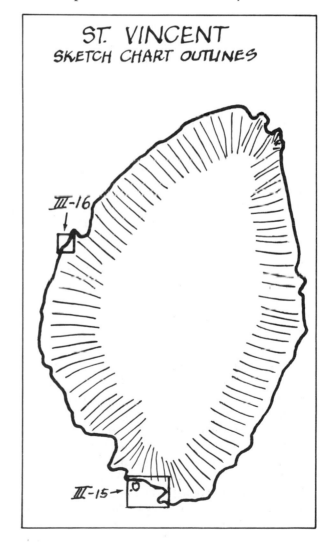

ST. VINCENT
SKETCH CHART OUTLINES

III-16

III-15 →

There are a number of good hotels on St. Vincent. The best thing to do is pick up a tourist guide to the island which lists all the hotels. They are varied, and you are sure to find a hotel to suit your taste and pocket.

The shopping situation, from a yachtsman's standpoint, is not too good. There is no really good big supermarket. Instead, you have to go from store to store and spend a day acquiring about half of what you really want. The open-air market is excellent and operates every day from 0800; if you want to get the best, arrive early. Ice is available at the ice cream factory. Fuel is obtainable by appointment with the Shell agent at Hazel's store, and arrangements can be made for it to be delivered at the steamer dock.

The dock was clearly not designed with yachts in mind. It is a miserable place to lie, especially when the ground swell is running. Unfortunately, this is the only place in Kingstown Harbor where fresh water can be had.

There is deep water all along the jetty. The best place to anchor at Kingstown, a port of entry, is around the northeast corner. Get your bow close to shore, drop anchor, and ease your stern into the dock right next to the steps where the small bum boats offload.

During Hurricane Klaus, in November 1984, a small freighter sank in the northeast corner of the harbor; it was in deep water and wouldn't have caused a problem except that its mast was sticking up to within six feet of the surface. As of January 1985, the obstruction was still there, marked by a tiny buoy that looked more like a fish-pot marker. The mast may have been cut off by the time you read this, but don't count on it. Once you have cleared, I would advise moving out of Kingstown to another anchorage as soon as possible.

I suggest you *not* spend the night in Kingstown—and so does no less a personage than the Honorable James "Son" Mitchell, premier of St. Vincent. He has told me that any yachtsman is crazy who does anything in Kingstown but clear and leave. The problem is that dinghy and outboard pilferage is rife, and the authorities so far haven't been able to do much about it.

One large yacht was victim of a particularly galling theft. Its St. Vincentian crew had a girlfriend ashore and he asked permission to take the dinghy and leave it tied up overnight to the St. Vincent Coast Guard vessel *Captain George McIntosh*. The yacht's skipper figured that would be safe and gave permission. Next day the dinghy arrived back, but the outboard was gone. The deck

watch on the *McIntosh* (which keeps a twenty-four-hour watch) gave the usual West Indian reply, "Me no know," and a shrug of the shoulders.

If you are coming from the north, I hardly think it worthwhile to clear through Kingstown at all. From Johnson Point it is a hard beat to the jetty in the northeast corner of the bay. Much time is lost in maneuvering your way safely to the jetty, and thence through Customs. Once cleared, you are required to leave, and from the jetty it is two and a half miles against wind and current to the nearest amenable anchorage, at Young Island. The better way by far is to take a beam reach from Johnson Point to Bequia and then a short sheltered beat up to Admiralty Bay. This is a fine (if crowded) anchorage where you may clear at your leisure and pass the night. If you then wish to visit St. Vincent, you can sail directly to the anchorage at Young Island or Blue Lagoon, thereby postponing indefinitely the suspect pleasures of the Kingstown jetty.

If, after all the above, you still decide to clear at Kingstown, call the lighthouse at Kingstown Harbor on VHF channel 16 and ask that a message be relayed to Customs and Immigration so they will expect you. The procedure then is to go alongside the landing stage on the northeast corner of the main ship jetty, not the small easternmost jetty used by the local schooners. There is usually a surge, so make sure you have plenty of fenders and strong spring lines. Customs is right there on the dock and they will usually get the Immigration officer by telephone. Otherwise, walk south along the front street; Immigration is found on the ground floor of the police department. Immigration nearly always insists on boarding the boat even if you are anchored out. They do so with boots that usually have gravel lodged in the soles—not too good for paintwork and teak decks.

One charter skipper had a solution to this problem—he always anchored out and dumped a couple of buckets of water into his dinghy before rowing ashore. When the police officers complained, he apologized, saying he had a leaky dinghy. By the time the officers came aboard, their shoes were somewhat cleaner and a bit squishy and somewhat less damaging to his paint and varnish. The next time the boat came in and he arrived with his "leaky" dinghy to clear, the officers, remembering their previous experience, cleared the boat without going on board.

Back in the early 1970s, St. Vincent levied a tax on all charter boats entering her waters. The tax itself was not too bad, but the precedent it set was scary. Since all the islands are semi-independent, a charter yacht visiting all the Lesser Antilles in a six-week cruise would have to shell out taxes to thirteen different governments. This would of course have to be passed on to the charterer, thereby increasing the coast of chartering.

Then, in January 1979, the St. Vincent government began to charge private yachtsmen huge fees. In order to make sure these were collected, Chateaubelair and Canouan were made Customs clearance stations, and the St. Vincent government bought a number of police launches. Predictably (since the life expectancy of a police launch in the Eastern Caribbean seems to be three years), the Customs stations in Chateaubelair and Canouan were closed three years later.

Over the winter of 1984–85, I had to stop off in the Grenadines to check on a few things for this revision of the *Cruising Guide*, and it cost me more than $99 E.C. to spend forty-eight hours in St. Vincent waters!

Now I'm glad to report that things have changed. James "Son" Mitchell, who was elected premier by a landslide in 1984, has done much to make St. Vincent's waters more hospitable to yachtsmen. Fees for charter boats have been much reduced, and there is *no* fee for visiting yachts; the head of Immigration has been replaced, and a more realistic attitude is being taken toward yachts stopping on the west coast of St. Vincent prior to clearing officially.

Mitchell, who is from a long line of seamen on the marine-oriented island of Bequia, pointed out to me that under certain weather conditions, for the safety of the vessel, the law allows a captain to anchor in an out-port prior to clearing. He also hinted that Customs and Immigration might turn a blind eye to any yachts stopping at Cumberland or Wallilabu bays before clearing, as long as they were not engaged in any illegal activity. I wouldn't take these suggestions as gospel, nor by any means expect to hold the premier to them, but they certainly are welcome indications that what has been a very difficult situation in St. Vincent might be improving.

St. Vincent is not without its oddities, although my favorite traffic sign was taken down sometime ago. This sign said, "Windward traffic, keep right. Leeward traffic, keep left."

The Catholic and Anglican churches in Kingstown are across the street from each other. The Anglican establishment is so high church it is hard to tell which church one has wandered into; if you hear what sounds like a good old-fashioned Catholic Mass, you're undoubtedly in the Anglican church.

Tourism is making its mark on the island. The hotels, restaurants, shopping centers, and cruise ships have arrived in the customary profusion. The expansion, however, has been hampered by the lack of a good airport. For years it was assumed to be impossible to build an airstrip on St. Vincent, until a young Grenadian engineer designed and executed a small one for DC-3s. To get around the space shortage, he built the strip uphill. The planes landed uphill and took off down, with gravity doing the extra work in both cases. Flying out in one of those old DC-3s fully loaded was the experience of a lifetime, and if it was blowing really hard in the wrong direction, you just didn't take off, occasionally for two or three days. Sometimes the stewardess would take the passengers from the last four rows and cram them up against the door of the cockpit so that, with the weight of the plane forward, the pilot could get the tail off a little faster. It worked fine in the Islands, but I wonder how an FAA inspector would have reacted to the procedure.

With LIAT Avro airplanes, there is no problem landing or taking off; it is more a question of when LIAT is motivated to dispatch a flight to St. Vincent. The St. Vincent government has extended the runway, night landings are regularly made, and LIAT's schedule has been rearranged so that one is no longer stranded in Barbados trying to get to St. Vincent, unless they have fouled up your reservations, which they do with alarming frequency.

It is interesting to note that Ron Smith, the young Grenadian engineer who in 1960 built the airport that could not be built on St. Vincent, was head engineer on Grenada's new international airport.

A taxi ride around St. Vincent is definitely worthwhile. One can rent a car, but it's better to take a taxi, for then the agriculture, customs, etc., of the island will be explained. Check with the hotels for a reliable and interesting driver.

The botanical garden in Kingstown is a must for those interested in flora, as it is by far the best botanical garden in the Eastern Caribbean.

KINGSTOWN BAY
(II 1, B, B-30, B-3; Sketch Chart III-15)
If possible, avoid, for the reasons described above. If you decide you must anchor in Kingstown Bay, do so in the northeast corner of the harbor, as that is the only place you will find water shoal enough to anchor. Beware of the previously

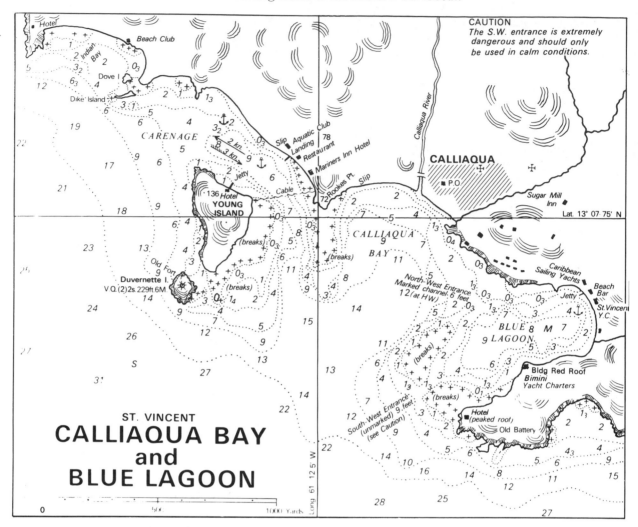

SKETCH CHART III-15   Calliaqua Bay and Blue Lagoon

mentioned wreck. The wind will box the compass, so set a Bahamian moor, or moor bow and stern.

YOUNG ISLAND
(II B, B-2, B-3; Sketch Chart III-15)

For many years this has been the most popular anchorage in St. Vincent, but anchoring here should be done with great care. It is frequently crowded, and when the tide starts running to windward the boats have a tendency to roam about a little erratically. Many a bow pulpit has been bent out of shape at the change of tide. The Bahamian moor is strongly recommended.

For many years we anchored with great success off the northeastern tip of Young Island, on a Bahamian moor in 10 feet of water immediately behind the submerged power cable. But when we sailed in there in 1985, we found 65 to 70 feet of water on our old spot. It turns out that the ground

swell that came in as a result of Hurricane Klaus in November 1984 completely changed the underwater topography of the area. We then spent three days dragging from one end of the anchorage to the other. The locals told us that the only decent anchorage now is in the northwestern corner of the Young Island anchorage, off the sand beach west of the Aquatic Club—if you can find room. Otherwise, you are anchoring in 70 to 80 feet of water and a rocky bottom.

I am told that the guns on the top of Duvernette Island are four 24-pound guns and two 8-inch mortars. They were mounted in two batteries facing landward to lob shells into the hills to keep the French and Caribs from attacking Calliaqua, then the major community on the island.

Once you do finally get anchored in the slot, as it is called, there are various facilities. If your anchors are well set and you can swing your stern in, you can take water on from the Aquatic Club, now run by Stilly Frazer, who also runs a nightly disco in a soundproof building; the noise supposedly does not disturb the neighbors.

Then comes a French restaurant, run by M. Simon Despointes; he has a lobster pound, so you can point to the lobster you want for dinner. Next is what I am told is a good and efficient laundry service. And there are Mariners Waters Sports, Mariners Windsurfing School, and Mariners Inn, a small hotel with bar, restaurant, and public showers.

Mariners Water Sports runs a sailboat for charter and offers diving trips, diving equipment, water skiing, and so on. They also have a boutique and a mail drop and they stand by on VHF channel 16. They also sell Imray-Iolaire charts and Street guides. This new organization, which has high hopes, is run by MacGregor Brisbane and Eric and Susan Holbrick, Box 639, St. Vincent. With difficulty, they can arrange to fill your water tanks and to have laundry done.

Youngs Island Hotel is extremely attractive; a wander through the buildings and gardens is well worthwhile. Check out the bar's excellent punches; there is evening entertainment some nights, and dinner is reported to be very good but expensive.

CALLIAQUA BAY
(II 1 B, B-3, B-30; Sketch Chart III-15)

An open, turbulent, and generally unattractive anchorage, unless you have it in mind to stop for a short while, row ashore, and watch the fishing boats being hauled up on the beach in the afternoon. These are interesting native boats, although not so well finished or maintained as the boats of Bequia.

In Calliaqua, one will also find Buhler's Fibreglass, a boatbuilding operation. They build multihulls on the foam-sandwich principle, and are apparently doing an excellent job, with orders coming from all corners of the world. It is a heartening example of someone bringing something to the Islands that is not only providing employment but also producing a product that is competitive in the world market. There are also always a couple of schooners in the process of construction onshore, and you'll have a good chance to see how these local schooners are constructed. Also on the beach is De Freitas' marvelous hauling rig, a great big rubber-tired cradle that looks extremely rough and ready and not capable of much; years ago, however, he did haul Mike Jarrold's *Lilly Maid*, a 54-foot cutter that drew nine feet of water.

BLUE LAGOON
(II B, B-3, B-30; Sketch Chart III-15)

With Caribbean Sailing Yachts' southern fleet of around forty-five boats based in Blue Lagoon, plus a few local yachts, Blue Lagoon is not the quiet anchorage it used to be. There is barely maneuvering room, much less anchoring space, and it is not run for visiting yachts or yachtsmen.

The only way a visiting yacht can use this harbor is to anchor bow-on to shore by the Sugar Mill Inn's beach bar. Approach shore slowly, throw out a stern anchor, and sail in until the bow nudges the sand; either bury an anchor in the sand or tie on to a palm tree. This means you can do without a dinghy.

There are two entrances to Blue Lagoon. The one most frequently used is the northwest entrance, which is strictly limited in draft. Basically it is a 6-foot channel (despite what other guides may say to the contrary), although greater draft may be *squeezed* through the channel at the right state of the tides, particularly in winter when the Caribbean is higher than in summer. (Similarly, at low-water springs, in late April, May, and June, one can touch with 5 feet!) It would certainly be a boon to all yachtsmen if CSY would set up a tidal gauge at each end of the channel so that with binoculars one could read the controlling depth at various stages of the tide.

There is another entrance on the southwestern corner of the lagoon which used to be marked with a stake; it is now completely unmarked. The sea has changed the channel slightly so that it is now rather a dogleg. The controlling depth in this channel has shoaled to around 9 feet. Approach this entrance from the southwest with a lookout in the rigging and you will spot the channel. Access to the channel is about 067. Run in on this course with good way on and sail between the breakers. As the reef to the northwest comes abeam, alter course to starboard, eyeballing it for the deepest waters. In periods of heavy weather, the swell breaks completely across this entrance, making entering somewhat like running a New Jersey inlet: only for the brave and the skilled.

Be wary of boat boys passing themselves off as pilots. In the winter of 1979, one boat picked up a so-called pilot in Kingstown and went hard aground trying to enter the southwestern channel. She was finally pulled off, but the salvage and repair bill was in the region of $15,000 U.S. Upon investigation, it was ascertained that the "pilot" never had been through this channel before. So many boats have bounced or gone aground sailing through the southwestern entrance that Alan Hooper, manager for many years of CSY, states categorically that boats must use the northwestern entrance at high water, proceed very slowly, and be very cautious if they draw more than 6 feet. I repeat that a depth gauge would save a lot of groundings.

From CSY, Bob Sacks and Bill Trewes run their diving operation, Dive Saint Vincent. I am told they are excellent divers; both are Australians who learned their diving on the reefs off Australia and Papua New Guinea.

The large, conspicuous house on the south side of Blue Lagoon offers water at a very reasonable rate, a facility regularly used by Stevens Yachts.

West Coast

CUMBERLAND BAY
(II 1, B-1, B-3, B-30; Sketch Chart III-16)

One of the few anchorages on the west coast of St. Vincent, this spot used to be a popular anchorage for boats bound from St. Vincent to St. Lucia. From Young Island to Castries, at the northern end of St. Lucia, it is an 80-mile sail, which is longer than most charter parties care to make. Hence, Cumberland Bay became the natural overnight layover. The bottom here drops abruptly from the shore. The best method is to ease in slowly, checking for bottom. As soon as you see it, drop a stern anchor and continue on ahead toward shore. Then you can either row the bow anchor into the shoal water or nudge your bow against the shoal, drop from there, and haul back on your stern line. Make sure your bow anchor is well set, or tied to a coconut tree, or you may find yourself drifting out to sea during the night. If you are entering the bay from the south, give the southwesternmost point a wide berth. There is a rock with 6 feet of water over it. A number of yachts have cut too close and have left behind large portions of their keels to commemorate the oversight.

Cumberland Bay has had a terrible reputation for years because of the rowdy and belligerent attitude of the boat boys on the beach and, tragically, because of the murder of Carl Schuster aboard his yacht there in 1976. Times change, though, and now it has been reported to me that the behavior of the local inhabitants has improved so much that the bay is an acceptable anchorage again.

One of the attractions of Cumberland Bay is Stevens' Bar, a disco and restaurant run by Girlyn and Elford Stevens (an ex-police officer who served in both Antigua and St. Vincent). In early 1985, it was serving meals at a reasonable price and, if you arranged beforehand, was offering island specialties. Like many new operations, the restaurant has had mixed reviews; make sure early on of the menu, the prices, and whether you are paying in U.S. or E.C.—this will avoid confusion and embarrassment later.

Mr. Stevens told me in early 1985 that he is planning to build a beach bar; if he does and staffs it with a couple of tough bartenders, that might ensure that the boat boys behave themselves.

The latest news, May 1986, is that a hydroelectric plant is being built in Cumberland Bay.

WALLILABU BAY
(II 1, B, B-3, B-3o; Sketch Chart III-16)

Because of the local problems in Cumberland Bay, nearby Wallilabu Bay has become the preferred anchorage within this area. The radio tower is incorrectly listed on the British and American charts but correctly placed on Imray-Iolaire on B-30. As you see on Sketch Chart III-16, it is on the hill forming the south corner of Wallilabu Bay.

About twenty-five years ago, the Stevensons (mistakenly referred to as the Livingstones in my previous guide) built a craft shop where they produced batik. The shop, on the water's edge, offered the batik at what was described as the best buy in the Caribbean. Now Mr. Stevenson's niece Jan and her husband, Steve Tattersall (no relation to the well-known doctor from Tortola), have taken over the operation. They are young and full of enthusiasm and are making a drive to improve everything.

The batik shop has elastic hours, since yachtsmen tend to have a few drinks at the bar in the evening and then buy some cloth—and then decide to buy some more before they leave at 0700 the next morning. Water is available, as is fuel in emergencies; batteries can be charged, and they have a certain among of welding equipment. The bus goes right by Wallilabu Bay and offers a cheap ride to Kingstown.

One of the nicest things about this anchorage is the beautiful small waterfall that's about a fifteen-minute uphill walk along the river road. Go about four in the afternoon; it will be a bit hot and tiresome, but then you can dive into the pool under the waterfall, take a shower, and wash your hair and clothes, and no one will complain about

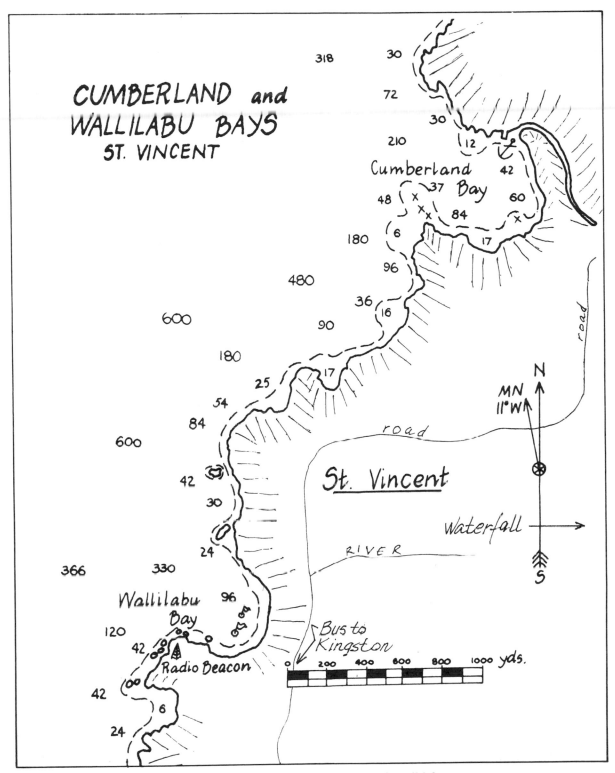

SKETCH CHART III-16 Cumberland and Wallilabu Bays

how much water you're using. By the time you're through, it's cool enough so that even after the walk downhill you're still feeling cool and fresh.

Another attraction is the freshwater crayfish (*écrevisse*, in Martinique) that the boat boys sell: beats saltwater shrimp seventeen ways to Sunday. The boys will ask astronomical prices, but they are negotiable; check with the Tattersalls for the going price. And since the boys sell the crayfish by the dozen and not by weight, check their size—which ranges from very big to tiny—before settling on a price. The boys spear the crayfish at night, so get your order in in the evening for the next morning. Since speared crayfish won't last as long as netted ones, you should eat them quickly.

Anchoring in Wallilabu Bay is straightforward. Sail in, drop a stern anchor about fifty yards off the beach, and coast on until you are about to run aground; one of the boat boys will immediately grab your bow line and run it up to a tree and then offer to do errands for you. Five dollars E.C. seems to be the going rate.

CHATEAUBELAIR

(II 1, B, B-3, B-30)

The northernmost town on the island of St. Vincent. Here again, although the charts do not properly show it, the bottom drops off very abruptly to 30 or 40 fathoms within a hundred yards of shore. The only way to anchor is with one anchor ashore and a second one to seaward. The best anchorage is on the small shoal north of the Fitzhughes estate as marked on the NOAA and Imray-Iolaire charts. This is good only in calm weather when the swell is down, but it's the best spot from which to set forth on an expedition of north St. Vincent. My good friend, the late George Freeman, told me that you can sail between Chateaubelair Island and the mainland; he did it a number of times in his *Rosemary V,* drawing 6½ ft. There are the ruins of an old estate at the village of Wallilabu. This is reputed to be one of the most primitive areas of the Lesser Antilles, by romantic accounts not unlike regions of darkest Africa.

In years gone by, as has been described in my previous guides, one of the interesting excursions when in St. Vincent was to climb to the rim of Soufrière volcano, see the lake below, and on a clear day look south the whole length of the Grenadines. It was a stiff uphill walk, not a mountain climb, but it was essential to bring a water bottle, good heavy shoes, and foul-weather gear in case it rained. Sometimes it was a great trip; other times a complete waste: you would arrive at the rim of the crater, the clouds would roll in, and you would see nothing but a good Maine pea-soup fog. The supposedly dormant volcano started sputtering off

and on in 1973, an island appeared in the crater lake, and then it all quieted down until it went off again with a bang in the spring of 1979, covering the island with ash and largely destroying the rich agricultural land on the east coast

The explosion of Mt. Pelé, on Martinique, is the one that always captured the imagination, but when Soufrière on St. Vincent blew up the day before Pelé 2,000 people were killed. Amazingly, some were killed all the way down in Kingstown by small pieces of flying rocks. People in Kingstown heard the explosion and rushed outside to see what had happened, and many were struck down.

You used to be able to climb to the rim of the volcano from the west coast by taking a dinghy up to the village of Morne Ronde, hiring a guide, and climbing. Alternately, the peak can be assaulted from the east by taking a cab to Orange Hill and following a fairly well-defined trail. I don't know if this is still possible and have not been able to find anyone who does.

There are undoubtedly other anchorages on the west coast of St. Vincent that have not been mentioned in this book, as I have done little exploring in that area. There is no wind along the lee of St. Vincent from 1600 or 1700 straight through to noon the next day, and even then it is a sometimes thing. However, if you have the inclination to explore, here are various anchorages that might prove attractive, working from south to north: the first cove north of Johnson Point (unnamed); then Questelles Bay; Anse Cayenne; the northeast corner of Buccament Bay; Laylou Bay; Anse Bonaventure; and, in summer when there's no ground swell, Petit Bordel, south of Chateaubelair Island.

A final place of interest to yachtsmen on St. Vincent is the waterfall at Grand Baleine at the north end of the island. The falls are quite spectacular and make for a good day-trip from Chateaubelair. One can go the six miles from Chateaubelair to Grand Baleine either by dinghy or under sail. If you sail, you must leave crew on the boat to stand off under shortened sail while the rest visit the falls. There is no hope of anchoring at Grand Baleine, as the cliffs are vertical to a great depth. In a way, this is typical of the problem faced by the yachtsman in St. Vincent. There is much to be seen ashore, but a definite shortage of dependable anchorages from which to set out.

NOTES

NOTES

NOTES

5

Barbados

II 1, B, B-2

Barbados lies 80 miles due east of St. Vincent. It is a hard windward slog to reach it, and very few of the boats that cruise the Lesser Antilles ever try to. As good as *Iolaire* is to windward, I've found that nothing goes into the wind quite as well as an LIAT plane, and to my mind this is the best way to get there. In most cases the yachts you will see in Barbados have arrived there from Europe.

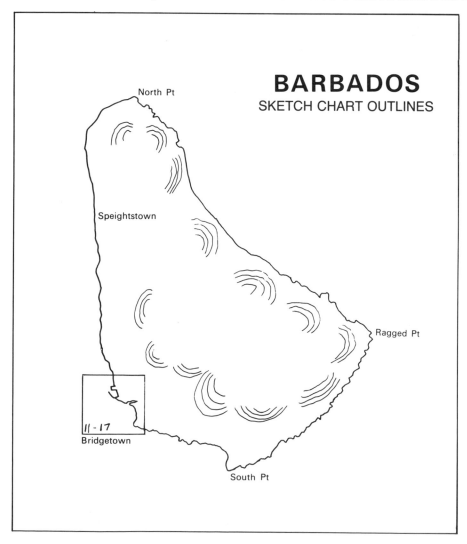

Too bad that Barbados is so far upwind (and has so poor an anchorage once you get there), because it is a very attractive island. Despite its being one of the most heavily populated areas in the world, with 1,400 people per square mile, it is neat, clean, and orderly. Certainly it is the best run of the Lesser Antilles. The people are polite, friendly, and helpful. They speak in the soft, musical tones of the Bajan accent and regard themselves as Englishmen rather than West Indians. For centuries Barbados has been referred to as "Little England," and justly so. The beautifully tended landscape little suggests a tropical island. There are neatly clipped lawns, a racing turf, a cricket field, and a proper little bandstand. The police are impeccably dressed, and the harbor police in their straw hats and white sweaters look like something out of another era. The spoken language is English; there is no patois or corruption with a foreign language. In short, the island shows clear signs of being the only one in the entire West Indies that has remained under a single flag.

The northeast trades have been its lifeblood, making travel from England a simple matter. By the same token the trades were its protection from rival colonial powers to the west. In those days of wooden ships and iron men, the windward ability of a warship was roughly that of a bathtub toy. It was impossible for the French to keep a fleet assembled through a long beat out to Barbados. They tried once or twice, became hopelessly scattered, and had to give it up.

Despite the generally low aspect of Barbados, its highest peak, Mount Misery, is 1,069 feet, and this is altitude enough to produce clouds that will often serve as a landmark well before the island itself comes into view. Barbados is well lighted and well charted; making a landfall at night presents no real difficulties. All corners of the island are marked with lights visible at great distances. While there are no off-lying hazards, bear in mind that there are a number of reefs on the coasts of the island, so do not hug the shore too closely. On the southeastern coast especially, the reefs extend offshore one and a half miles in places, and the current sets onshore. The current can mount to 2 knots at times, so, again, do not approach too closely. There are a number of small-boat passages through this reef, but a good deal of local knowledge is required.

Barbados was for years the traditional landfall for yachts crossing the Atlantic. In the winters of 1978–79 and 1979–80, it was estimated that roughly 300 yachts cleared through Barbados during the periods of December through early March. However, that huge influx of yachts has dried up almost completely in recent years for various reasons.

In years gone by, when a yacht rounded Needham's Point, lighthouse keepers spotted the running lights and reported to the harbor police, who came out immediately and were waiting when the anchor went down. The harbor police, picturesquely dressed in the costumes of sailors of Nelson's day, were efficient and cheerful; the yacht was cleared instantly, and the crew was free to go ashore within an hour after dropping the anchor.

Then a new deep-water port was created, and the harbor police were pretty much disbanded. Skippers who went to the deep-water part were usually chased out and had to anchor off and go around trying to enter at the various government offices that were often less than interested in taking care of yachtsmen. I have heard tales of people spending *three days* in Barbados trying to enter.

In addition, the government began slapping all sorts of clearance fees on yachts, to the point that if you cleared at the wrong time of day or on the wrong day (i.e., Sunday) you could get stuck with approximately $100 U.S. in Customs, Immigration, and landing fees. This was bad enough, but rumors through the yachting grapevine made it worse, jacking the cost up to $300 U.S. (it probably was $300 E.C.—a little more than $100 U.S.), so that in the winter of 1985, yachts avoided Barbados like the plague.

Furthermore, Antigua is now well lit, and Guadeloupe now has an excellent marina, so yachts are now heading for those two islands rather than to Barbados. The Barbados government has made the first step toward reattracting the trans-Atlantic set by reducing the fees, so that if you enter between 0600 and 2200, seven days a week, the total fee for entering and clearing is about $25 U.S.—not cheap but not too bad. In addition, the Knowles brothers have established a little boatyard that caters to the yachtsmen.

If you arrive outside of clearing times, drop anchor in Carlisle Bay, hoist your "Q" flag, and go to bed; then first thing in the morning call the harbor authority on channel 12 and request permission to proceed to the deep-water harbor for clearance. If you do not have a radio telephone, get a neighboring yacht to call for you.

Once you have cleared, move back and anchor in Carlisle Bay wherever is convenient.

From the Antilles, Barbados is best approached from a point north or south of the island, depending on the season. In the spring and summer, when the wind is in the southeast, the best place to start is from the south end of Grenada. Put to sea on the starboard tack, and check your progress by RDF (Barbados Radio at Black Point: 705 mHz; Sewell Airport Beacon: 345 kHz) or celestial sights. The current runs to the northwest, so watch that it doesn't set you north of the island. Barbados is low-lying and it is possible to miss it. Native schooner captains have a way of returning to their home ports in the Islands with the explanation that "Barbados done sunk. We was where she is, but she ain't dere no more."

In the winter months, with the wind in the northeast, it is best to set out from Martinique or St. Lucia. Here is the method used by the schooners from St. Lucia: Stand north from Castries until the light of Îlet Cabrit—the southeastern corner of Martinique—is abeam; go about on port tack, and stay as close to the wind as you can; if you don't see Barbados in twenty-four hours, turn around and try again. These are not the most explicit sailing directions in the world, but they seem to work one way or the other.

In 1986, a cruising race was organized from the Canary Islands to Barbados. The race was sponsored by Mt. Gay Rum and *Yachting World*. Barbados waived all Customs clearance fees for the race entrants. As of fall 1986, 280 yachts have entered the race. Providing for the needs of 280 yachts arriving over a ten-day period will certainly be good for business, but will stretch Barbados' facilities to the maximum.

CARLISLE BAY

(II 1, B, B-2; Sketch Chart III-17)

The major anchorage in Barbados is off Bridgetown in Carlisle Bay, due north of the fort on Needham's Point. It is a relatively poor anchorage because it is open to the rollers from the northwest, and the normal trade-wind sea hooks around Needham's Point. When the northwest swell is severe, it is well nigh impossible to land ashore in a dinghy. Anchor off the Boatyard pier (see insert in II Chart B-2). That's where the Knowles brothers have opened the Boatyard (Carlisle Bay, Bay Street, St. Michael's, Bridgetown, Barbados). To provide something for the yachtsman, they have built a dinghy dock, so you no longer have to land through the surf. They have showers, ice, water and wholesale drinks, and an inexpensive and informal bar; communications are good, and they monitor channels 06, 08, 09, 11, 12, 16, 67, 72,

77, 78—the call sign is 8 PKM (eight poppa kilo mike).

They stock Imray-Iolaire charts and Street guides, and are only a short walk to the center of town.

It's hard to list exactly what's available in Bridgetown, as many things are scattered around the city and are hard to find without the aid of a tourist map. I recommend that you go to the Boatyard, where they will point you in the right direction for hauling (a twenty-ton crane, I am told, is available at the port authority dock), sail repair, or excellent machine shops throughout the island. International calls may be made via Barbados radio, which can be contacted through VHF channel 16 or 8269.3 SSB. People wanting to contact yachts through Barbados radio can direct dial from most areas in the world; telephone: 809-427-5200.

No sailor should miss the carenage. It is chockful of vessels of every shape and size. There are always a couple of schooners being loaded at the pier, water taxis shuttling about in every direction, and the harbor police maneuvering to keep the mayhem under control. In years gone by, during rush hour one of them stood in a dinghy ceremoniously directing traffic.

Formerly, everything was lightered out to the ships anchored offshore, and passengers were brought in by rowing wherries. It was a picturesque sight, and the arrangement provided needed employment for the locals who built and ran the little boats. Now, as in all the Islands, a large deep-water dock has been built. The boatmen are unemployed, the wherries are rotting away in the carenage, and the people who were dependent on them for their livelihood are looking for work.

Recently there has been talk of building a marina in the carenage, but that kind of talk has been going on for years. Much of the commercial traffic has been moved out of the carenage to the deepwater harbor. In February 1985, I found a number of yachts moored stern-to in the carenage: a nice bar and restaurant opens directly onto the carenage in a kind of Mediterranean-style operation; you can jump off the stern of your boat and sit down at a waterfront pub.

Bridgetown is a major transfer point for passengers and cargo. Many freighters stop here, as do most of the cruise ships and airlines. Whatever you may have heard of cargo lost in Trinidad holds true of Barbados as well.

There are a number of good hotels within walking distance of the anchorage, and regular bus service to the heart of town. If you are an early riser, for a change of pace try watching the trainers

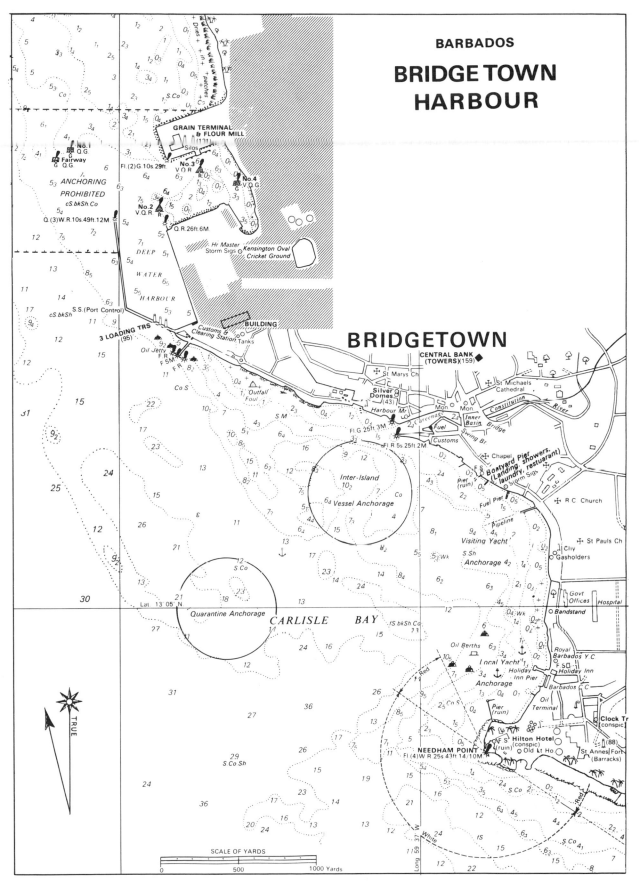

BARBADOS

BRIDGE TOWN
HARBOUR

GRAIN TERMINAL
& FLOUR MILL

Silos

No.1
Q.G.
Fairway
G. Q.G.
Fl.(2)G.10s.29ft.

No.3
V∩R

No.4
V.Q.G.

ANCHORING
PROHIBITED
cS.bkSh.Co

No.2
V.Q.R

Q.(3)W.R.10s.49ft.12M

Q.R.26ft.6M.

Hr Master
Storm Sigs

Kensington Oval
Cricket Ground

DEEP

WATER

HARBOUR

S.S.(Port Control)

cS.bkSh

3 LOADING TRS
(95)
Oil Jetty
F.R
F 5M F.R

Customs &
Clearing Station

BUILDING
Tanks

BRIDGETOWN

CENTRAL BANK
(TOWERS)(159)

St Marys Ch

St Michaels
Cathedral

Silver
Domes
(43)
Mon   Mon

Harbour Mr
Careenage
Inner
Basin

Constitution   River

Fuel

Swing Br

Customs

Fl.G 25ft.3M

Fl.R 5s.25ft.2M

Chapel Pier
Boatyard Pier
(Landing, showers,
laundry, restuarant)

Inter-Island

Vessel Anchorage

F S

Pier
(ruin)

Storm Sigs

Co

Fuel Pier

R C Church

Pipeline

Visiting Yacht
S Sh
Anchorage

St Pauls Ch

Cly
Gasholders

Wk

Quarantine Anchorage

CARLISLE   BAY

IS bkSh Co

Govt
Offices   Hospital

Bandstand

Wk

Oil Berths

Local Yacht

Red

Holiday
Inn Pier

Holiday Inn

Barbados C C

Anchorage

Royal
Barbados Y C

F S

Pier
(ruin)

Oil
Terminal

Clock Tr
(conspic)

(88)

Hilton Hotel
(conspic)
Old Lt Ho
St Annes Fort
(Barracks)

NEEDHAM POINT
Fl (4)W R 25s 43ft 14/10M

S.Co Sh

White

Long 59 37

TRUE

SCALE OF YARDS

0   500   1000 Yards

SKETCH CHART III-17   Bridgetown Harbor

give their horses a workout every morning at dawn at the racetrack.

Many small-boat fittings can be obtained on the island, but it is practically impossible to locate fittings for larger boats. Basic marine supplies such as paint are much cheaper here than in the rest of the Islands, since no duty is paid on any marine supplies at all. For the most part, you will find supplies that you were unable to find anywhere else. The major distributors of engines, mechanical equipment, paints, tools, and what have you are based on the island, usually in Bridgetown. It is indeed a pleasure to deal directly with the supplier.

The machine shops and hauling facilities for large yachts are really excellent. Their mechanics are used to working on boats. The screw-lift dock can lift yachts of any size. In fact, this screw lift is well worth a look around, even if you don't need to use it. It was installed by a Scottish designer sometime in the 1880s. The original steam engine has been replaced by diesel. Each section of the dock assembly disengages and lowers away to allow access for bottom and keel repairs.

There are two yacht clubs—the Barbados Yacht Club, north of the Holiday Inn Pier (marked Aquatic Club on some charts), and the Barbados Cruising Club, south of that pier. The Barbados Yacht Club looks like something right out of an Edwardian novel—with large, cool reading rooms, tennis courts, a monumental bar, and just the sort of quiet atmosphere one expects of a well-heeled British club. It was formerly the *Royal* Barbados Yacht Club and it is still listed as such on the charts. The reason for the change, I am told, dates back some years to a time when Prince Philip was paying a visit to the government of Barbados. He had immensely enjoyed the company of Barbados' pre-

mier and, discovering that he, too, was a yachtsman, invited him to the Royal Barbados for a drink. The premier replied that he was not a member of the club and furthermore was not permitted to become one. A day or two later, the story goes, the Royal Barbados became just the Barbados Yacht Club. They have loosened up. In the past, they used to feed visiting sailing teams on the beach out front instead of in the clubhouse proper. But this attitude has changed entirely, and visiting yachtsmen from other clubs are now welcome.

The Barbados Cruising Club seems to be more actively used by yachtsmen. Its friendly bar is nearly always crowded on the weekends. During the week, quite a few members come by for a sundowner. The Bajans are very hospitable and will do their best to solve whatever problems a yachtsman comes up with.

The former lack of a dinghy landing used to cause much grief to yachtsmen. Trying to land dinghies in the ground swell was especially trying when rowing ashore all dressed up for a night on the town (the Bajans tend to be formal). Many women went ashore in the skimpiest of bikinis, with long dresses, high heels, etc., packed carefully in a plastic bag. Once ashore, they dressed for the big night out on the beach. One young woman I know took this a step further. Pointing out how uncomfortable it would be to sit all night in a damp bikini, she took the trip ashore *au naturel*, with dress, etc., tied on her head with a bandanna. Returning to the boat about 0200, she reversed the procedure. Needless to say, all this made the damp landing conditions a lot less unpleasant.

Now, with the building of the Boatyard dock, these difficulties have become nostalgic memories.

NOTES

NOTES

6

Northern Grenadines

II B-3, B-31, B-311

The Grenadines comprise a string of small islands stretching 45 miles from Bequia to Îlet de Ronde. They are a varied lot, ranging unpredictably in size and topography. While the Tobago Cays are low and flat, neighboring Union Island soars high into the air. During the popular charter season in the winter, most of the islands are dry and windswept, but in the rainy season their colors change abruptly from dull brown to a bright, lush green. In sailing the Grenadines, the runs are very short; most passages can be made in two hours and the longest ones never last more than five. There are anchorages virtually everywhere, but these must be carefully negotiated. What distinguishes this area from the rest of the Antilles—and the Virgin Islands in particular—are the vast reaches of shoal water. There is an indescribable thrill in sailing across these banks with only 2 or 3 feet of water below the keel, and in watching the bottom slipping by from your place on the spreaders.

Most of the islands lie along a northeast-southwest axis, allowing a weatherly yacht to lay a course close-hauled going north. This contrasts with the Virgins, where you are either dead before or dead against the wind. There is very little chance of getting becalmed in the low-lying Grenadines. Soon, however, the days of the unspoiled tropical cay will have passed. Many of the islands are undergoing the throes of long-term development ventures.

In 1978, under the direction of the Canadian Hydrographic Office, the government of St. Vincent established lights and buoys throughout the Grenadines. These are marked on the latest British charts. However, it is universally agreed by yachtsmen who are familiar with the area that the installation of the lights, buoys, and ranges is—to

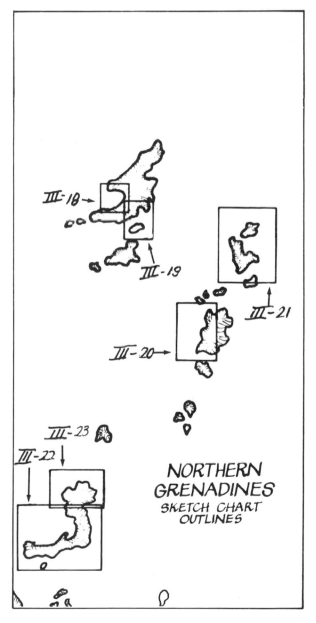

III-18→

III-19

III-21

III-20→

III-23

III-22

NORTHERN GRENADINES
SKETCH CHART OUTLINES

say the least—a mixed blessing. The ranges, as will be noted, are often not as marked on the charts and often are poorly placed.

For instance, in the Tobago Cays they will tend to put the yachtsman trying to sail into the anchorage right on the rocks. Further, the buoys at Montezuma Shoal and Grand de Coi are practically booby traps, likely to put the yachtsman right on top of the very danger he is trying to avoid.

The lights are unreliable and are frequently not lit. It is sometimes months if not years before they are relit. Needless to say, all this creates a dangerous situation.

Visiting yachtsmen have always been told not to sail at night in this area. Now, with lights and buoys supposedly there to warn the unknowing, some yachtsmen do attempt to sail after dark. Many of them have gotten into serious trouble. So, despite the buoys and lights that have been installed in the Grenadines, the old rule still applies: *Under no circumstances should you sail in this area at night.* And we can add another rule: *Night or day, treat all buoys with extreme skepticism.*

Bequia

The island of Bequia has been celebrated by sailors for hundreds of years. I have read glowing first-person accounts of Admiralty Bay by officers of the Royal Navy during the Napoleonic Wars. Esteemed by legend and heralded by song, it has always been a fine place to careen a ship, muster a crew, or replenish stores. There is a good deal of Yankee blood in the people of Bequia, harking back to the New Bedford whalers who took wives and settled here. In Paget, on the western tip of the island, are the descendants of the early French settlers, a group that has remained remarkably separate from the rest of the island.

Bequia is the last refuge of the sailing fisherman. Even now, the sail-fishermen outnumber the motor-fishermen by a large number. An attitude still prevails there that a motor is an auxiliary to the sail. When the fishermen gather for the sailing races on the major holidays, the level of the competition is as high as you will find anywhere. These people think nothing of sailing down to Grenada in a 17-foot open boat.

Bequia is one of the major yacht centers of the Grenadines. There are usually fifty to sixty yachts anchored at any one time in Admiralty Bay. Some are visiting yachts, many are semipermanent. Bequia is an extremely attractive island that in a

way time has passed by. The only way to get on and off Bequia, at least as of April 1985, was via local schooners, basically motor-sailers, plus a small steel freighter. They leave Bequia about 0645, do the one-hour run to St. Vincent, and leave about 1500, arriving in Bequia about 1600. If you go over for the day, don't miss the boat back, as they all leave at the same time. If you miss the boat, the next stop is a St. Vincent hotel, where you wait for the following day.

Needless to say, this lack of communication has hampered the development of Bequia. To some people this is deplorable; others feel it preserves the wonderful charm of Bequia. One thing is certain: The Bequians and St. Vincentians are two different peoples, though both are under the same government. The Bequians, in fact, do not like the St. Vincentians, and always blame any crime committed on the island of Bequia on them.

That may or may not be fair. Certainly there is crime on Bequia, and neither the local populace nor visiting yachtsmen seem to have much faith in the ability of the St. Vincent police force to do anything about it. This is made clear in the book by Betsy Hitz-Holman, *Sitting Ducks*, the story of the burglary of her boat and the near killing of her boyfriend, and the difficulties she had with the St. Vincent police and legal authorities afterward.

Yet Bequia is an extremely attractive island, and I hope not too many sailors are scared off by *Sitting Ducks.* I think it's clear that a singlehander or a couple cruising in this and many other parts of the world are vulnerable to marauders. Many people don't like carrying guns—and much of the time they have to be locked up in port anyway. As I've said before, I think the best answer is to have a dog aboard. Even a small dog, as long as it is yappy, will work. Barking of any kind will normally send a would-be burglar rowing off into the night. In all the years I have talked to yachtsmen worldwide, I have never heard of a single boat with a barking dog aboard that has been boarded and burgled.

In any case, there's no doubt that dinghies disappear all the time in Bequia. Of course, Admiralty Bay is open to the west, and I am convinced that about one-third of the missing dinghies are improperly secured and drift off; another third are taken by other "yachtsmen," and the final third are stolen by Bequians or St. Vincentians. Incidentally, the latest ploy is to steal an inflatable dinghy, deflate it, put it and the outboard below, and sail to the next island and sell them.

I have been in the insurance business for twenty

years and have read a lot of reports on stolen dinghies. Not once in my experience has the police department of St. Vincent offered any help in retrieving or searching for the stolen dinghies. In some cases they were actually obstructionist when the dinghies were found.

One might argue that the police have better things to do than look for yachties' lost dinghies, but the attitude is pretty unpleasant nevertheless. I am hopeful that Premier Mitchell, as a Bequian and as a sailor, will do something to improve the situation.

ADMIRALTY BAY
(II B-3, B-30, B-31; Sketch Chart III-18)

A beautiful anchorage and excellent in all normal weather; but it is an absolute death trap in hurricane season. Witness Hurricane Klaus in November 1984, which passed *north* of the Virgin Islands but still sent a swell into Admiralty Bay that put numerous boats on the beach.

Admiralty Bay is the major anchorage and the port of entry for Bequia, and is easily entered in daylight, although one should be wary of Wash

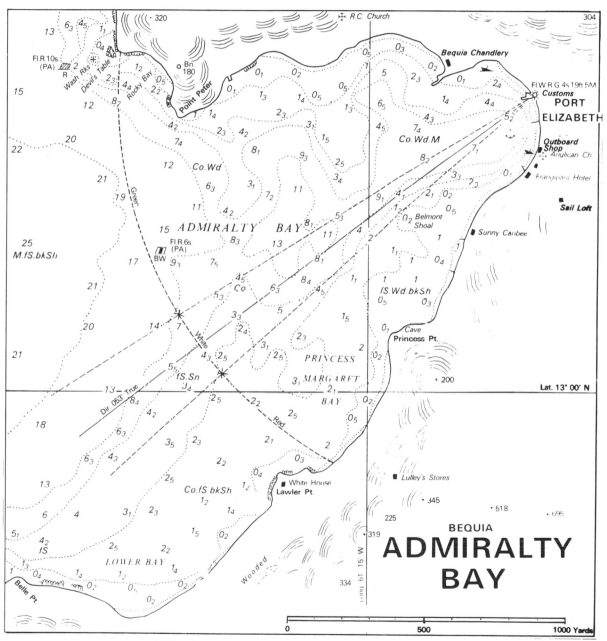

SKETCH CHART III-18 Bequia, Admiralty Bay

Rock off Devil's Table. Give Devil's Table a good 150-yard berth.

Devil's Table is supposed to be marked by a lit buoy that may or may not be there; even if it's there, it is so far off Devil's Table that one can actually pass well inside the buoy and still clear Devil's Table. There is another buoy right in the middle of Admiralty Bay that can be disregarded by the average yacht. Once around Point Peter (Fort Point), a course can be laid for the church in Elizabeth Town (106 magnetic), providing you draw less than 9 feet. If you are tacking in, care must be taken to avoid Belmont Shoals, which is foul ground and full of coral heads. If you are approaching from the west, a clear course can be set from West Cay directly to the town dock.

The best anchorage can be had due west of the church. There is deep water quite close to shore, so allow plenty of scope. The hard, sand bottom is excellent holding. It may take a moment or two to set, but once it has, you won't budge. Do not anchor south of the line of boats extending southwest from the church, as these are moored right on the edge of the shoal. Admiralty Bay is a popular spot, and there may be as many as sixty boats anchored within. As always, space is on a first-come basis, which may require anchoring well offshore, leaving you a long row into town. A way of avoiding this problem is to sail right up to shore just north of the church. The bottom drops off so steeply here that it is possible to lie close in, with a stern anchor out, and run up and bury a bow anchor on the beach.

This arrangement, however, has at least one liability. There is a large, bronze bell in front of the church. Now, I don't mind a bell for calling the faithful, but when every village drunk takes to clanging it at all odd hours of the morning, it gets to be too much. On one Whitsunday weekend, I counted 103 rings in the noisy course of one night and early morning. The next time I hit Admiralty Bay, I'll be packing a hacksaw! In any case, the bell is rung at 0600 every morning to wake up people in time to catch the 0645 boat to St. Vincent.

Bequia was once one of the major centers of schooner traffic, and was active in owning, crewing, and building them. Right behind where the Frangipani Hotel now stands, the Mitchell family built a 120-foot three-masted schooner, which they launched with only jack iron (rum), rollers, muscle power, and song. Premier "Son" Mitchell, who is also the owner of the Frangipani, used to be glad to show visitors a half model of his father's schooner.

Some years ago, the voices of doom cried that the last of the schooners had been built, that boatbuilding would become a lost art, never to be revived. Nothing could be further from the truth. A young American, Chris Bowman, can probably take credit for part of the present revival of boatbuilding in Bequia, as he built "by eye" (the traditional method) a rather nice 40-foot gaff-rigged cutter. Then he went to work supervising the construction of a 70-foot traditional schooner for a pop music star. This turned into the beautiful double-topsail gaff-rigged schooner *Water Pearl of Bequia*, a classic Bequian cargo schooner built as a yacht. She is usually seen during the winter season day-chartering out of Marigot, St. Martin.

In the 1980 edition of this book, I mentioned that young Bert Ollivierre of the extensive Ollivierre family (famous as schooner captains, fishermen, boatbuilders, and smugglers) was building traditional double-enders—locally referred to as two-bow boats—and was talking of modernizing the construction with steam-bent or laminated frames, possibly clinker construction. This would certainly make the boats much, much lighter, but nothing came of the idea; they are still building their beautiful little two-bowed boats, excellent sailors but certainly not light. They build them in various sizes and race them very competitively; some are working fishermen, others are small two-bowed boats from 13 to 18 feet long and built as yachts. If you are anchored on a Saturday or Sunday in Bequia Harbor, you'll see the two-bowed boats zigzagging back and forth across the harbor, many of them in races sponsored by the Bequia Yacht Club. In fact, everyone in Bequia seems to sail. Now, of course, instead of the old flour-sack sails they use Dacron sails, stainless rigging, and bronze fittings.

While anchored in Admiralty Bay, you may notice many boys chasing model yachts through the water to and fro across the harbor. Model-boat racing has been a pastime here since time immemorial. The kids used to make models of the charter boats that frequent the area. A feature of the big holiday weekends is racing these models. Each model is attended by its young owner swimming furiously to keep up with it, as the rules provide for one person to adjust sails, rigging, or direction. Those not strong enough to keep up with the boat follow in a dinghy, diving in to make adjustments whenever necessary. Without the aid of self-steering gear, these model yachts manage to hold a true course and stand up well to the breeze.

These models are to my mind the best souvenirs that can be brought back from the Caribbean. And it is interesting to note that only in Bequia do the children have the skill and interest to build model yachts that can really perform. No wonder they grow up to be such fine seamen.

To see the next generation of boatbuilders, go to Bequia Slipway, walk across the road, and ask for the model shop. Here you will find beautiful models of the various charter boats that visit the area. More interesting, they also build complete models of the traditional Bequia whaleboats, complete with all their whaling gear. It is very interesting to see how, over the years, the quality of these models has improved. Years ago, the models were very crude—now they are extremely skillfully done and not far below the quality of work by top model makers in the States. Needless to say, their prices have also "improved" with the passage of the years.

Lawson Sargeant, who heads the shop, started making models of the Bequia whaleboats complete with all equipment when he was sixteen years old. Now in his thirties, he is still building models and has quite a little industry going, employing approximately sixteen boys. One of the boys who worked with him years ago, Marvin Hutchin, has set up a rival shop, which is located behind the small supermarket across from the petrol station in the main part of town.

If someone really wanted to help the economy of Bequia (and also yachting, since the model makers of today will become the shipwrights of tomorrow), he or she could locate and send books on model making to these enterprising young boys. Books should be sent to: Bequia Model Shop, Bequia, St. Vincent, West Indies. I am sure the quality of the models will improve if this is done.

For many years the economy of Bequia was going down, and yachts did not visit the island too frequently; but now things are picking up, more and more yachts are coming in, and the marine economy in Bequia is developing.

Missy and Daniel Foulon have Hodge Taylor's old building and call it Grenadine Yacht Equipment. They have mainly outboards but are trying to get in stock the bits and pieces needed by the average yachtsman.

Lincon Simmons, whose sail loft was just south of the anchorage by the church, has built a sail loft on the hill overlooking the Frangipani Hotel. King of the sailmakers of the lower Caribbean, Lincon has been making sails for well over half a century. He is also the whale butcher on the island, so don't expect him to be there when a whale needs to be dealt with. Lincon is a fund of information about Bequia, and by talking to him and his son Nolly, you can find out everything there is to know about the island. If Lincon gives you advice, it will be blunt and to the point—take it, even though it may be bitter.

Bequia Slipway has been open for fifteen years; Bill Little took it over a few years ago. Bill is an ex-Marine sergeant who served from 1939 to 1949, not only through all the Pacific campaigns but also with a company of marines who were dropped by parachute into Burma to help Stilwell retrieve his troops the second time he was kicked out of Burma. After he left the Marines, Bill became a race car driver, then a yacht skipper. Being an old marine top sergeant (as he says, "had three up, three down, and a diamond in the middle"), he is an excellent raconteur and an excellent friend, but definitely not one to be pushed around.

Bill runs the shipyard, which, he states (I think rather optimistically), will haul 150 tons in ten feet of draft. Basically, he hauls your boat; you hire your own labor. Bequia has an abundance of good labor to do your work, and then Bill drops you back down. He has installed a water maker and has a quarter of a million gallons of water storage. So water is available at Bequia Slipway—but it is not cheap. Similarly, ice is also available. Bill's wife, Barbara, runs a restaurant, the Harpoon Saloon, which overlooks the harbor. Hodge Taylor provides marine supplies you need when hauling, i.e., paint, seam compound, carpentry materials, etc., from his Bequia Chandlery right at the Slipway.

Getting a shower is Bequia is difficult. You can have one at Mitchell's Guest House in the middle of town, but it's not too cheap and I would say not necessarily the friendliest of operations.

Southwest of the Frangipani, the Bequia beach is peppered with small restaurants and bars, all ready to take care of the needs of the yachtsman. The Frangipani Hotel is not only a hotel but also a mail drop and message center. The Whalebone Bar and Restaurant, adjacent to the hotel, also has a boutique run by Angie and Albert Hinkson, of the old Bequia Macintosh family. There is also Mac's Pizzeria, which sells bread, cakes, cookies, quiche, muffins, pies, and other baked products. Geoff Wallace's Fig Tree Bar is an old standby that goes back donkey's years. Although the Sunny Caribee's management and ownership changes, the place has been the major hotel of the Admiralty Bay area for four decades. For women's clothes and accessories, there is the Crab Hole, a nice, simple West Indian boutique right next to the Sunny Caribee.

Ross Lulley is back in business near his old location up on the hill high above the western end of Princess Margaret Beach. He first went to Bequia thirty-seven years ago at a time when there were practically no roads, and he built his house and shop 300 feet in the air, miles from the nearest harbor—I had always wondered why, since his business concerned the sea and fishing. It was some years later that I discovered the answer: Lulley's shop was situated equidistant, via backwoods trails, from the fishing communities at Friendship Bay, Paget Farm, and Admiralty Bay. Thus he drew business from all three communities.

For many years his shop was a little two-by-four shack jammed full of fishing goodies. As yachting began to expand in the area, Ross branched out into the chandlery business, selling gear at extremely good prices. As the years went by, Lulley's Knife Shop (it was so called because he sold some of the best knives in the world) became known not only throughout the entire Caribbean, but also in Europe and even as far away as the Pacific. The shop expanded, and he installed a big kerosene deep freeze, so he served the coldest beer on the island.

Then Ross sold the business, but being the kind who can't stay retired, he decided to start up again, selling fishing supplies and some yachtsmen's gear, including Dacron and nylon line at very competitive prices.

To get to Lulley's shop, take a taxi. Or take your dinghy around to Princess Margaret Beach and you will see a small path running up the side of a rock with a cave through which you can see the water on the other side; follow the trail and you'll end up at Lulley's—with a considerable thirst which can be taken care of at Lulley's store with an ice-cold Heineken. The view from the shop is magnificent, the gear superb, and Armina, Ross's longtime Bequian assistant, is as efficient as ever. To top all this, the conversation is always entertaining. In fact, I recently heard from Ross on the subject of the caliber of yachtsmen in Bequia these days. He has a strong opinion: "I don't call the majority of the present group afloat 'yachtsmen' any longer. 'Waterpeople' is what I call them. I spent one year in Shanghai on the Wong Poo anchorage back in the forties, and I know waterpeople when I see them."

We used to get fresh food from the late Sidney Macintosh, who had a farm on the south side of the island. We all remember him with affection for his wonderful sense of humor. In his hen house was a big sign that read, "Remember, girls, an egg a day keep the butcher away." They must have been able to read because they produced an awful lot of eggs. His chicken farm is nearly the most efficient operation on the island, second only to a visiting dentist I once found pulling teeth, forceps in hand, under the large shade tree south of the church. His dental chair was an empty whiskey case; the anesthesia was a shot of rum. He pulled fifty-five teeth in one day.

This was the well-known Australian sailor-dentist Bill Howell, who was giving free dental care in exchange for an engine repair. He complained the next day that he had a sore wrist from all the work he did—and a sore head from all the rum he drank while pulling the teeth. The locals had sore heads from the rum anesthetic and sore jaws where teeth had been.

Near the western tip of Bequia on the north side is Moon Hole. This is a cave that passes directly through the island and in which one Tom Johnson built a house. He decided that he needed a proper, safer house after a rock fell out of the roof of the cave and demolished his fourposter bed—which was unoccupied. Now the whole area around Moon Hole has expensive houses built by wealthy individuals who want to get away from it all. They have succeeded, since there is no road (you arrive by foot, donkey, or boat), no electricity (except what is provided by wind generators), no piped water, and, best of all, no telephones!

There are three good beaches, the one in front of town and two on the south side of the harbor. The easternmost is called Princess Margaret (formerly Tony Gibbon) Beach; the western one is called Lower Bay. Both beaches are beautiful and frequently deserted. At the western end of Princess Margaret Beach is a cave through the rock which leads to another small beach about twenty feet wide with overhanging cliffs on all sides. Presumably this, too, was a favorite of Princess Margaret.

In Lower Bay on Sundays there is always a good Sunday barbecue / beach party well populated by locals, visiting yachtsmen, and expatriates living on the island; it's a good way to spend a Sunday and feed everyone. During the course of the day there are usually small-boat races off the beach.

On the westernmost beach is a new small bar and restaurant called the Reef. When visiting any of these bays in a dinghy, be warned that at certain times of the year getting ashore in a dinghy is a major operation unless you are very adept at handling a dinghy in surf.

In 1985, a young Canadian named Stephen Price, with the aid of the Honorable James "Son" Mitchell, was in the process of collecting bits and pieces of gear, whalebone, photos, letters, and the like to set up a whaling museum in Lower Bay. This museum should be well worth a visit, as the Bequians still go after whales the same way that Captain Ahab in *Moby Dick* did.

PIGEON ISLAND
(II 1, B, B-3, B-30, B-31)

Southwest of Bequia, little more than a rock sticking out of the water with no harbor, no beach—and no reason to stop.

On the west side of the northeastern point of Bequia is Anse Chemin, a cove seldom visited by yachtsmen. With the wind south of southeast, this

anchorage is a calm one. It is 3 fathoms close to shore. There is good snorkeling, and ashore are the ruins of an old sugar plantation.

On the south side of the western end, there is an anchorage off Paget Farm. It is usually calm here and undisturbed by the ground swell, but there is always a wind, which tends to put you onshore. Care should be taken when anchoring in this bay.

FRIENDSHIP BAY
(II B-2, B-3, B-31; Sketch Chart III-19)

Well worth a visit by boat or taxi from Elizabeth Town. It is easy to enter: merely stay in the middle of the entrance to the harbor, steering 035 magnetic for the Friendship Bay Hotel flagpole. Anchor in the eastern corner of the harbor, where there is the best protection from the ground swell. This is a smooth anchorage for the most part, although it

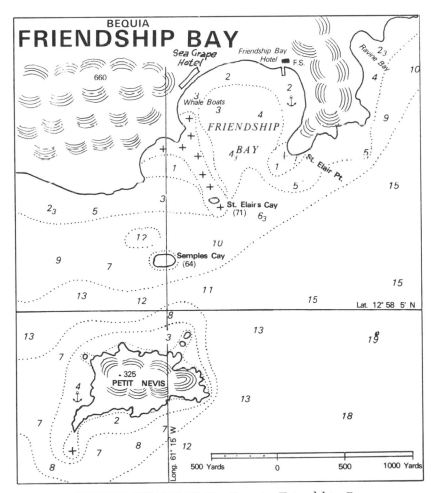

SKETCH CHART III-19   Bequia. Friendship Bay

is prone to some turbulent periods. The dock at the Friendship Bay Hotel is for dinghies only. The beach bar is to the west of it. There is good snorkeling on the reef out front. The hotel discourages spearfishing. A long, white-sand beach extends from the hotel west to the settlement at Friendship. The beach is lined with pretty manchineel trees whose fruit, which resembles apples, is deadly poisonous.

On the western side of Friendship Bay is a new, small guest house called the Sea Grape Hotel, run by Sylvester. I am told the food is good and the prices are right; it is an economical place to spend a few days ashore.

At the western end of the beach are the whaleboats. These are big, heavy boats, weighing as much as a ton each, and it's worth rising before dawn some morning to watch the Bequians launch them swiftly from the shore; they drag them back up in the evening. It's a rough way to earn a living. They go out after the humpback whale, a variety that usually travels in pairs, so that when one is caught, the second can be caught also. Often the charter boats will come racing down to watch the whaling boats after the first whale has been taken, making it very difficult to capture the second. The humpback is very fast and sharp of hearing. It is easily scared off, so it is best to stand off while the whalers conduct their business. Whaling in Bequia is the livelihood of an impoverished people and should be distinguished from the reckless plunder carried out every year by large nations. Only occasionally is a whale caught out of Bequia, but when it is, the entire animal is used. The oil is sold to the States, the meat is eaten by the poor, and the bones are sold to the tourists as scrimshaw. What could be neater?

Despite the fact that the whaling industry has almost completely died out in Bequia, they built a new whaleboat in 1984. Now there are two boats whaling during the season.

PETIT NEVIS
(II 1, B, B-3, B-30, B-31; Sketch Chart III-19)

The island where the whales caught by the Bequians are brought to be butchered. Whale bones are strewn along the shore. Most of the time you will find the island deserted, except during weekends and holidays, when the people of Bequia come across to let the good times roll.

There is a good anchorage off the western shore of Petit Nevis, but the bottom falls off so steeply

here that you must nearly set your bow ashore before dropping anchor. When the anchor's down, feed out plenty of scope. It is always calm here when it's windy. You can walk over to the windward side, where the beach varies from white sand to loose gravel, depending on the storms that year. This is an excellent picnic spot, and regardless of the condition of the beach, it is always cool, with the trades blowing through the palm trees.

In 1974, there were the beginnings of a great land development scheme on Petit Nevis, but after a few buildings were completed and a few roads started, the scheme fell flat. Too bad for the developers; a break for yachtsmen.

ISLE QUATRE
(II 1, B, B-3, B-30, B-31)

Pretty to look at, but one must be something of a mountain goat to appreciate it. Anchorage is below the house on the northwestern shore in 3 fathoms of water. The house is perched on a ridge 400 feet above the sea and facing directly into the trades. It must have one of the best views in the entire Caribbean.

The southwestern cove of Isle Quatre can be entered by boats drawing 6 feet or less—both Ian Cowan of Stevens Yachts and John Corbet of *Freya* use this harbor. However, the older Imray-Iolaire charts are wrong in showing 2 fathoms and no reefs; there is a maximum of a fathom and a half in the cove. The cove is completely reef-encumbered and should be attempted only by an experienced reef navigator under ideal conditions. Both Cowan and Corbet say it is impossible to give detailed sailing directions: just enter on the eastern side of the cove and feel your way in, *but only under ideal circumstances with good light.* A Stevens Yachts charterer tried to get in at 1800, ran aground, and knocked his rudder off, and was extremely lucky not to lose the boat.

Mustique, Baliceaux, and Battowia
MUSTIQUE
(II 1, B, B-3, B-30; BA; Sketch Chart III-20)

This has always been a favorite of mine, but the times they are a-changing. Out to windward of the rest of the islands, it was seldom visited by the charter yachts. For many years the island was owned by the Hazel family of St. Vincent. The first time I visited the island there was a small fishermen's camp on the northwest beach and a small

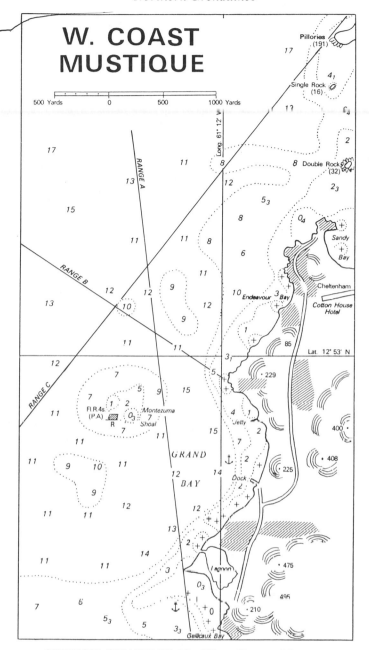

SKETCH CHART III-20   West Coast—Mustique

Range A: S.W. point of Mustique in line with N.E. point of Petit Mustique 006–186 magnetic cleans
           Montezuma Shoal to the East.
Range B: Rocks N. end of Grand Bay bearing 136–316 magnetic cleans Montezuma Shoal to the North-
           East.
Range C: Western Pillories in line with N. summit of Baliceaux 051–231 magnetic clears Montezuma
           Shoal to the West.

community of farmers barely scratching out an existence.

The fishermen who formerly camped at Cheltenham would row their six-oared double-ended boats down to Grand Bay to shoot their nets at twilight. If there was a yacht around, they would race, and it was quite a sight to see—twelve huge fishermen heaving away and bending the huge, crude West Indian oars. That is all gone now; the fishermen still fish in Grand Bay, but they camp on the beach in the northeast corner and do most of their fishing under power.

All the O.W.I.H. (Old West Indian Hands—sailors who have been here twenty years or more) bemoan the fact that the formerly uninhabited islands of Palm, Petit St. Vincent, and Mustique, and semi-inhabited Gannouan and Meyreau, are all in the hands of developers. However, one must look at the other side of the coin. In the late fifties and early sixties, the inhabitants of the middle Grenadines were practically starving to death, as there was literally nothing for them to do. The islands were too dry to grow anything but sea-island cotton, and the bottom had dropped out of that market. Fish were plentiful, but the economies of St. Vincent and Grenada were in poor shape, which meant that the fishermen could not get a decent price for their fish.

Then the developers arrived: Hazen Richardson and Doug Terman, backed by Mr. Nichols at Petit St. Vincent; and Johnny Caldwell, his wife, Mary, and his two sons on Prune (now Palm) Island. Their efforts were followed by significant developments at the Anchorage on Union Island, Salt Whistle Bay, and Mustique, all of which provided a lot of continuing employment. Most important, remember that the taxes paid by these five establishments in the Grenadines—Mustique, Palm, Petit St. Vincent, Salt Whistle Bay, and the Anchorage—go a long way toward supporting the government of St. Vincent.

One must also admit that all these developments have been tastefully done, and have destroyed neither the landscape nor the independence of the people.

As for Mustique, the old ruins have been restored, and the Cotton House, originally an old warehouse, is now a splendid restaurant and one of the most magnificently restored buildings in the whole region. Numerous guest cottages around the Cotton House are so well restored that it is hard to tell which ones are original and which are new. A pier has been built, and an airstrip accommodates assorted charter and private planes, as well as LIAT, which flies to St. Vincent, Grenada, Union, and Barbados. Basic supplies can be had in the grocery store across the street from Basil's Bar, which is built out over the water near the pier and provides lunch, dinners, and some nightlife.

Mustique takes its name from the French for mosquito. Although a valiant effort has been made to eliminate this pest, my advice is to get off the beach before sundown—from 1730 to 2000 the mosquitoes are out with a vengeance. Apparently they go to sleep at 2000.

Mustique should be approached cautiously. The off-lying Montezuma Shoal has done in any number of ships, including the yacht *Lord Jim*, which might easily have become a total loss had a tug not hauled her off. The shoal bears 309 magnetic from the dock at Grand Bay. If you are beating up from Bequia against the easterly trade, under no circumstances should you fall eastward of Range C on Sketch Chart III-20 until you have passed clearly north of Range B, which bears 135 magnetic on the rocks at the north end of Grand Bay. Staying northeast of Range B, stand in toward shore until east of Range A before working down into Grand Bay.

Here is the first booby-trap buoy installed by the St. Vincent government. It is not on Montezuma Shoal, but is off to the southwest of it; depending on the direction you're heading, the buoy could mislead you into going right on the shoal. Thus, check the ranges on Sketch Chart III-20 and disregard the buoy. There are only 3 feet of water over Montezuma Shoal, so why did they not simply mark it with a day mark on top of the shoal?

The best anchorage in Grand Bay is off the new dock. Feel your way in and anchor where the depth suits you. The current here is not particularly strong. It comes and goes at intervals, and frequently during the night you will find yourself rolling for a few hours as the current swings your beam onto the wind, but I have never found it too uncomfortable.

Now that Mustique has become fairly popular with charter yachts, there is usually a cluster of boats anchored in Grand Bay, off the pub built out over the dock. It's just a short row ashore in the dinghy. The Cotton House is either a long walk or a short taxi ride away; the latter is expensive. The manager of the Cotton House, Robert B. Hoflund, who cut his teeth in the Caribbean tourism business at Petit St. Vincent, is doing an excellent job in Mustique. He stocks Imray-Iolaire charts and Street guides.

A tour of Mustique is certainly worthwhile, but since taxis are fairly expensive, it may be smart to rent one of the little mopeds for the day. Explore the island and admire the beautiful houses, which obviously have been built without regard to expense. Most of them are in the old West Indian style.

Amazingly, we discovered in March 1985 that a place called Charlie House was doing European

bed and breakfast at $40 U.S. a day per couple—
not cheap by European standards but reasonable
around here.

It is best to avoid Mustique on Sundays, as a
schooner arrives from St. Vincent with a mob of
day-trippers hell-bent on a day at the beach.

Besides Montezuma Shoal, which I have mentioned and which is difficult to spot even on a clear
day, there is a second hazard at Mustique that
must be reckoned with. This is the shoal at the
south end of Grand Bay, which extends much
farther to the southwest than old charts show. This
shoal is growing continually and must be given a

wide berth. South of this shoal is a white-sand
beach under a steep cliff in Gelliceaux Bay, a
favorite anchorage of John Corbet of *Freya*. Princess Margret has a house on the hill above. The
southernmost bay, known as Shark Bay, has a roly
anchorage and does not sound too appealing.

BALICEAUX
(II 1, B, B-3, B-30, B-31; Sketch Chart III-21)

A small island one and a half miles long and a
quarter mile wide, north-northeast of Mustique.
This high, rugged, seldom-visited island is inhab-

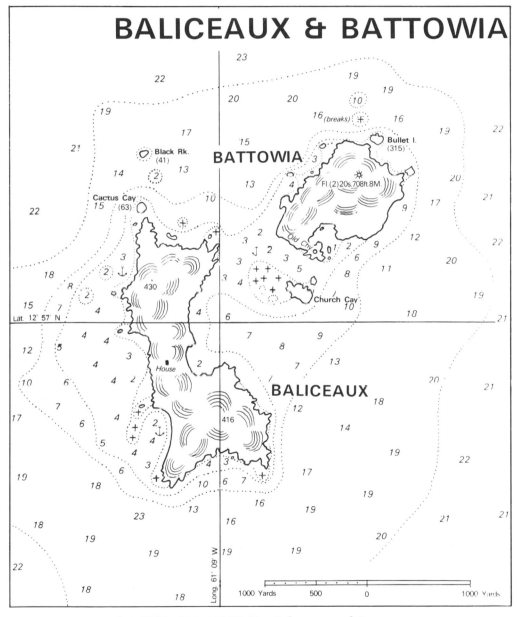

SKETCH CHART III-21   Baliceaux and Battowia

ited by transients—fishermen who camp on the beach for weeks or months at a time. There is a nice little part-time anchorage in the cove on the southwestern corner of the island. With the ground swell running, this is a totally impossible anchorage; the surf breaks so heavily onshore that even the fishermen cannot launch their boats. But during the spring and summer, it can be a great spot.

As you approach from the south, feel your way up, favoring the eastern shore. The reef to the west is extremely difficult to spot. There is only room enough for one or two boats, so if it is crowded here when you arrive, other anchorages can be had anywhere along the western side of the island, after you have skirted the reef. Once anchored, go ashore and enjoy the view from the top of the hill.

The fishermen here are a hardy lot. Many come down from Bequia for the day only. They leave Paget on the southwestern coast of Bequia early in the morning in their 20-foot boats, beat 8 miles out to Baliceaux, arriving before dawn, fish through the early morning, and then reach over to St. Vincent to sell their catch. Late in the day they beat around the eastern end of Bequia and finish up with a final run down to Paget. This amounts to an eighteen- or twenty-hour day of sailing, fishing, and rowing. It's small wonder that the Bequians are such a lean breed. I have the greatest respect for them.

BATTOWIA

(II 1, B, B-3, B-30, B-31; Sketch Chart III-21)

So far as I know, this, too, is seldom visited by yachtsmen. There is no harbor whatsoever. If the trades are not blowing too hard, an anchorage can be had west of the reefs extending to the west of Church Cay. A Bahamian moor will be required here, since the current runs strongly through the break between Battowia and Baliceaux. I am told by the fishermen that a landing by dinghy can be made in the cove on the southeast corner of the island. Here, in the past, small boats would land to drop off and pick up supplies. The island was a sugar island, the only reminder of which is a ruined smokestack at the head of the cove. This is the island where the British detained several thousand Carib tribesmen captured on St. Vincent in the eighteenth century. Now Battowia is uninhabited, but it remains a delightful place to visit when the weather permits.

PETIT MUSTIQUE

(II 1, B, B-30, B-31)

A small steep island south of Mustique with no anchorages and of little interest. It is not visited by yachtsmen, so far as I know.

SAVAN ISLAND

(II 1, B, B-30, B-31)

Well to windward of Petit Canouan. If you are heading south from Mustique, this is a possible place to anchor for a night in settled conditions. But the only person I know who has spent the night here is Richard Scott Hughes, a famous charter skipper, who stopped here when skippering *Boekanier,* a 65-foot schooner. John Corbet of *Freya* claims that you are likely to rock and roll here so much that your charter party will be seasick in a hurry. He advises making it a day stop; go ashore and have a beach party rather than staying on the boat.

One can anchor on the lee of this island, or between the islands with one anchor on the windward of the two and a second anchor on the reef to leeward. The current runs strongly there, which no doubt accounts for the excellent fishing. Without the fishing, I suspect that this little pile of rocks known as Savan Island would be totally uninhabited. The people charge visitors for the right to camp or fish. If it is not blowing hard, a north-to-south passage between the islands makes for a spectacular sail. Be sure to have your camera ready on the starboard side as you emerge from the channel. You will see a massive stone arch that the tides have formed.

PETIT CANOUAN

(II B-3, B-31)

Four miles northeast of Canouan, this is steep-to and offers no anchorage possibilities.

Canouan Island

The British island of Canouan is one of the largest in the Grenadines and remains one of the least known and least populated. It offers a variety of good anchorages to visiting yachtsmen. If you are approaching from the south, the westernmost peak of the island, Glass (or Glossy) Hill, will appear detached from the rest. The narrow, low-lying, sand spit that separates it from Taffia Hill is hard to spot from any distance. When approaching from the north, Canouan is the first sizable island after Mustique or Bequia. Its main anchorage is Charlestown Bay.

In the last century, Canouan was a major outpost of the whaling ships. During winters in the 1890s as many as twenty New Bedford schooner-whalers could be seen anchored in its lee. Although whaling finally died out in the 1920s, one still encounters scattered remains of whaleboats in the area. Canouan is covered by Imray-Iolaire Charts B-3, B-31, and 25042, and Sketch Charts III-22 and III-23.

Canouan was owned for roughly 100 years by the Snagg family as a private estate. They raised cotton, corn, pigeon peas, and fish, and evidently made a lot of money. You can see for yourself by taking the path from the northeast corner of Charlestown Bay across the hill—it's about a twenty-minute walk—to the carenage. Here you will find the remains of the old estate buildings, and one of the largest old cisterns I've ever seen. It must have held about 40,000 gallons of water. There is also a beautiful old church, one of the biggest I have seen in the Eastern Caribbean outside the towns. The church was built in the 1860s, completely paid for by the resident Snagg. It has beautiful bronze bells, which were cast in England in 1867, but these, sadly, lie on the ground outside the church. The east wall, now bricked in, probably had a stained-glass window. The roof blew off in the 1921 hurricane, and the window was most likely blown in at the same time. Repairs were then made to the wall by bricking it in and to the roof by covering it with corrugated iron.

From the look of the buildings and the church, this must certainly have been a prosperous island, even after the slaves were freed in 1838. You can see traces of wide roads with good retaining walls, drainage systems, and other signs of careful planning. Horses were raised and used by the manager, the owner, and his family, oxen were used for plowing and hauling carts. (The only other island in the Caribbean where oxen are found is Marie Galante.) Each laborer had a section of fence to maintain so that the donkeys, goats, and sheep didn't chew up the crops.

There were two whaling fisheries on this island, besides the offshore whaling operation based here. These all died out just prior to the First World War. The estate was obviously still relatively prosperous by the 1920s, because the church was repaired after the 1921 hurricane. Unfortunately, the windmill-powered cotton gin went with the hurricane, as did the school, which was in the same area as the Snagg estate. The new school was built down in the main part of town at the south end of the harbor.

Henry Snagg died in 1924, and things started going downhill, to the extent that the majority of the estate was sold to the St. Vincent government in the 1930s.

At the present time, there are only 600–700 people on the island. They are mainly supported by money from family members working overseas. As late as 1980, there were just three vehicles on the island—one tractor, one pickup owned by the Crystal Sands Hotel, and the police Land Rover.

The St. Vincent government has built an airstrip; Island Air comes on schedule, and there are charter flights. The field is unfenced and untended—occasionally planes can't land until the waiting passengers chase livestock off the runway. I have also witnessed a dog chasing a landing airplane. What one doesn't see in these islands!

There is a very nicely designed small hotel, the Crystal Sands, right on the excellent beach at Charlestown. The hotel was run by Mrs. Phileus De Roche. (Her husband originally got into the tourist business as crew on Walter Boudreau's boat *Ramona*, a 112-foot schooner, which was subsequently lost on Bermuda's northeast breakers, with a number of crew.) Unfortunately, the Crystal Sands Hotel encountered financial difficulties and in the winter of 1985 it was closed. Rumor has it that it will reopen.

CHARLESTOWN BAY
(II B-3, B-31; Sketch Chart III-22)

When entering Charlestown Bay, carefully check Sketch Chart 22, as both the British Admiralty chart and the chart in Julius Wilensky's *Yachting Guide to the Windwards* are wrong. The Admiralty chart shows the range in the northeast corner of the harbor bearing 055 magnetic; this range is actually 073 (checked December 1978). This leads to within 20–25 yards of the conspicuous white-topped rock in the northeast corner of Charlestown Bay.

The range in the southeast corner of the harbor is listed as 158 true (168 magnetic), but this was not operating in December 1978 when we were there. The red spar buoy in the middle of the harbor was there.

When approaching Charlestown Bay from the

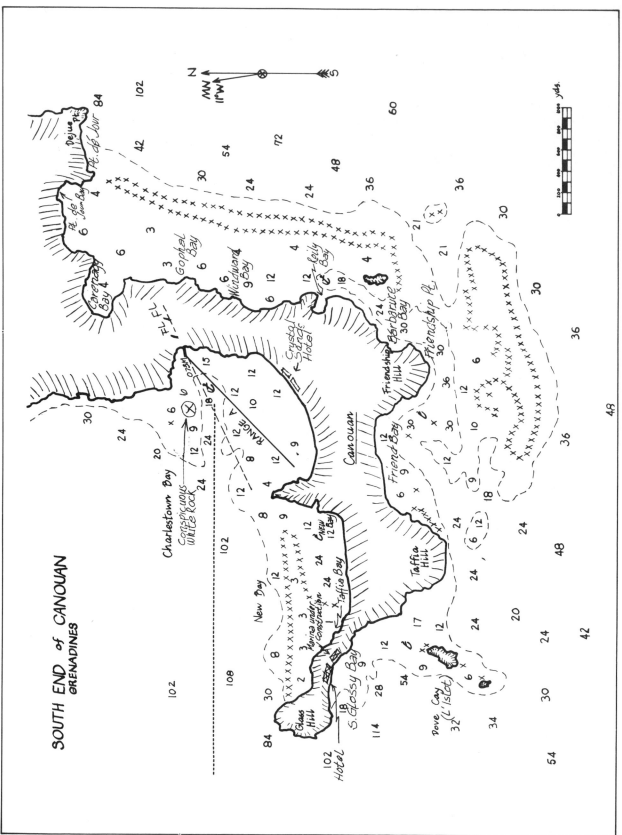

Range A: Forward range tower brought to bear 045 magnetic. *Note: Disregard aft range tower, as it is misplaced. Lining up both range towers (073 magnetic, not the 055 shown on the government chart) places one extremely close to the conspicuous white rock.*

SKETCH CHART III-22   South End of Canouan—Grenadines

north, sail down the lee coast of Canouan and head for the dock on the south side of the harbor until the conspicuous white rock in the northeast corner of the harbor bears 070 magnetic. Then come to a course of 100 magnetic, and hold this course until the *forward* range mark bears 045 magnetic. Then run in on this course, disregarding the back range mark entirely. Anchor somewhere in the corner according to your draft.

One can anchor off the Crystal Sands Hotel in 10 feet of water, but the wind loops over the hill, making you lie stern to the beach. Sometimes it is calm, but when a ground swell is running it would be most uncomfortable, sometimes dangerous. Make sure when anchoring that you drop the anchor in a patch of sand and not in the grass. If it is blowing hard, you will be well advised to use two anchors out in a "Y" to the northeast.

NEW BAY
(II B-3, B-31; Sketch Chart III-22)

According to the charts, there is a seemingly good anchorage in the bay due north of Taffia Hill, New Bay. From an airplane it also looks like an ideal anchorage. I have visited this spot only once, and I was rocked all night long. The reef on the north side of the bay affords less protection than the charts indicate. There are 3 or 4 feet of water over the reef, enough to let the ground swell from the north come rolling in. For the winter months, therefore, I would have to rule out this spot. Only in the summer, when there is no ground swell and the wind is in the southeast, is this adequate for anything more than daytime stops. The bottom is grass, and the holding wretched. The night I spent there, I had to dive to the bottom, dig a hole, and bury my anchors before they would hold. The reef appears excellent for snorkeling, and in the cove on the eastern side of the bay there is an attractive small beach. Over the bar at the entrance the water is 8 feet deep. You must stay within 50 yards of the eastern point as you enter. When the sand beach falls abeam to port, bear off toward the middle of the harbor. There is plenty of water inside the reef—anchor anywhere, but don't plan to spend the night. It is only a short walk west from this anchorage to the new hotel and marina.

CORBEC (CORBAY)
(II B-3, B-31; Sketch Chart III-23)

Corbec provides a small anchorage, only slightly larger than L'Anse Goyeau. There isn't much of a beach ashore, but again there is good snorkeling. If you want a white-sand beach to walk on, go over a small spit of land to the north end of Rameau Bay. This beach, although fine for sunning and exploring, is not good for swimming, as it goes from white sand to rock. However, the snorkeling is good.

L'ANSE GOYEAU (GUYAC)
(II B, B-3, B-31; Sketch Chart III-23)

There are a number of other anchorages northwest of Charlestown Harbor, if you'd rather be alone. L'Anse Goyeau is a very attractive small cove for room for just one boat. It's probably best to moor bow to stern. The beach ashore is not too good, but the snorkeling is excellent and you may find small lobsters.

South of Cor Point, the point that forms the southern end of L'Anse Goyeau, one can find a moderately good anchorage if one moors bow to stern and on a northwest-southeast axis. There are 10 feet of water quite close to shore, and everyone can go snorkeling directly from the boat. Thus it makes a good lunchtime stop.

RAMEAU BAY
(II B, B-3, B-31; Sketch Chart III-23)

This bay is really too exposed for anchoring, but along the shore are a number of very small white-sand beaches, ideal for honeymoon couples landing with a bottle of wine, a picnic lunch, and hopes for an all-over suntan. You are just a short dinghy ride from the anchorage in Charlestown Harbor.

SOUTH COAST OF CANOUAN

There is good exploring along the south and southeast coasts of the island. If the ground swell is not running or if it is not blowing too hard, there is sometimes an anchorage between Dove Cay and the mainland. Due north of Dove Cay is excellent. Sail in and check it out. If it looks calm, drop the hook and enjoy yourself. Farther east, between Taffia and Friendship hills, is another anchorage. The approach requires careful eyeballing. Post someone in the rigging and stand in cautiously under power or on starboard tack. There is good holding here on a white-sand bottom, excellent swimming, and not too much of a swell unless the wind is from the southeast.

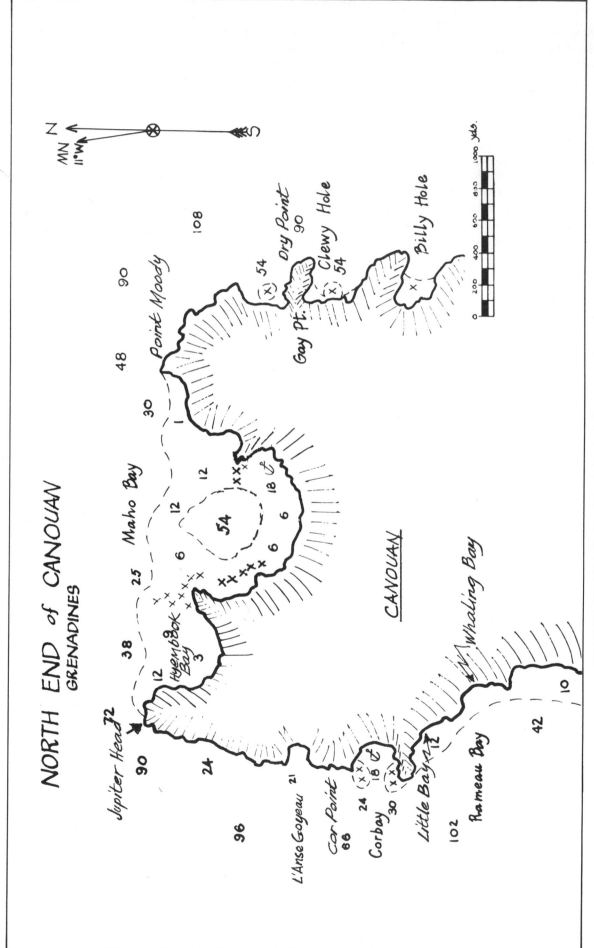

SKETCH CHART III-23   North End of Canouan—Grenadines

SOUTH GLOSSY BAY (SOUTH GLASS BAY)
(II B, B-3, B-31; Sketch Chart 22)

This anchorage varies. I have anchored here, rolled my guts out, stayed for an hour, and picked up my anchor and moved. But the last time we were there, in February 1985, there was only a slight roll and we happily anchored for the afternoon, evening, and following morning.

We also went ashore to the new Canouan Beach Hotel, which finally appears to be making it. It was built a number of years ago, but succumbed to the usual problem faced by a West Indian project: undercapitalization. It went bust three times over the last few years, but now seems to be properly financed and will be a major development in years to come. It has a nice big dining room, many cottages under construction, and a suction dredge standing by to start dredging the swamp east of the hotel to create a marina with ten feet of water in it. The plan is for fuel, water, electricity, and ice to be available, plus a specialty shop that imports French wine, cheese, and cold cuts from Martinique, plus a boutique. It may well become a must stop for charter yachts heading north and south through the Grenadines in years to come.

South Glossy Bay has crystal-clear water, a white-sand bottom, and long stretches of beautiful beach.

EAST COAST OF CANOUAN
(II B-3, B-31; Sketch Chart 22)

For the seasoned sailor, deep water can be carried to windward around Friendship Point and a good way north inside the reefs (Sketch Chart III-22). Boats drawing 8 feet have gone up through here. Within the reefs the current is always running south and at times too strongly for a person to swim against. You will find complete privacy here, good swimming and snorkeling, and great shelter. A boat drawing 5 feet or less can easily make its way north all the way to the head of the bay—carefully. Marcy Crow took his *Xantippe*, drawing 6 feet 3 inches, all the way to the village at the very end of the basin. A good deal of skill is required. The deepest water is fairly close to shore off the beaches and at the points of land no more than 30 yards offshore. It is a matter of feeling the way with a boathook or with someone leading in a dinghy. When you reach the head of the basin, there is an old church ashore, which is worth a look.

It has been claimed possible to enter this basin from the north through a break in the reef, but I tend to discount this as a local boast of derring-do. I have observed the area from the air, and the approach looked quite impossible, although I suppose one or two boats may have done it. I am pretty certain that where the charts say 3 fathoms there are no more than 2.

The other bays on the northeast corner of Canouan are not feasible, as they face out into the eastern wind and swell.

NORTH COAST OF CANOUAN
(Sketch Chart III-23)

Maho Bay, on the north end of the island, can be a beautiful summer anchorage when the wind is in the south. I would advise against using it in the winter. If you do, rig two anchors and be prepared to move out if the swell makes up. There is a beautiful white-sand beach in the southeast corner of the bay. The best spot to anchor is in the extreme southeast corner, very close inshore. The cove is seldom visited; it is a good place to get away from the herd.

NOTES

NOTES

NOTES

NOTES

7

Southern Grenadines

II B-3, B-31, B-32, B-311

IMPORTANT: When in the area between south end of Canouan and north end of Carriacou (including Petit St. Vincent and Petit Martinique), use Chart II B-311.

TOBAGO CAYS

(II B-3, B-31, B-311; Sketch Charts III-22 and III-22A)

The Tobago Cays (pronounce it "keys") have been without a doubt the most popular, photographed, and publicized cruising attraction in the entire Caribbean. They are low, dry, uninhabited, with palm trees and white sand, surrounded by miles of fabulous reef—the *pièce de resistance* of an Island charter. Now, though, the cays are so overcrowded that they are losing their charm, fast.

First, there's simply the matter of too many boats and too little privacy. I suppose this is inevitable, and is a familiar lament among yachtsmen almost everywhere these days.

More serious is the garbage problem: As the years go by, the quality of yachtsmen seems not to have kept up with the quantity. People used to be very careful about not polluting the area with garbage. (If a few bits and pieces got scattered around, the charter skippers would get together and organize a cleanup—and then have a celebratory party on one of the boats.) For the past few years, the cays have begun to resemble a garbage dump; the problem seems almost insurmountable. Unless *every* visitor learns to carry all trash back to the boat, or unless the St. Vincent government sets up a disposal or collection scheme—which would be a good way to spend some of the income generated by the yachts—the area may well be ruined before too long.

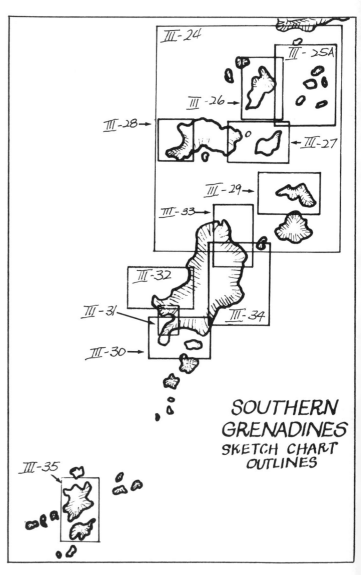

SOUTHERN GRENADINES SKETCH CHART OUTLINES

Furthermore, the cays are almost fished out. Years ago, Bequian fishermen started to come down to the Cays and camp out on the beach, diving on the reefs to provide lobster for the visiting yachts. As the influx of yachts grew, the Bequian fishermen spent more and more time in the cays; now they've even built a permanent house on Petit Rameau. To make things worse, the French from Martinique discovered the cays as a cheap source of fish and lobster and began to buy up everything they could. Now, although you can still be lucky, most of the lobster are taken at 60 feet down—well below most amateur divers' range.

Still, there's no denying the beauty of the cays, and if you're lucky or are cruising in the off season, you'll find a lot of pleasure in the Tobagos. Even if the fishing's not so good, you're sure to find the shelling on the shoals surrounding the keys profitable. Put on a pair of sneakers to protect your feet as you wade about. And finally, for the complacent, a fine time may be had just lazing about under a deck awning, listening to the water slapping against the hull, or ashore under the shade of a palm tree. In the evening some visitors like to have a barbecue on the beaches.

The tides run swiftly through the cays, and your movements and activities—especially diving—should be planned accordingly. A swift tide can take you by surprise; and every season at least one insurance claim is made for yachts colliding in these narrow straits. If you are approaching a crowded anchorage, you may be wise to drop sail and motor in.

Once into the cays, you may anchor anywhere along the slot between Petit Rameau and Petit Bateau in a full 2 fathoms. I prefer to moor on the south side of the slot near the shoal forming the western end of the beach on Petit Bateau. Best to use a Bahamian moor; otherwise, when the tide runs to windward, it will swing your stern into the wind, even when blowing 20 knots through the slot. The effect will be to waltz a boat in a 300-foot circle. This could present a problem when there are other boats in the area. Large boats usually anchor leeward of the cays. If the anchorage within the slot is too crowded, a good anchorage can be had close to shore southwest of Baradal. There is plenty of room here and no need for a two-anchor rig.

For those who value privacy and wish to be close to a reef, an anchorage can be had close behind Horseshoe Reef. It is cool, breezy, calm, and bugless. If you are planning to stay more than a few hours, two anchors are recommended: a Bahamian moor during full or new moon if the wind is light; or during a small moon—neap tides—and heavy weather, use two anchors ahead in a "Y." Given the crowded condition of the cays, this in my opinion is now the only place to anchor. It may be a little choppy and certainly will be very windy but you will be guaranteed privacy and good snorkeling.

The true adventurer in a centerboarder or a bilge-keel boat can anchor behind the reef east of Petit Tabac. A boat drawing 3½ feet can enter the break in the reef at the northwest corner of the island. There are about 5 feet of water in behind the reef.

Really experienced divers, and good small-boat handlers who want some exciting diving, should go to the other edge of Horseshoe Reef and to World's End Reef. If the weather is not too rough, they may be reached by dinghy through the small-boat pass through Horseshoe Reef (Sketch Charts III-24, III-25A). This range should be very carefully lined up, i.e., the southeast end of Petit Rameau should line up with the cut in the hill that is north of the low area of Mayreau Island. It is easy enough to remember this range when going out, but when you are coming back and tired and wet, it is easy to miss as you are coming downwind through the surf. And if you miss this pass you will be swamped. This I know from personal experience, when I became confused coming downwind from World's End Reef and was swamped; luckily we got through without serious damage.

On this subject, I would strongly advise that you trace the profile of this range and take it with you in a plastic bag. Furthermore, I suggest that all cameras and loose gear be packed in waterproof bags and tied down individually or in a bag whenever you are landing a dinghy through surf or passing through surf-surrounded reef areas. Then if the dinghy capsizes or swamps, the bits and pieces will still be attached to the boat and can easily be retrieved. If everything is lying loose and the boat capsizes, then fins, spears, guns, cameras, face masks, and all are spread over a wide area and will usually be lost.

World's End Reef, east of the Tobago Cays, provides a good anchorage under its lee if it is not blowing too hard. However, this anchorage should be attempted only by yachtsmen who are very experienced and can handle their boats in tight situations. You must be good at eyeball navigation and have plenty of ground tackle. If you want to spend the night at World's End Reef, you should be moored on a chain with at least two anchors out—if you started to drag during the night you'd be in serious trouble, as eyeball navigation simply doesn't work in the dark even with a full moon.

Approaching the Tobago Cays from either the north or south should not be difficult. However, new buoyage and ranges have been installed (see Sketch Chart III-25A), and these do little but confuse the issue; they serve no useful purpose except for a boat that uses engine only. The marked entrance from the west along the top of Mayreau Island is one that a sailboat can lay only if the wind is well in the north; this course *cannot* be laid under sail in normal conditions. Below are described some of the approaches used by yachtsmen in this area since time immemorial.

Approaching the Tobago Cays from the North: Coming from the north, you should pass to windward of Baline Rocks, trim sheets, and skirt to leeward of the reefs southeast of Baline Rocks. Take care here, as a number of boats have clipped this reef too close and have bounced off. Luckily there is an inner and outer reef and the outer reef breaks most of the swell, so the boats were not badly damaged. Hold a course of approximately 160 magnetic to the southwest tip of Petit Rameau and all will be well.

If, however, you approach the cays from the north but wish to pass through them and on down direct to Palm Island or Petit St. Vincent, it is best to follow Route 6 (all routes are shown on Sketch Chart III-24): Sail to windward of Baline Rocks and hold a course of around 200 magnetic to the reefs to windward of Mayreau; pass between the reef east of Mayreau and the reef to the east again of that. The channel is narrow but deep; there is no water, port or starboard, but about 40 feet beneath. Continue on this course with a crew in the rigging, not just on the bowsprit—this is essential, as the channel takes a sharp turn to port and you enter the channel on a beam reach. Start sheeting in halfway through the channel. At the end, you will be practically hard on the wind, since the axis of the south end of the channel is southeast-northwest. Once clear of the reef to starboard, you can ease sheets and head for Palm Island, Petit St. Vincent, or wherever.

This route is very useful when sailing direct from Bequia or Canouan to Petit St. Vincent and Palm Island, for if you pass *leeward* of Mayreau, you have to beat back eastward to reach Palm and Petit St. Vincent.

If you are sailing through the cays from south to north and do not intend stopping, pass between the reefs on Range 9 (Sketch Chart III-A, Chapter 1), then ease sheets and follow Route 3 northward (Sketch Chart III-25A), joining up with Route 4 and exiting to windward of Baline Rocks.

Approaching the Tobago Cays from the West: If coming under power—no problem—just head for the buoy southwest of Baline Rocks and pick up the newly established range. The course is 139 magnetic, established under the direction of the Canadian experts. This leads directly to the anchorage, in the slot. If, however, you are beating to windward under sail and cannot lay the range, be careful of the 9-foot spot approximately 800 yards south-southwest of Baline Rocks—really a case of eyeball navigation.

Approaching the Tobago Cays from the South: When approaching from the south, you should work well to the east until you find Range 9 (Sketch Chart III-A or II B-311). The middle hill on Palm Island should be directly under High North (also known as Mount St. Louis) on Carriacou. This leads between the two disappearing sand islands on Route 1 (Sketch Chart III-25A), and into the Tobago Cays. This is a dead accurate range which I have used for years. However, you can get in trouble if as you approach this narrow channel a rain squall blocks out either Palm Island or Carriacou. Thus a bow range is useful. One that Mike Forshaw has given me (which was given to him in 1938) also leads to the same opening. Put the southeast corner of Petit Rameau just closing with the northwest corner of Petit Bateau and you are set to go through the channel between the two disappearing sand islands. Once through the channel it is again a case of eyeball navigation, following one of the routes described in Sketch Chart III-25A. One trouble with this range is that unless the wind is well around to the south it will be impossible to use under sail; you will have to motor-sail to use this range. Do not attempt to use Range 5 when entering the cays from the south, as there is no range leading to this route; it is an exit route only.

Leaving the Tobago Cays: When leaving the cays to the north, just reverse the entry procedure. For boats heading south, Routes 1 and 5 (Sketch Chart III-25A) are the most popular; Route 5 is most favored for boats heading directly to Petit St. Vincent and passing to windward of Palm Island, since if you use Route 1 when going to Palm, you will throw away a quarter mile of windward ground.

The St. Vincent government has established a buoyage system that I think acts like a booby trap system to nail the careless yachtsman. What the government ought to do is to establish a buoyage

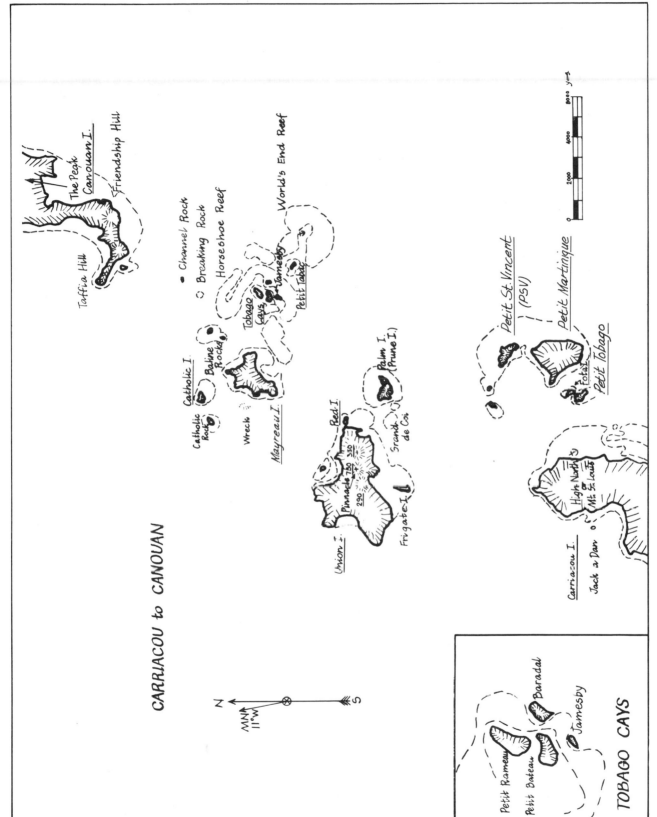

CARRIACOU to CANOUAN

The Peak
Canouan I.
Taffia Hill
Friendship Hill

● Channel Rock
○ Breaking Rock
Horseshoe Reef

Catholic I.
Baline Rock
Catholic Rock
Wreck
Mayreau I.

Tobago Cays
Jamesby
World's End Reef
Petit Tabac

Union I.
Red I.
Pinnacle 750 350
290
Grand
de Coi
Palm I.
(Prune I.)
Frigate I.

Petit St. Vincent
(PSV)
Petit Martinique
Fota I.
Petit Tobago

Carria-cou I.
High North or
Mt. St. Louis
Jack a Dan

N
MNW
11°W
S

TOBAGO CAYS

Petit Rameau
Petit Bateau
Baradal
Jamesby

SKETCH CHART III-24 Carriacou to Canouan

0 2000 4000 8000 yds

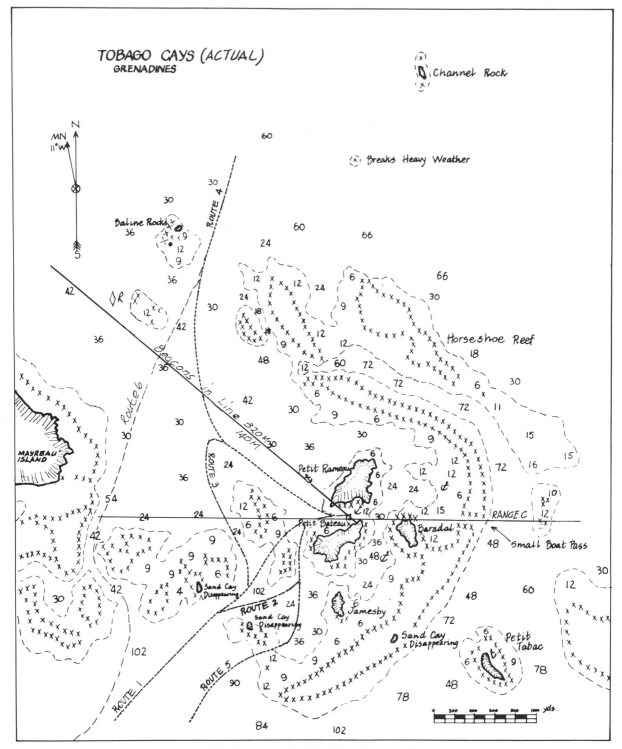

SKETCH CHART III-25A Tobago Cays

Range A: North end of Petit Rameau in line with north end of Mayreau clears shoal south of Baline
           Rocks, 120-300 magnetic.
Range B: Baline Rocks in line with east end of Mayreau leads over shoals south of Baline Rocks, 215-
           035 magnetic.
Range C: North or Baradal in line with north end of Petit Bateau in line with south edge of flat land on
           Mayreau leads through boat pass.

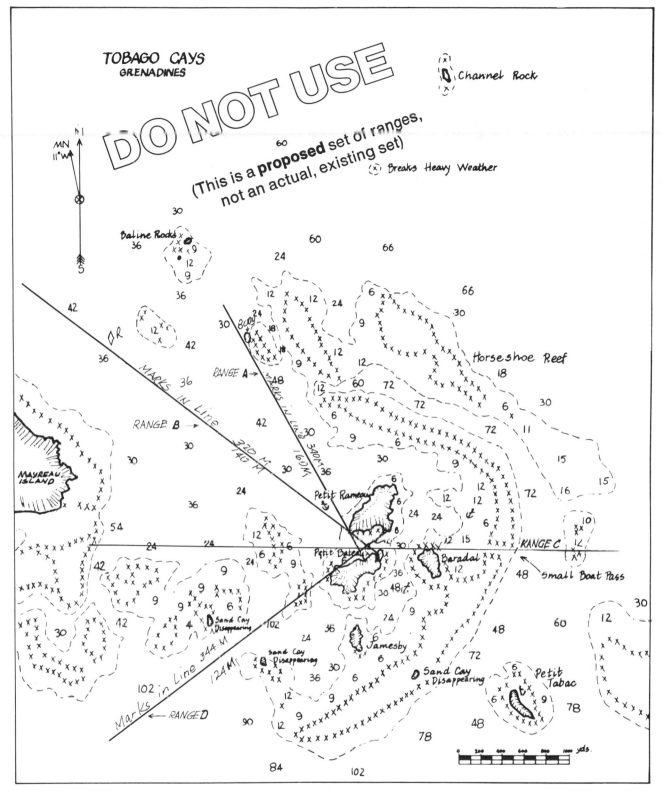

SKETCH CHART III-25B   Tobago Cays

Range A   (northern entrance to the cays): Marker on southwest end of Petit Rameau (existing mark) in
           line with mark (to be installed) on north side of Petit Bateau in line with 340-160 magnetic.
           Possibly a buoy should be placed as noted on chart to lead clear of reefs northwest of the cays.

Range B   (western entrance): Existing range and buoy.

Range C   (small-boat pass through the outer reefs): Establish marks at north end of Petit Bateau and
           Baradal—in line lead through boat pass.

Range D   (southern entrance to the cays): Mark on northwest corner of Petit Bateau in line with mark
           on southeast corner of Petit Rameau (both marks to be established), 344-124 magnetic, plus
           possibly buoy as marked on the chart to keep boats in really deep water instead of having them
           reef-dodge on Routes 1 and 2 in Sketch Chart III-22.

system that would lead the yachtsman clear of all dangers. Many yachtsmen feel that range marks should be established in the Tobago Cays as per Sketch Chart 25B.

Elsewhere in the Grenadines, Grand de Coi should certainly be marked by a day marker, perch, or what have you, directly on top of the reef, which bares at low-water springs. This Johnny Caldwell has been volunteering to do for many years, but the St. Vincent government has never accepted his offer.

Similarly, Montezuma Shoal should be marked in the same fashion. I would think that the developers of Mustique, like Johnny Caldwell, would be willing to do it for free.

Union Island Harbor should have a clearly defined entrance range, and if lit, should be well lit with reliable lights.

If the above were done, perhaps yachtsmen would not be so resentful of the taxes imposed on visiting yachts.

MAYREAU ISLAND
(II B-3, B-31, B-311; Sketch Chart III-26)

Mayreau is three miles south of Union, and its peaks should not be confused with those of Union, which are only half as high. Some years ago the people of Mayreau were living at a bare subsistence level. Today the island appears much more prosperous; the old houses are being fixed up and painted, and some new ones built. (Tourism has certainly brought some advantages to these small islands.) Saline Bay is a large open bay on the southwest side of the island, with a dock on its northeast corner. Deep water extends much closer to shore than some old charts show. This is a beautiful spot with a half-mile-long white-sand beach that is usually deserted. Best to spend your time on the beach, as the ground swell hooking around the point makes laying-to a roly affair.

I've been told that if you tuck up in the northeast corner of the harbor, west of the sand beach, you'll be almost completely out of the swell, which of course creates that beautiful white-sand beach on the southern end of the bay. There is talk of a restaurant and bar being constructed in this corner of the bay.

For a superb view of the Islands, tie your dinghy up at the jetty in Saline Bay and walk up the hill for a panoramic look at the Southern Grenadines.

When leaving for the north, give a wide berth to the shoal extending from Grand Col Point. It has a longer reach than some charts give it credit

for, one that has dented a surprising number of boats in recent years.

One of the new buoys has been placed off Grand Col Point; pass to westward of the buoy and you'll clear the shoal. But the buoy is so far from the reef that boats are tempted to pass between it and the reef, and end up clipping the reef. Why the buoy wasn't placed close to the reef only the Lord—and the Canadian government—knows. A safe range is discussed in Chapter 1.

North of this reef you will find the submerged wreck of the World War I gunboat *Paruna*. I am indebted to Jol Byerly and Desmond Nicholson for the story of the wrecking of the *Paruna*. She was a Royal Navy gunboat, stationed in the Lower Caribbean during World War I. Royal Navy food not being too good, they frequently anchored in Mayreau's southern bay so the crew could go out in small boats to fish. While they were so engaged late one afternoon, a steamer coming out from behind Union Island was spotted and the captain decided to investigate, in spite of the lateness of the hour. He figured he knew the area well enough to operate at night.

Thus he weighed anchor, the rudder was put to port, and the ship kicked ahead, making a hard left turn. About the time she had a head of steam up, a hard gust of wind hit and, having a lot of windage aft, the poor old *Paruna* could not bear off enough to clear the reef. She evidently hit the bricks going at about 8 knots, which took the whole bottom off her; she sank on the other side of the reef.

This should be a cautionary tale to anyone who fancies sailing at night, for if a Royal Navy gunboat that had been in service in the area for many years didn't make it, you probably won't either.

And even by daylight, pay attention to the ranges shown on Sketch Chart III-26 for locating the wreck. The current is very strong, so plan your diving expeditions for slack water.

The bay directly east of the wreck is a nice lunchtime spot when the swell is down. The beach is beautiful here, but is definitely not recommended for overnight stops.

At the north end of Mayreau is one of the most attractive anchorages in the Grenadines—locally called Salt Whistle Bay. As Sketch Chart 26 shows, the shoal extends south and east from the northern point of the harbor; however, there is a full 5 feet of water south of the reef, and this depth can be carried inside the reef well up into the northeast corner. Proceed slowly, as the bottom comes up gradually. Anchor bow and stern; otherwise, when the wind dies down in the evening, the swell

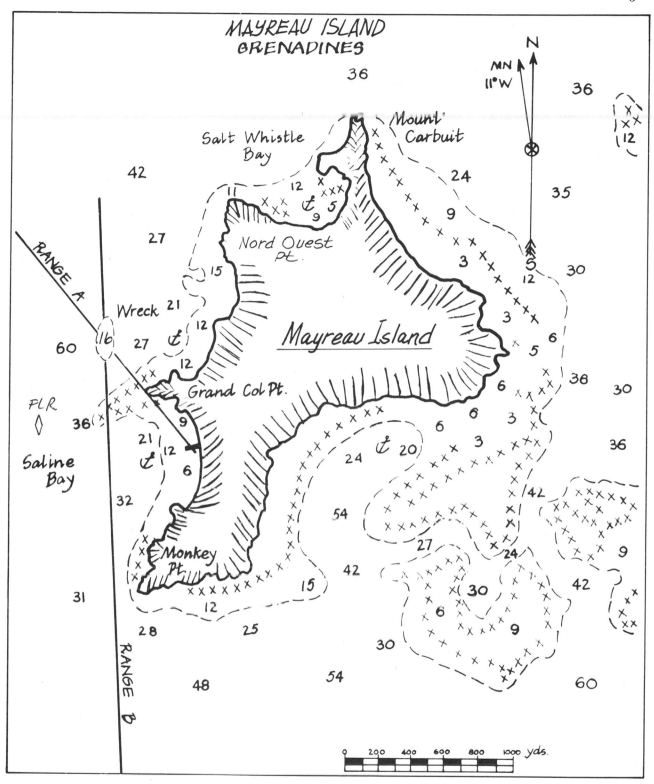

MAYREAU ISLAND
GRENADINES

36

N

MN
11°W

36

35

36

12

Salt Whistle
Bay

Mount
Carbuit

24

42

9

12

5

27

9

Nord Ouest
Pt.

3

15

Mayreau Island

3

12

30

Wreck 21

12

3

6

60

16

27

5

12

6

36

30

FLR

9

Grand Col Pt.

6

6

3

36

Saline
Bay

21

12

6

24

20

3

36

32

42

54

27

24

31

54

42

9

Monkey
Pt.

15

30

12

6

28

25

9

30

42

48

54

60

0   200   400   600   800   1000 yds.

SKETCH CHART III-26   Mayreau Island

Range A: Cliff of Grand Col Point in line with midpoint of Saline Bay dock leads over wreck.
Range B: Peak of Petit Martinique over western low land of Palm leads over wreck.
Note: Use ranges cautiously and only for finding wreck; otherwise you may become one yourself.

hooking around the point will throw you beam-to to the sea and you will roll badly. Note the condition of the tide: If you sneak too far in and the tide goes out from under you, it may be a few hours of rough bumping before you get out. Beware that the ground swell does not make up while you are inside, as this would make getting out a hazardous proposition. This is a good anchorage in settled weather only.

I would estimate that eight is the maximum number of boats for the anchorage, but they tell me that one New Year's Eve they had twenty-two happily jam-packed yachts.

The cove has been beautifully developed by Tom and Undine Potter. I say "beautifully developed" because when you sail into the anchorage and look ashore you see little or no sign of the cottage-type hotel that has been built; the cottages are all hidden completely in the trees. The only fly in the ointment is a horrible square concrete house at the northernmost point of the bay—which the Potters refer to as "instant disaster." Originally the staff cottage was hidden among the palm trees along with the guest cottages, but it seems the staff, after quitting time, continued partying until the small hours and were keeping the guests awake. Hence the sudden building of "disaster."

You used to be able to walk across the sandspit and find a lovely beach on the windward side, with sheltered rock pools for warm-water bathing. Unfortunately, what garbage yachtsmen don't leave in the cays they apparently throw overboard as they leave, and it all drifts down onto Mayreau's windward beaches, which have become foul with litter and hardly worth the walk anymore.

The Salt Whistle Bay Hotel can be contacted on channel 16; they can arrange diving and fishing trips. They also have a small boutique.

Mayreau used to be so poor that there was a main catchment and cistern where most people got water. It was built by a Father Dionne, who, because water was in such short supply, kept the key to the cistern on his person. Father Dionne worked hard to improve the lot of the islanders, but with the money that has come in from Palm and Petit St. Vincent and the Anchorage, people are better off and most have their own cisterns. Father Dionne has gone and there is no longer a resident priest.

There is one good anchorage on Mayreau's windward side. On the southeast coast there is deep water inside the reefs. Sail up inside, round up, and anchor close behind the reef where Sketch Chart III-26 indicates. Use two anchors to keep you off in case the wind dies. A final note on the chart: A 1-fathom passage is shown around the eastern point of Mayreau. Looking at it from the hill it does not seem to exist, but *Brabantine* with a 6-foot draft succeeded in getting through at high tide.

CATHOLIC ISLAND
(II B-3, B-31, B-311)

There is nothing to attract yachts to this small island northwest of Mayreau. It is noteworthy only as a hazard for boats working north from Mayreau. Jondell Cays, extending well to the east of Catholic Island, threaten boats beating north against a leeward-setting tide. Low-lying Catholic Rocks to the west are unlit—no place to investigate after dark.

PALM ISLAND
(II B-3, B-31, B-311; Sketch Chart III-27)

Formerly called Prune Island, Palm Island is under a long-term lease to John Caldwell. In American folklore, Johnny Appleseed planted apple trees from coast to coast. Here in the Islands it was Coconut John who planted palm trees throughout the Caribbean. For this reason Prune Island was renamed when John Caldwell took over.

Caldwell has had an interesting career. He was married in Australia during World War II. When the war ended, he found himself in Panama with no means of returning to his wife in Australia. Although he was not a sailor, he bought a small sailboat, and with more guts than brains set out for Australia. He got as far as Fiji before wrecking and damn near losing his life. The fiasco resulted in Caldwell's first literary effort, *Desperate Voyage*.

He and his wife moved to Los Angeles, where he received a graduate degree in sociology, thereafter setting out in a gaff-rigged Tahiti ketch for Australia. The passage was successful and resulted in a second book, *Family at Sea*. He worked in Australia for several years before building his present boat, *Outward Bound*. With his family on board, he sailed westward halfway around the world to the Caribbean. He has been in the Islands ever since.

It has been a long pull for John, his wife, Mary, their sons, John and Roger, and their wives. With nothing but sweat and guts they have built huge cisterns, vacation homes, well-designed rental cottages, a beach bar, restaurant, boutique, etc., thus developing a mosquito-infested island into a popular resort that draws people from all over the world.

As if this weren't enough, John and his sons

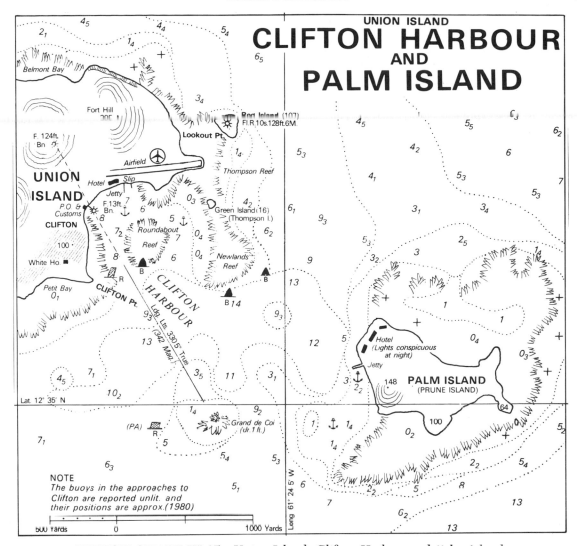

SKETCH CHART III-27   Union Island, Clifton Harbor, and Palm Island

have, incredibly, salvaged close to 100 boats over the years. At least ten of them would have been total losses had it not been for the Caldwells. And they have never charged a cent for their efforts. Would there were more people like them around!

Outward Bound was finally replaced by a 41-foot Carib bought from CSY; with a few other boats John for a while ran a bare-boat operation but finally thought better of it. For years he has dreamed of dredging through to the salt pond and building a marina at Palm but his project seems to be in the land of dreams till such time as a financer can be found.

The boys and their wives finally decided they'd had enough of life in the Grenadines and have moved to the States, where they have successful careers.

Palm Island can always be reached on VHF channel 16 and has a telephone that works with a fair degree of regularity. There are parties some nights of the week—check on channel 16. Lunch and dinner are always available. There is a dive operation and you can arrange diving trips in the Grenadines; they will also charge tanks and provide equipment. A boutique, attractively located on the beach and originally set up by John's daughter-in-law Cindy, is loaded with attractive locally made jewelry, clothes, bikinis, etc. This shop also stocks Street guides and Imray-Iolaire charts. A commissary can supply the basics if you run out.

One of the sights to see when anchored at Palm is *Sea Cloud* running down from Mustique. It is only a 20-mile run from Mustique to Palm, but frequently when the winds are favorable *Sea Cloud* will set everything to her royals for the short run down.

When anchoring at Palm, get as close to shore as possible, let go your anchor, back her down with mizzen or engine, and let out plenty of scope: It is much deeper off Palm Island than the chart shows; there is 30 feet right off the docks. Once the anchor is in, it will not drag; but be sure it is well set or you will back right off the shelf into deep water. More than one bare-boat skipper has anchored at Palm and gone ashore for a cool drink only to be told that his boat was heading for Carriacou. This causes instant panic and a hasty pursuit of the runaway boat in a dinghy.

In periods of heavy weather, the anchorage at Palm Island can be roly, but it is never dangerous. Just be careful and *make sure the anchor is properly set.*

The north shore of Palm is completely surrounded by reef. There is very little water inside the northeasternmost reef. You would need a shoal boat drawing less than 4 feet to penetrate safely inside. (Such a boat, in fact, could circumnavigate most of the island *inside* the reef.) By the way, when anchoring off the southwest corner of the island watch out for the detached coral head 300 yards to the southwest. You can carry a full 9 feet between the coral head and the main reef, but keep a sharp eye for the former.

Grand de Coi is a very dangerous reef approximately one-half mile west of Palm Island. This reef bares at low-water springs and one would think it is extremely easy to see—but unfortunately it is not. Numerous boats have piled up on this reef— the 70-foot schooner *Mollihawk*, after she was sold by the Nicholsons, ran hard aground on Grand de Coi; after a lot of work, she was eventually gotten off. *Annamarie* was not so lucky. This 70-foot Baltic trader succeeded in running up on Grand de Coi right at the top of the high-water spring tide, and although the motor vessel *Meteor* made a valiant attempt to haul her off, it was not good enough— *Annamarie*'s bones remain on the reef. With great regularity boats pile up on Grand de Coi and are rescued by John Caldwell and his assistants.

Now a buoy has been placed to mark Grand de Coi—but it lies so far to the west of the reef that one is tempted to pass between the buoy and the reef. Don't! To be in the clear you should always pass west and south of the buoy. However, when beating out of Union Island heading to Petit St. Vincent under sail, clearing the buoy properly means you're throwing away a good deal of windward distance. So it may be worth cutting the buoy and eyeballing the reef. Grand de Coi should be marked by a day marker or perch on top of the reef.

When heading north or south, check Ranges 3 and 4 on Sketch Chart III-A.

When sailing northwest from Petit St. Vincent to Union or Palm in the afternoon with the sun in front of you, it is virtually impossible to see Grand de Coi. In this case, pass between Pinese and Mopion and head for the peak on Frigate Island until you pick up Range 4 or 5 (Sketch Chart III-A or II B-311). Follow Range 5 if heading for Palm Island, Range 4 if heading for Union.

UNION ISLAND
(II B-3, B-31, B-311; Sketch Chart III-27)

As the Grenadines go, Union Island is fairly large. Its population is sparse, with only two small villages, Clifton and Ashton. It is easily spotted from a distance by rock pinnacles that bristle the sky like large spikes. The island is three miles long and two miles across at its broadest.

A beautiful hotel, the Bougainvillea, was built in the northeast corner of Clifton Harbor by André and Simone Beaufrand. They also build a dock, ice plant, slipway, and airport. The place is now called the Anchorage Hotel and Yacht Club, and is run by Carlos Brouard. It still serves delicious French meals, and you can get water and diesel—but no gas. It's also a good place to pick up fish, as fishermen come into the hotel to have their catch air-freighted off to Martinique—a practice that has helped denude the entire Grenadines of lobster. If I ever see a lobster in these waters, I'll probably die of shock. It has, however, put money into the local economy.

The boutiques, run by Carole Gueson, stocks not only jewelry, bikinis, pareus, and the like, but also the Street guides and Imray-Iolaire charts.

There are saltwater pools behind the dock where you will find lobster, turtles, fish, and also sharks (nurse sharks, not the man-eating kind).

The slipway is interesting in that it is one of the few in the Caribbean with side tracks, i.e., they can haul you and slip you off to the side and thus get four or five boats out at once. As in the old days at Beef Island, you can hire a gang of bottom scrubbers and a few carpenters who are used to working on local schooners and sloops, but they are certainly not yacht carpenters. There are no marine supplies or decent lumber on the island, so you must bring everything you need with you. As to the price, I have inquired a number of times and decided it was too expensive. On the other hand, I have talked to people who have hauled there and paid a lot less than I had been quoted. So it seems the price is negotiable—a chance for a bit of good old-fashioned horse trading.

Behind the hotel is a concrete airstrip, which,

while not as hairy as the one at St. Barts, is certainly one whose approach can weaken the knees of even experienced pilots on their first landing there. One of the first planes that tried to come in ended in the harbor, and other accidents have occurred since then. Now the runway has been expanded and the airport is busy from dawn to dusk.

Customs and Immigration is difficult: there is a Customs and Immigration office in town at the post office, and also one at the airport. Whenever I go to town, I discover I have to go to the airport and whenever I go to the airport, I have to go to town. In many cases, the officials have been less than friendly in telling me I am very dumb in going to the wrong place!

Garbage is a bit of a problem, as the only dump is an open pit in town near the post office. Do not leave your garbage at the Anchorage Yacht Club.

Although there are no marine supplies available in Union, if you ask around you will discover that CSY usually has a mechanic based at Union who in an emergency can help out with mechanical problems.

Food supplies have improved greatly in the last few years in Union; the supermarkets, although not really "super," do supply the basics—including fresh, hot bread baked every morning.

There are now numerous places to get food and drink, such as the Anchorage Yacht Club, good but expensive, and the Clifton Beach Hotel and Boutique. The yacht skippers seem to hang out at the Sunny Grenadines, farther south along the beach from the Clifton Beach Hotel, where you'll also find Gil, the French sailmaker. Wander through all three, have a beer at each, and decide which one suits your needs best.

Union is served by Island Air, from Grenada to St. Lucia; by Martinque Air, running from Martinique and St. Lucia; by Tropic Air; and by other charter organizations from Barbados.

CLIFTON HARBOR
(II B-311; Sketch Chart III-27)

The entrance to Clifton Harbor will be confusing to the newcomer. The charts are inaccurate in many respects and the buoys simply cannot be trusted. In March 1986, both outer buoys were unlit and the range shown on the British chart was not working. The American chart shows solid reef extending all the way to the shoreline to the north. In fact, this is middle ground, and it is possible to sail to windward of the reef and to anchor directly behind the outer reef. Use II B-311.

Formerly Roundabout Reef was marked by a large concrete block in the middle of the reef with a light on it—this has fallen over and will probably have disappeared within a few years. Now the southwestern corner of the middle ground is marked by a black buoy that is—supposedly—lit at night.

When approaching Clifton Harbor, it is easy to spot the outer reef. Round the outer reef close aboard to starboard, sail north toward the gap between Fort Hill and Red Island (eyeball navigation), and round up behind Green Island (also referred to as Thompson Island on some charts and guides). Anchor at a depth suitable for your draft. The bottom is hard sand, and once the anchor is dug in, the holding is extremely good. Make sure you are on the shelf, though, because the bottom drops off very steeply to 35–40 feet.

The water here is always calm, while the wind whistles past the anchorage, making it cool and bug free. Take the dinghy to the hotel dock, where you will be less tormented by small boys than at the main dock. Walk along the shore to town, the post office, and the small supermarket.

Anchorage in the main part of the harbor is not too good, as one finds 40 or more feet of water, which makes hauling up the anchor a back breaker.

At night there is supposed to be a range by which to enter Clifton Harbor, but it was not operating the last time I was there; and in any case, I would not under any circumstances enter Union Island at night. Rather, I would anchor in the lee of Palm Island and wait until dawn.

Ashton, west of Clifton and the main town, has no harbor for boats carrying more than 3 feet. A path leads up from Ashton or Clifton to the Pinnacle (Mount Taboi), the highest peak on Union. Coming from Clifton, according to John Clegg, the best approach to the peak is from the east, heading for the smaller pinnacle northeast of the main one. From the small one to the summit of the large there are two or three routes, and which one is more convenient depends on where the century plants have been growing that year. None should present any problem, but beware the Jack Spaniard wasp. He won't kill you, but he gives one hell of a nasty sting. He looks like the North American wasp, only a mite larger.

FRIGATE ISLAND
(II B-3, B-31, B-311; Sketch Chart III-24)

This is the small island just off Union, and behind it there is a good anchorage indeed. Deep water extends much farther north than some charts indicate. I normally anchor with the high hill on

Frigate bearing approximately southeast. It is always sheltered and cool here. There may be some chop, but this is more than made up for by the total seclusion. It is pleasant in the evening to lie back and watch the frigate birds circling lazily around the peak towering above you. The harbor behind the reef is a perfect place for dinghy sailing. The water is shallow and the wind is always good. If

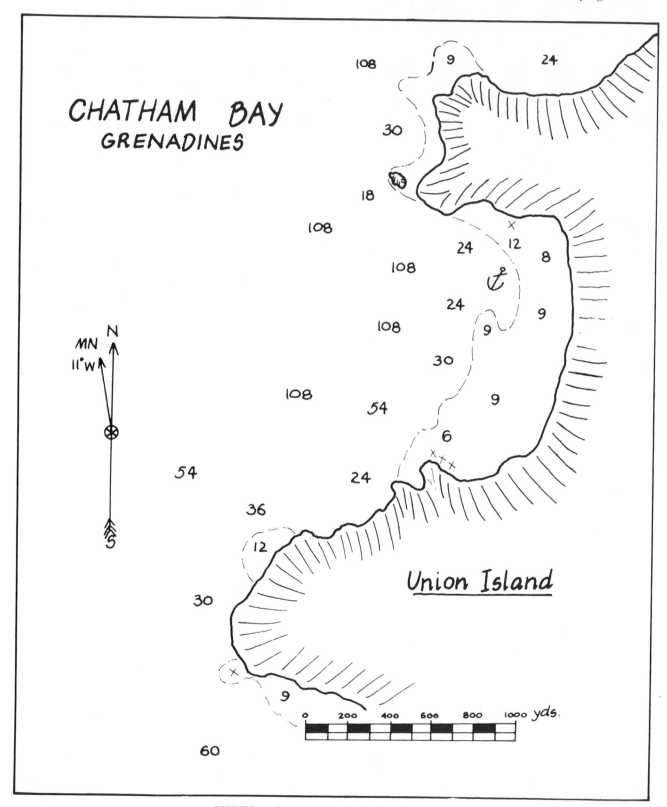

SKETCH CHART III-28   Chatham Bay

the kids capsize, they can stand in the shallows and right the boat.

CHATHAM BAY
(II B-3, B-31; Sketch Chart III-28)

The other good anchorage of Union Island, Chatham, was uninhabited until some years ago an individual in search of privacy built a small cottage. He is seldom visited by anyone except a few of the local fishermen. Inside Chatham Bay, hard gusts have a tendency to blow out of the hills with surprising force. They are not dangerous in themselves, but they may lead you to believe that it is howling outside. Boats have hung back timorously in the harbor for days on end expecting raging gales outside. Finally venturing out, they have found it blowing no more than 10 or 15 knots. Don't be deceived. From here you can travel to the northeast tip of the island, where the reef diving and spearfishing is of the very best. Yachts seldom anchor in the area, but it is good nonetheless. The best place is in the northeast corner in 2 fathoms. The southeast corner is shoal and exposed to the wind.

Doug Terman and Hazen Richardson served together in the Strategic Air Command. With their mustering out pay, they bought the 77-foot Crocker-designed schooner *Jacinta* and tried to make their fortune in the charter trade. They did not succeed in that, but they found and fell in love with the uninhabited island of Petit St. Vincent. They managed to buy it, and with financial backing they built Petit St. Vincent into the world-famous resort it is today.

Haze and his wife stayed on to run Petit St. Vincent, and Doug went on to become a successful novelist whose books include *First Strike, Free Flight, Shell Game,* and the children's book *By Balloon to the Saraha.*

They have decided to join forces again and with backers are planning a multi-million-dollar facility in Chatham Bay similar to Petit St. Vincent and with a VHF relay station on the top of Union Island. This is certainly needed and will give good VHF coverage to the whole Grenadines. As at Petit St. Vincent, they will do their level best to cater to the needs of the true yachtsman. Needless to say, those types that Ross Lulley refers to as "waterpeople" will not be catered to.

We lose another deserted anchorage, but you cannot stop progress, and if the area is going to be developed, I cannot think of anyone better equipped to do it than Haze and Doug.

Island Dependencies of Union

PINESE AND MOPION
(II B-3, B-31, B-311; Sketch Chart III-29)

These are the two sand cays off Petit St. Vincent. Mopion means crab louse, and the translation of Pinese is bedbug; perhaps both are distant relatives of Las Cucarachas (the cockroaches) off the northeast tip of Puerto Rico. When passing to leeward of Mopion, be careful of the shoal, since the island is continually extending to the south and southwest farther than is shown on the chart. Many yachts have struck this shoal, as several Lloyd's underwriters will attest. There is a channel east of Mopion, known among experienced Islands yachtsmen as Crazy Corrigan's Crooked Channel, named after Dave Corrigan of Mariner's Inn, St. Vincent. It is perfectly safe for the experienced reef pilot, but there are no ranges whatsoever. I will give the general gist of the directions, but you will have to eyeball it for yourself. Head a little bit to windward of Mopion until you spot the break in the reef. Enter and head roughly southeast, following the color of the deep water. As Mopion comes abeam, the channel curves to the south, and as you pass Mopion, it curves again to the southwest. Follow the channel around, and once clear in deep water, head for Petit St. Vincent. In the annual race between the Tobago Cays and Petit St. Vincent, this channel saves about half a mile of windward work.

As of May 1986, Pinese broke water a low, low water, only in May, June, and July.

PETIT ST. VINCENT
(II B-3, B-31; Sketch Chart III-29)

The island is commonly referred to as PSV. It was formerly a beautiful deserted island, but I am not particularly surprised that it has been built up. It is an attractive island with good anchorages and beaches. The hotel on PSV is spectacular in every respect, right down to the bill that will be tendered you at the end of your stay. Lunch or dinner reservations can be made by radio on VHF channel 16. Ice and fuel are available on the island; water is hard to come by, although you could probably get some in a real emergency.

PSV has always catered to the yachtsman, helping out in emergencies, throwing excellent weekly jump-ups during the winter charter season, and hosting the four-day PSV Thanksgiving Regatta, which features good racing and even better parties.

Unfortunately, the free showers PSV used to

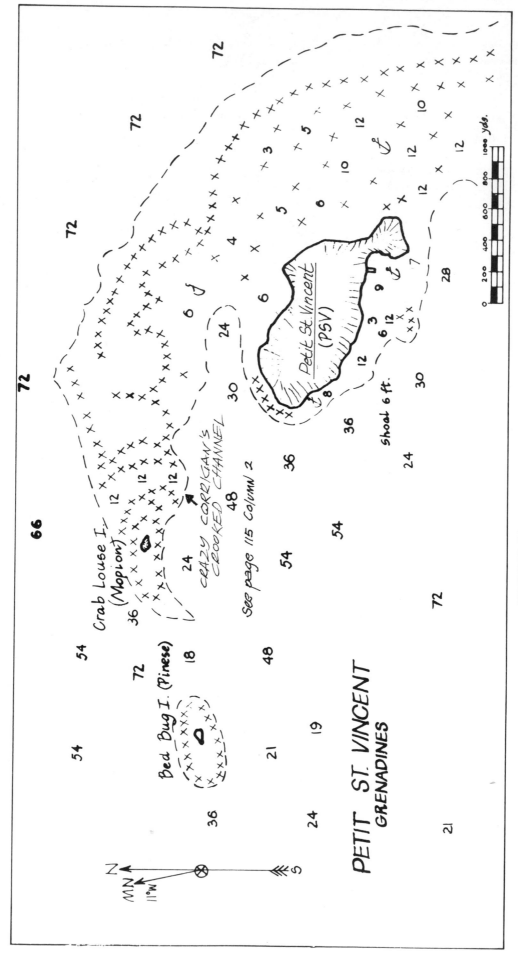

PETIT ST. VINCENT
GRENADINES

Bed Bug I. (Pinese)

Crab Louse I.
(Mopion)

CRAZY CORRIGAN'S
CROOKED CHANNEL

See page 115 Column 2

Petit St. Vincent
(PSV)

Shoal 6 ft.

72 72 72 72 72 66 72

54 54 54

54 36 72 18 24 12 12 12 12 6 4 5 3

36 48 30 24 6 9 6 5 10 12 5

19 21 24 48 54 54 36 12 8 3 12 6 9 7 10 12

36 24 21 72 30 28

N MN 11°W S

0 200 400 600 800 1000 yds.

SKETCH CHART III-29   Petit St. Vincent

offer visiting sailors are no longer available because so many so-called yachtsmen aren't. But the fruit drinks sold on the terrace, with or without booze, are still terrific, and the view is likewise.

PSV is part of St. Vincent. If you are headed north from Petit Martinique or Carriacou, you're supposed to clear through Clifton Harbor, Union before anchoring in PSV. Considering the number of yachts visiting PSV now, it would make great sense to make it a port of entry. But as of 1986 it isn't, except during the November Thanksgiving Regatta.

At one point, Customs officers from Union used to raid PSV and make any yachts there that hadn't cleared properly sail over to Union in the dark to enter. There isn't an operating Customs launch at the moment, though, so there's little chance of being nabbed. (If Haze Richardson needs a policeman on PSV these days, he has to provide transportation!)

Furthermore, as mentioned earlier, it seems likely that even if a yacht hasn't properly cleared, it won't be jumped on by Customs (as long as it's doing nothing illegal) if the skipper says he has gone into a harbor of refuge, i.e., couldn't reach a clearance port before dark.

Fishermen from St. Vincent and Bequia camp at the western edge of the beach below the Petit St. Vincent Hotel. They are *not* employees of the hotel or in any way connected with it. Many of them are the finest old-time Bequian fishermen —hardworking, honest, and helpful—who are a pleasure to meet, talk to, and do business with. Others, unfortunately, of the younger generation are rough, tough, broke, and out to get everything they can. That could include your dinghy. The fishermen who camp on Petit St. Vincent beach always maintain that dinghies are stolen by smugglers from Petit Martinique; the Petit Martinicans insist that the dinghies are stolen by the Bequian fishermen. Either way, lock your dinghy to the mother ship or to the dock.

The shoreline of PSV is a string of beaches, separated one from another by intermittent outcroppings of rock. It is possible to walk around the rocky points, but I would suggest wearing a pair of sneakers unless your feet are more leathery than most. The shelling on the rocks is unusually abundant; diving expeditions can be made to the reefs windward of the island; small boats can be rented from the hotel.

The normal anchorage is off the south coast. The larger boats favor a location due south or slightly east of due south of the highest peak on the western end of the island. Smaller boats can tack farther east between the reef and the island, ending up at anchor south of the saddle formed by the two hills. The bottom is hard sand and good holding. The current reverses along here so I would recommend a Bahamian moor, especially when the anchorage becomes crowded. Since the completion of the new dock, the shoals along the shore have been growing and shifting—proceed with caution. When leaving the anchorage, boats drawing 8 feet or less can pass to windward of the shoal, before turning to the south and west. This is sometimes an easier way out than threading downwind through a crowded anchorage. (In March 1985, we bounced going out with *Iolaire*, drawing 7 feet 6 inches. So the channel has shoaled a bit.)

The chart shows a ragged sort of channel through the reef between PSV and Petit Martinique. Some of the work sloops sail this channel, but you would have to be one hell of a seaman to make it through, and I strongly urge newcomers not to use it. The first time I saw a boat in this channel with seas breaking all around, I thought I was watching the preliminary maneuvers of an elaborate suicide. Haze Richardson, manager of PSV, ascertained from the local fishermen how they manage to thread their way through these reefs going downwind: "The highest land on Union, the Pinnacle, is sighted through the lowland of PSV. Stay on this range until the southeast corner of Carriacou comes out from behind Petit Martinique. Then take a short tack to the east, eyeballing it to find a narrow gap between the reefs." Sailors who use this channel are either good or aground—there is no room for error.

Some boats in search of privacy anchor north of the island or else work their way along the south coast through the reef to an anchorage east of the island. Both possibilities are indicated on Sketch Chart III-29.

Island Dependencies of Carriacou

PETIT TOBAGO AND FOTA
(II B-3, B-31, B-311)

No anchorage and little of interest except to the geologist at either Little Tobago or Fota, although in calm weather there is a marginal anchorage off the latter's lee shore. They do provide a number of helpful ranges, which are drawn on Sketch Charts III-A and III-24.

PETIT MARTINIQUE

(II B-3, B-31, B-311)

If you visit this dry, windswept island, you will notice rows of houses like the wooden salt-box houses of Nantucket. Back in the old days the locals must have learned house building from the New England whaler crews. High in the hills on the northern top of the island is the Catholic church, whence the view is stupendous.

The islanders make a living by going to sea for legitimate trade or illicit smuggling. At times the Customs inspector comes over from Carriacou, but his visits are always well advertised and the people have time to put their island in order. I suspect that if the government chose seriously to crack down, Petit Martinique would soon be uninhabited. Basically, the people of Petit Martinique are hardworking and honest, with a strong streak of independence.

There is an interesting story told about Petit Martinique smugglers of the past; perhaps, like many good yarns, it has very little to do with what actually happened, but it has been repeated so often now that most people take it for the truth.

It concerns a Petit Martinique smuggler who killed a rival smuggler from Venezuela who was poaching on his patch. The Grenadian government sent the chief of police to investigate the murder, and after sorting things out a bit, the chief ordered one of his sergeants to go and arrest the Petit Martinican.

"I am sorry, I am not going," replied the sergeant.

"Then I am holding you for direct disobedience," replied the chief, to which the sergeant responded, "Sir, I have just resigned from the force."

After a lot of shouting, everyone returned to Grenada.

Months later the chief went himself to make the arrest. Arriving by boat off the island about four in the afternoon, he noticed that every soul on the island was assembled on the beach near the burial ground, dressed for a funeral. As the anchor went down, a man came swimming out from shore and said, "Oh, commissioner, sir, please hurry ashore immediately."

"I don't want to interrupt a funeral. I'm here on official business."

"But, sir, we don't like to bury someone after dark."

"Well, who died?" asked the mystified chief.

"No one, yet," the messenger replied. "It's your funeral; the coffin is ready and the grave is dug. But please hurry—because it will be dark soon."

The chief decided to up anchor and go back to Grenada, and history does not record what happened to the smuggler from Petit Martinique who killed the smuggler from Venezuela.

The Gairy administration tried to do in the smugglers of Petit Martinique and Carriacou by drastically reducing the duty on liquor, hoping to make it unprofitable to smuggle. That didn't work out—it just reduced the profits and changed the smuggling products. Now instead of rum, whiskey, and gin picked up in St. Barts and smuggled into Grenada, they go only as far as Martinique and load up on good Dutch Heineken beer (as opposed to second-rate St. Lucia and Trinidad Heineken beer) and smuggle that. At the same time, when the exchange rate is favorable (when things are cheaper in Martinique than in Grenada), they also load up with various household items and bring them to Carriacou. Many imported French items are much cheaper in Carriacou than they are in Grenada. While heading north, they smuggle milk from Grenada into St. Vincent. The previous St. Vincent government established a dairy and made it illegal to import milk; but the dairy doesn't produce a sufficient quantity and so the smugglers provide it.

Good smuggling stories abound. Bill Stevens of Stevens Yachts, a very active fisherman, points out that it is easy to tell Petit Martinican, Carriacouan, or Venezuelan rum smugglers from true fishing boats: Just look at the rail cap. If the rail cap is clean and unscarred it is a rum smuggler. If it is a fishing boat, the rail cap will have gouges where the fishing lines dug in. Bill tells another story. When he first arrived in Grenada, he and his wife, Barbra, ran a small hardware store that specialized in supplying nets, hooks, and lines to the fishermen. Bill was often away up on the north end of the island, where he made friends with a Catholic priest. Bill dropped by one afternoon about 5 o'clock and the good father offered Bill a scotch.

While the good father was in the kitchen getting glasses and ice, Bill went to the liquor cabinet, pulled out a bottle of scotch, and noticed that there was no grenada tax stamp on the scotch bottle, and said,

"Father, I am glad to see that even the priests buy their booze from the smugglers."

The father said, "No, Bill, you are mistaken. I am a poor priest in a poor parish; the farmers bring me produce, the butcher drops off meat, beef, or goat, the fishermen drop off fish, and needless to say my parishioners who are rum smugglers keep me well supplied with beer and booze. When they bring it to me, I can hardly ask them to go into town and pay the duty on it before I accept it!"

Petit Martinique is, needless to say, an excellent place to buy liquor at the right price. It is also the place to buy a fiberglass dinghy that tows well, again, the price is right. Linus Belmar, who learned to work with fiberglass in various boatbuilding companies in England, has returned to Petit Martinique and set up a shop making splendid dinghies, using as a mold the standard Grenadines rowing boat.

Neither the People's Revolutionary Army (PRA) nor the People's Revolutionary Government (PRG) made much of an impression on Petit Martinique—the Petit Martinican is an out-and-out capitalist. The PRA officially ran the island, but I am told they always left before dark. Apparently the PRA teacher was singularly unsuccessful in trying to convince Petit Martinique children that communism was great. But, with European financing, the PRG built a generator on Petit Martinique. The Petit Martinicans had had plenty of money but never before had electrical power; once power arrived, there was instant civilization—everyone immediately installed lights, refrigerators, TV sets, video-tape machines, the works. Now the island is lit up like a neon sign.

A good daytime anchorage can be had so long as the ground swell is down, due west of a small jetty at the northwest corner of the island. From here to Petit St. Vincent is a short hop, but watch out for the shoal marked 1½ fathoms between the two islands. I sailed across it in *Iolaire* some years ago, heeled over and drawing no more than 6 feet, and I touched repeatedly. I advise sailing around this spot altogether.

Carriacou

This is the most populated of the Grenadines. At first one wonders how the inhabitants support themselves, much less maintain so many respectable homes. As it turns out, for many generations the sons of Carriacou have made their living by going to sea or to the oil fields of Venezuela and Aruba. They stay away for many years, sending money home to their families; eventually they come home themselves to marry in middle age and raise a family.

An alternate source of income for many years used to be the smuggling trade, as on Petit Martinique, which was carried out with surprisingly little government interference. It was argued that as long as the government did not intervene, a sizable part of the population was kept off the public dole.

In Tyrell Bay it used to be not a rare occurrence at night to hear a sloop working its way into the harbor with no running lights. It would anchor silently close to shore; the headsails would come down with the main left sheeted flat—the marine equivalent of the idling engine of a getaway car. You could hear the motors of unlit cars and the slapping of dinghies shuttling back and forth to shore. After fifteen minutes or so, she'd bring in the anchor and sail off around Cistern Point to Hillsborough, there to be found the next morning, anchored docilely off town, legally entering a regular cargo.

ONE TREE ROCK
(II B-3, B-32; Sketch Chart III-30)

If you are beating up to the windward side of Carriacou from the south, a good anchorage may be had inside the reef extending northeast from Little Mushroom Island. Enter to the west of Mushroom and anchor behind One Tree Rock. This is a wonderful spot. Approach Mushroom Island from the south, keeping Little Mushroom and One Tree Rock on the starboard hand; round up north of One Tree and anchor in 1½ fathoms over white sand. The many coral heads to windward break the worst of the swell and are a good area for spearfishing. In one hour we took ten fish and three lobsters. The times I have stopped there have been during the summer in calm weather, but the Bequia fishermen tell me that even in winter it never gets too rough through here. The only problem they speak of is the winter swell that pours over the reef and pours out again through the south entrance, setting up a stiff current that could give a swimmer quite a scare. Incidentally, a boat drawing 4 or 5 feet of water can sail up inside the reef to Manchioneal Bay and get away from the heavy swells.

TYRELL BAY (HARVEY VALE BAY)
(II B-3, B-32, Sketch Chart III-31)

This is the customary anchorage for boats coming to Carriacou from the south, and it is excellent in all weathers. Plenty of breeze and good holding over a white-sand bottom. The U.S. chart is incorrect: The shoal in the middle of the harbor marked

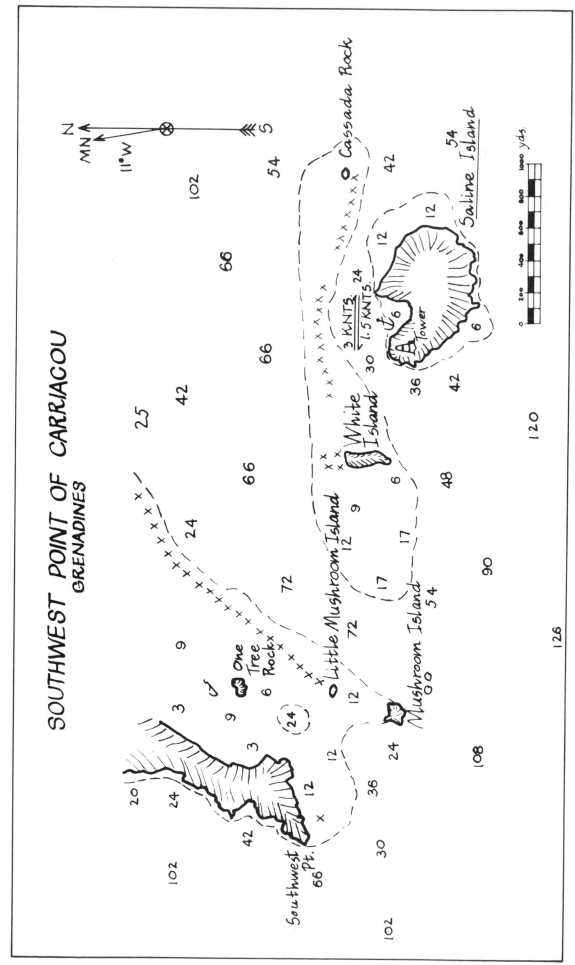

SKETCH CHART III-30   Southwest Point of Carriacou

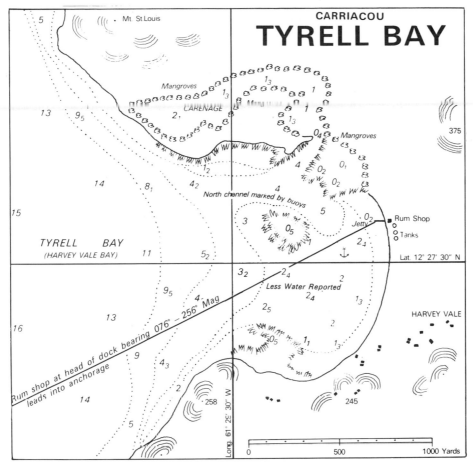

SKETCH CHART III-31 Tyrell Bay

1½ fathoms is actually shallower. *Iolaire* brushed it at 7½ feet, as have others with even less. The spot is easily seen in good light, and it is safe and advisable to steer north or south of it. The north side is probably the better route, but as you tack in along the north shore, watch out for the shoal in the corner of the harbor near the entrance to the carenage. Similarly, if you tack in along the south shore, you must watch out for rocks 200 yards offshore below the cliff. If the rum shop at the head of the dock is brought to bear 075 magnetic, you will safely pass south of the middle shoal and north of the rocks.

If you must enter at night, which I don't advise, the rum shop is usually lit by a kerosene lamp until late. Most nights the open-air theater south of the rum shop is easily spotted. If this is brought to bear 085 magnetic, you will also pass clear. The best anchorage is off the dock or south of it. Do not go farther inshore than the end of the dock or you will run aground.

An interesting diversion is to sail a dinghy into the carenage, where the old, wrecked schooners lie. You can tie up among the mangroves and fish in total solitude. The mangroves are alive with birds that will flit close around you. The whole carenage area has shoaled; send the dinghy in with a sounding pole or lead line before taking the mother ship in.

There is talk of establishing a slipway and marina on the south side of Tyrell Bay. This would be a great asset to yachting in the Grenadines, as charter parties could join bare boats in Carriacou and thus avoid the long slog up from Grenada, which can be a rough trip if the wind goes around to the north.

L'ESTERRE BAY
(II B-3, B-31)

Lies south of Sandy Island, southwest of Hillsborough. It is shallow, and the wind tends to sweep in from the north. All but the shallowest draft boats must anchor far from shore. I can recommend it for daytime use only.

SANDY ISLAND
(II B-3, B-31)

The island is owned and protected from development by the government of Carriacou. The people of Hillsborough frequent the island on weekends and holidays. Charter boats often anchor off its southwestern corner, their parties going ashore for lunch and snorkeling. Spearfishing is prohibited. This is a good and justifiably popular daytime anchorage.

In recent years, more and more boats have been spending the night in this rather exposed anchorage. Since you are sheltered by Carriacou 1½ miles to the east, the sea can't get too rough, but the wind can whistle across Hillsborough Bay. If you are going to spend the night, make sure you are well and truly anchored—probably two anchors set in a "Y" to the east would be best.

HILLSBOROUGH
(II B-3, B-32, B-311; Sketch Chart III-32)

The principal town on Carriacou. The inter-island schooners can be seen off-loading cargo from a dock at the eastern end of town.

Carriacou was for many years opposition territory for the ruling Gairy government in Grenada, so zero money was spent here. The Bishop government wasn't much better. The dock fell down, the airport terminal rotted, the telephone system became practically nonexistent, as did the cable service. Carriacou was basically incommunicado. The roads, once adequate, deteriorated very badly. The piped water system in Hillsborough was left to rust, leaving only the catchment area and cisterns as they were twenty years ago. (Even if the population of an island stays the same, or even decreases, as here, the water consumption per capita rises drastically as the people become more "civilized." The West Indian who in the fifties kept immaculately clean using a bucket of water now usually has built a shower and uses twenty gallons of water to do the same operation.)

The present Grenada government is headed by Herbert Blaize, who is from Carriacou. The government is trying to rectify the fifteen years of Carriacou's neglect—witness the rebuilding of the dock, a new airport terminal, and a telephone system as modern as any in the world—the instruments were made in Ireland, and some swear the bell has an Irish lilt! The new dock has a dinghy landing on the south side, but because of the surge, be sure to have a stern anchor to hold the dinghy off if you leave it there.

Customs and the post office are at the head of the dock, and Immigration is across the street. If they are closed and you really want to clear after hours, swing into the nearest rum shop and they will send you off in the proper direction.

Except for frozen and chilled food, the shopping situation is much better than it was in the past, and some people maintain it is better in Hillsborough than in St. George's. This has been brought about by two factors. First, the fishermen have discovered it is more profitable to sell fish in Martinique than in Grenada. Once they sell their fish in Martinique, they load the boat with French dry goods and bring them back to Carriacou. Second, the National Marketing and Import Board has been completely refurbished and has fresh vegetables and fruit from the north end of Grenada. Thursday is the best day to shop.

The old Mermaid Tavern has been renovated as the Mermaid Beach Hotel. It serves excellent meals, lunches and dinners, has a few rooms to rent, and is only a short walk from the dock—a traditional yachtsman's stop for the last twenty years, having been famous in the old days by the late Linton Rigg (who, among other achievements, designed the late Alf Loomis' pretty little cutter *Hotspin*). The Tavern continued to enjoy its popularity under the management of the late Tom Vickery—both he and Rigg were enthusiastic yachtsmen.

The Silver Beach Hotel, a cottage-type establishment with an open-air dining room, located east of town, has also been renovated. Various small guest houses, boarding houses, and small restaurants open and close in Carriacou with too great a frequency to report here, but just wander up and down the streets of Hillsborough, take a look, and find one that appeals.

The Carriacou Historical Society operates a mini-museum across the street from the Mermaid. Amazingly, despite its small size and arid climate, Carriacou also has a botanical garden in Hillsborough, within walking distance of the jetty.

Next to the Mermaid is an ice plant of uncertain heritage. I have never been able to find out who built it or when, but periodically some clever and industrious soul takes it upon himself to overhaul the machinery and get it operating. To everyone's amazement the plant actually makes ice. This goes on for a year or so, then the ancient plant breaks down, no one can repair it, and it lies doggo for a while—sometimes years—until another genius comes along to resurrect the beast. Presently, the beast is alive and well, producing ice. I wouldn't

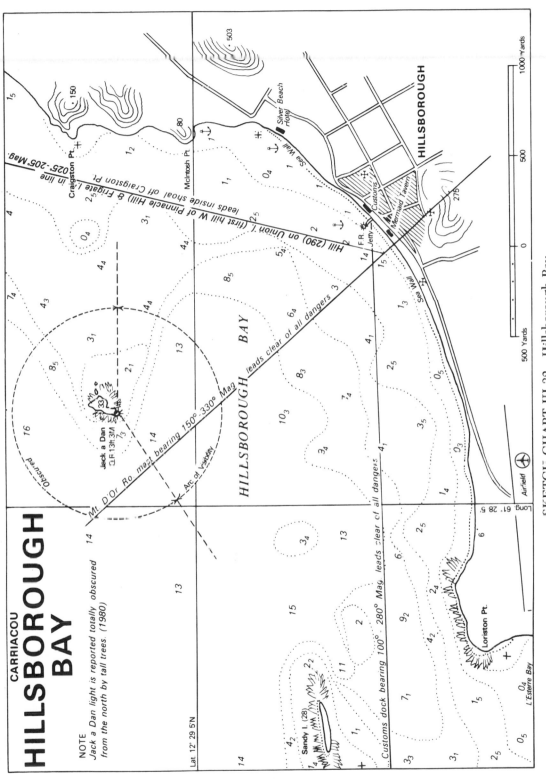

SKETCH CHART III-32 Hillsborough Bay

Range 1: Course 150-330 magnetic on cable and wireless tower leads clear of all dangers.

Range 2: Course 100-280 magnetic on Customs dock leads clear of all dangers

Range 3: Hill on Frigate Island in line with the 290-foot hill on Union (the hill is west of the Pinnacle, which is the highest on Union, 750 feet) leads a clear inside shoal spot (4 feet) inside Jack a Dan, 023-203 magnetic (see Sketch Chart III-1, Range D, in Chapter 1).

hazard a guess as to what the situation will be when you arrive in Carriacou.

A taxi will take you around the island, and a trip up to the hospital is a must, as it gives a fantastic view of Hillsborough Bay. It's a wonderful place for a hospital—cool and airy, with no need for air conditioning. Then take the taxi down the windward side, where you'll find commercial schooners and small sloops being repaired on the beach.

Francis Brinkley, who knows Carriacou intimately, feels that a stop at Belair or Doctor's House or Camp Mashie (three names for the same place) would be a better spot for a visit. The view there is all around instead of just Hillsborough Bay: north to the Grenadines, south to Grenada, and also Hillsborough. In the same area there are also the ruins of a 1809 great house, sugar mill, tower, etc. In recent history it was the PRA headquarters.

Despite what is said to the contrary, schooner and sloop building has not died out in Carriacou. One continually reads articles written by misinformed individuals stating that boatbuilding will die out because the young men are unwilling to work and are not learning the trade. Well, we were over at the windward side in March 1985 on what was supposed to be a legal holiday and we saw at least a dozen shiprights ranging in age from twelve or fourteen years right up to twenty-five hard at work building and repairing boats.

It is interesting to see the changes that have taken place in the Carriacou sloops over the years as the Carriacouans race, crew on yachts, and salvage the remains of wrecked yachts. The good Carriacouan fishing boats, trading schooners, and smugglers now sport stainless steel rigging, Barient winches salvaged from wrecks, and Dacron sails—recut throwaways from yachts. The lines of the boats through the years have changed drastically. They have become much more yachtlike—narrower, deeper, and better constructed and finished. Many builders are switching from gaff- to jib-headed rig, but they have not yet gone to outside ballast, as that would make it impossible for them to careen their boats as they presently do.

Before they fell apart due to lack of maintainance over the last fifteen years, the roads in Carriacou were well above the norm for this part of the world. They date back to the days when the British and the French were squaring off for control of the Islands. The British ruled the sea around Carriacou and the French the land. The French built roads to give their ground forces mobility against the British fleet wherever it tried to land. If the British fleet, thwarted at one landing, decided to haul up and sail down to the next inlet, the French would simply hitch up their cannon and follow them overland. So it went for many years, until an elaborate set of roadways crisscrossed the island.

The first weekend in August, known as August Monday, is one of the big weekends of the year in Carriacou. The workboat race in Hillsborough and yachts coming to watch from Grenada fills the island with people. A good chartering idea is to take a boat in late July through the Grenadines, timing your arrival in Hillsborough for August Monday—races start Sunday afternoon. The spectacle of some forty Grenadine workboats vying for cash prizes is really stunning.

The anchorage in Hillsborough tends to be roly; in the winter it can get all but impossible. The usual anchorage west of the dock is not the best—northeast of the dock is far better. Work your way as far northeast as your draft will permit, and anchor tucked in as close to shore as your draft will permit. Boats drawing 7 feet will have to anchor outside the shoal off the small hotel. Those drawing 6 feet or less can sneak in behind the shoal and anchor close to shore. The channel leading into a natural basin east of the shoal is best approached from the north—an eyeball proposition. The sand bottom is good holding in front of the hotel.

Northeast of Hillsborough you'll see an old dried-out stream bed running down into the harbor at McIntosh Point. This forms quite a nice little cove and is actually the quietest anchorage in the whole of Hillsborough Harbor. There is limited draft for boats drawing 5½ feet. Deeper draft may be squeezed in, but at low-water springs you would probably be touching bottom.

If the ground swell is rolling in, or if the wind is well in the north, be careful. It is easy to drag and the swell sets you onshore. That is how I came close to losing *Iolaire* here many years ago. The wind was well in the north, blowing hard, and a fair-sized sea was rolling in. I thought the anchor, my trusty old Herreshoff fisherman, was well set, but we suddenly found ourselves drifting back on the beach. By backing the mizzen to port and the staysail to starboard and cutting the rode we managed to fall off, gather way, and get out just as we bounced off the bottom. It turned out that the anchor had landed in a rusted old ham can; the tip pierced the tin part way, but the bulk of the can had prevented the fluke from fully burying. *Moral:* Be *sure* your anchor is set. Wishful thinking won't do it.

As has been frequently stated, one should not enter harbors at night. However, if you decide to be foolish and do so here, remember that the Jack a Dan light is obscured from the north. If you come from the north or northwest, bring the cable and wireless relay tower (a tower with two bright red lights) to bear on 150 magnetic, which will lead right into Hillsborough Harbor, clear of all dangers (see Sketch Chart III-32). This radio mast forms a very good point of reference in general. This is clearly marked on II Charts B-31 and B-32. It makes a good landmark when you approach from the south.

Don't forget, incidentally, that the cable and wireless tower is lower than Chapeau Carré Mountain and will therefore appear and disappear as you sail up the west coast of Carriacou.

When approaching Hillsborough from the southwest, round Cistern Point and short-tack up between Mabouya Island and Cistern Point, and between Sandy Island and Loristan Point. Just be careful not to sail too far into L'Esterre Bay, which is quite shallow. Staying inside Mabouya and Sandy islands keeps you out of the swell. If you are powering in, a bearing of 100 magnetic on the town dock will keep you in deep water all the way.

If you are approaching from the north, sail right on down the coast of Carriacou, as there are no dangers except for the 4-foot spot between Craigston Point and Jack a Dan. This spot is easily avoided by getting on the range as shown on Sketch Chart III-32.

The coast of Carriacou north of Hillsborough provides no overnight anchorages. There are one or two places where you might put in for lunch and a swim, and some spectacular beaches. Standing north from Hillsborough, don't forget the 4-foot spot inside Jack a Dan.

PETIT CARENAGE BAY
(II B-3, B-31, B-311; Sketch Chart III-33)

Due east of Rapid Point, locally referred to as Gun Point, is a cove called Petit Carenage Bay, where there is an anchorage for shoal-draft boats behind the reef, and a good beach. It is best suited for multihulls, centerboards, or shoal-draft motor sailers.

WATERING BAY AND GRAND BAY
(II B-3, B-31; Sketch Charts III-33, III-34)

On the east coast of Carriacou, locally called Windward Side, is Watering Bay, still called Bay à L'Eau. The entrance to the bay is slightly intricate and should be made when the sun is right overhead. If you are lucky, you can follow one of the local sloops that frequent the area. When coming from the north, proceed until Sail Rock is three fingers open on the northwest corner of Petit St. Vincent (West Indians say two fingers, but their hands are bigger). Then turn west on this range, 248 magnetic, until Fota joins Petit Martinique. When these two join, you should be close to the channel entrance; put a man in the rigging to con you into the channel, which first heads south, then west, into the basin.

Or else you can sail south along the outside of the reef, heading for the stone marker at its south end. Leave it to starboard and sail north into the anchorage (Sketch Chart III-33).

This is where you'll often find local sloops under construction—boatbuilding is very much alive in Carriacou.

You can then head south, leaving the marker to port, and sail through Grand Bay, exiting Windward Side at Kendeance Point (Sketch Chart III-34). The best water is near shore, but you will have to eyeball it yourself. On the chart there appears to be a break in the reef off Jew Bay, but I have tried twice to enter through here with no success. If you are entering at Kendeance Point, proceed carefully with a man aloft and you should have no problem. The channel is narrow, deep, and easily spotted by the breakers on the reef to windward. Because the wind and current will be setting you to leeward, hold high and stay as close to the weather side of the channel as the color of the water will permit. Inside, it is calm and secluded. You can sail in a rail-down breeze against no more than a light chop. Anchor close to the reef and stay there for days undisturbed by traffic of any sort, just as Jim Squire of the 55-foot schooner *Te Hongi* frequently used to do.

SALINE ISLAND
(II B-3, B-32; Sketch Chart III-30)

Just south of Carriacou lies Saline Island, seldom visited by yachts and one of my favorite islands in the Caribbean. It is possible to anchor between Saline and the reef to the north, but the tide runs a solid 3 knots down this channel, requiring a heavy anchor and a Bahamian moor. Inside the cover on the north side of the island, however, is a superb anchorage for shoal-draft boats. The southeastern portion of the bay is completely out of the tide. The shelf is 1 fathom, dropping off

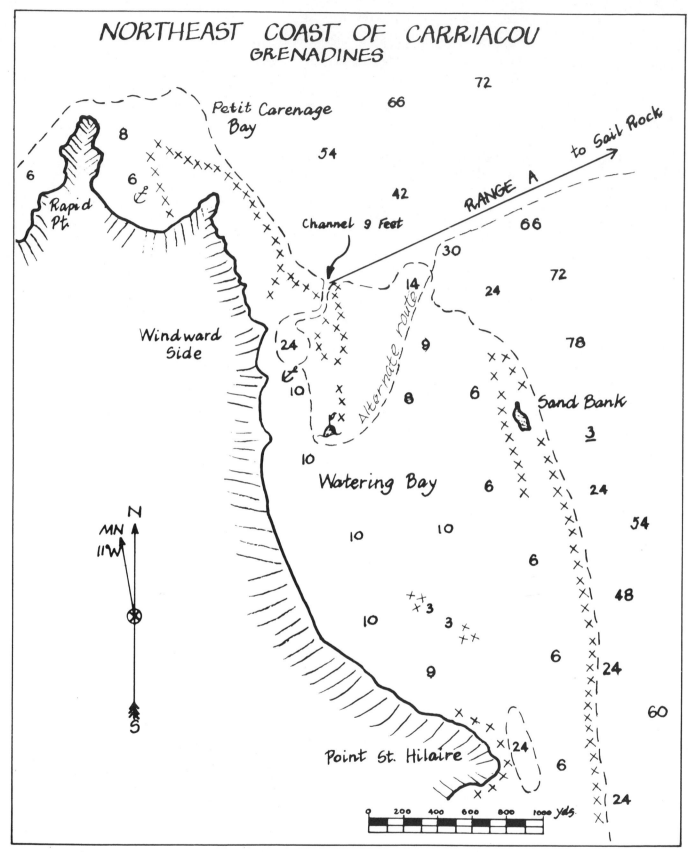

SKETCH CHART III-33   Northeast Coast of Carriacou

Range A: Sail Rock three fingers open to the northwest of Petit St. Vincent leads to channel into Wind-
            ward Side, Carriacou.

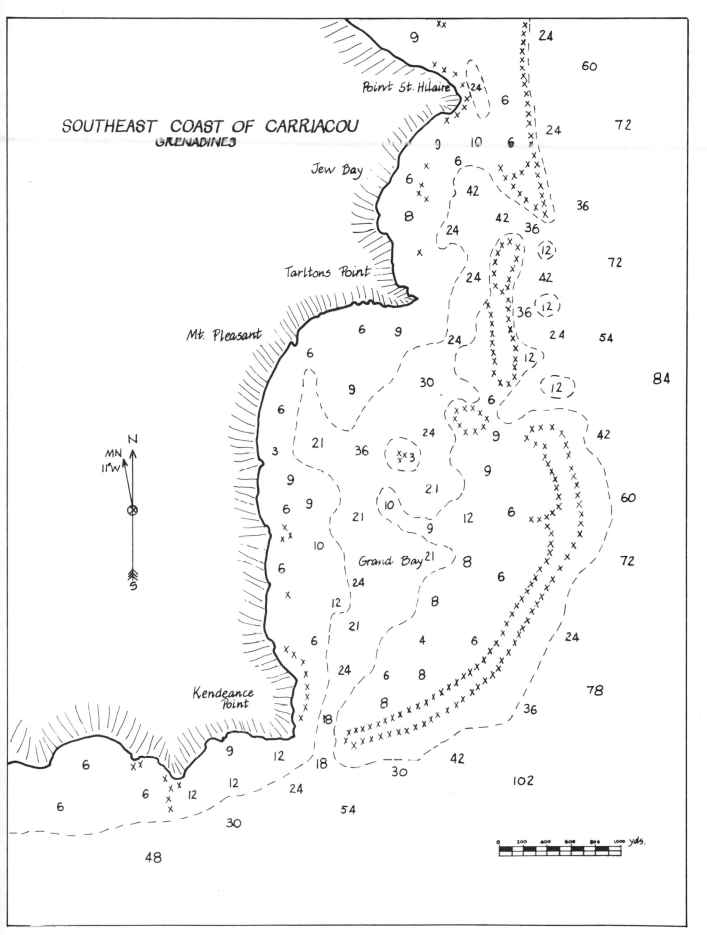

SKETCH CHART III-34   Southeast Coast of Carriacou

steeply at the northwest corner of the harbor near the old lime kiln. Good holding can be found by nosing right up to the shoal, dropping a bow anchor onto it, and setting a stern anchor to hold you off. With the kiln bearing southwest, you will find yourself out of the tide in 3 fathoms of water. Exercise caution in making your approach, as the bottom shoals from 2 to 1 fathom within 30 feet. The western tip of the island drops off so steeply that you can dive from the beach straight down into the sea. The snorkeling on the southwest corner is as fine as anywhere in the Caribbean. Stay close to shore and make allowance for the tides; once you are caught by the current off Saline Island, there is no swimming back to shore.

In summer, be prepared to be completely engulfed by mosquitoes as soon as the sun goes down.

FRIGATE ISLAND
(II B-3, B-32)

This is one of two islands so named in the Grenadines, the other being south of Union Island. Strong currents and narrow beaches are its drawbacks. Some have found it convenient to anchor off the western shore of Frigate. From here the dinghy can be taken around the northwestern tip and into the bay on the north. The bay is extremely shoal and should not be entered except by dinghy, the chart notwithstanding. There is good shelter on the southeast corner of the bay, but I cannot recommend this. Even a very shallow-draft boat (3 feet maximum) would have a rough time of it.

LARGE ISLAND
(II B-3, B-32)

The chart shows an anchorage in the northwest corner of this island, but the beach facing it is not particularly good. There is an abandoned estate ashore, but a strong current makes the approach difficult.

BONAPARTE ROCKS
(II B-3, B-32)

This is the small pile of rocks south of Large Island. I have never heard of anyone making a landing here, and I can't imagine anyone wanting to. The tide rips by them at 4 knots at times. They are best avoided.

ÎLE DE RONDE
(II B-3, B-32; Sketch Chart III-35)

From Grenada north to Carriacou is 38 miles; if the current is running to leeward and the wind is in the north, this can be one of the longest beats you will encounter coming from the south. Many break the trip by stopping off at Île de Ronde. The island is particularly vulnerable to a northwest ground swell, but in settled weather you couldn't find a better lunch spot. The fishermen keep their boats on the beach on the southwest shore. Here, if you sail in close and anchor on the edge of the shelf, you will find a passable anchorage. The tide runs swiftly and it is likely to be a bit rough, but the great attraction is a really beautiful beach.

A path, marked on Sketch Chart III-35, leads past the lake (which is a pond in the dry season) to the beach and reef on the windward side. From this anchorage you can also visit Île de Caille, the tiny island south of Île de Ronde made famous by Fritz Fenger's *Alone in the Caribbean*. Whale Bay on Île de Caille is recommended only for dinghy trips in calm weather.

Corn Store Bay in the northwest corner of Île de Ronde is perfectly adequate in settled weather. However, a ground swell can force your stern ashore. Two boats have been lost here in this way. If you elect to pass the night here, be certain to use a Bahamian moor. Feel your way in with the lead line and anchor off the little beach in 3 fathoms, with the hut bearing northeast. The snorkeling is fairly good, and with any luck you should be able to spear a few pan fish for lunch. The cove on the north face of the island may be visited by dinghy. The swimming and snorkeling are good here, but I would not recommend taking the boat inside unless you are very adept at reef navigation and your boat draws no more than 3 feet. As it stands now, the reef does not afford enough protection from the sea; no doubt some enterprising developer will soon arrive on the scene to remedy this.

LONDON BRIDGE
(II B-2, B-32)

This small island is about 1 mile north of Green Island and noteworthy only for the hole that the sea has washed through it. It is a fascinating and picturesque rock formation, a good view to bolster your photo album.

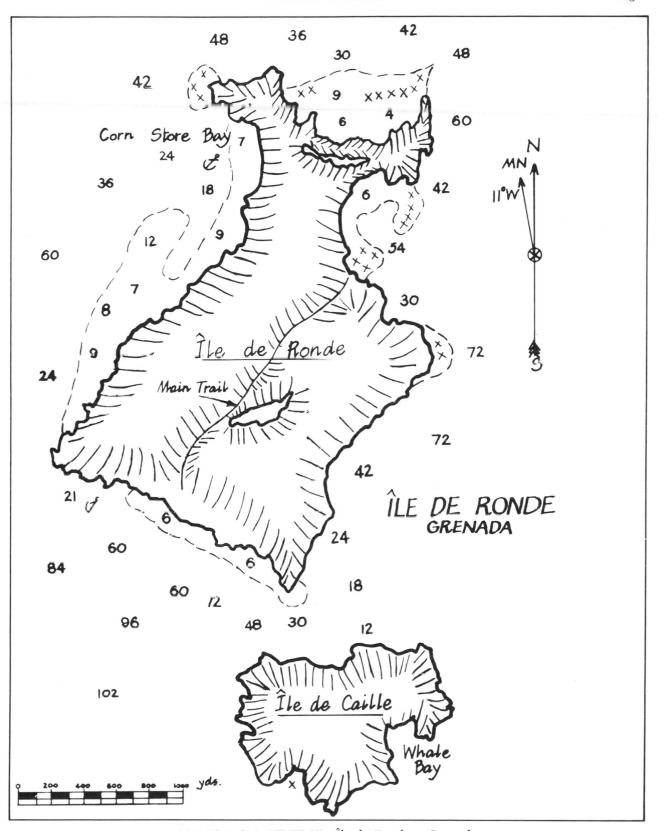

SKETCH CHART III-35   Île de Ronde —Grenada

DIAMOND ISLAND (KICK 'EM JENNY)
(II B-2, B-32)

The etymology of the variant is a mystery; it is probably some untraceable corruption of a French place name. There is no landing here at all. A strong current north of the island frequently sets up in a direction against the wind and kicks up quite a chop. It should also be noted that the shelf drops off steeply from 25 to well over 100 fathoms.

In sailing between Diamond Island and Carriacou, always hold well high of the course. Although it is only a 6-mile run, it can get very rough at times. Flying over this area is a real eye-opener. Tide rips can be seen cropping up in every sort of unpredictable place. If it is possible, you should carry the dinghy on deck to avoid a swamping. If the current is setting you to windward, you will have no trouble laying the course, but it will be rough going. A set to leeward will give smoother water, but then some tacking will be required.

LES TANTES
(II B-2, B-32)

To windward of Diamond Island and Île de Ronde, Les Tantes is a series of uninhabited islands. A rough anchorage can be had off their western shore, but I recommend it for the adventurous only. The swell and a stiff current are invariably a problem. Transient fishermen camp on these islands from time to time; otherwise they are deserted.

NOTES

NOTES

8

Grenada

II B-3, B-32

Formerly a British colony but independent since 1974, Grenada is a large, lush, populous island of about 90,000 people. Situated roughly 460 miles southeast of San Juan and 90 miles north of Trini-dad, it is 18 miles long and 8 miles wide. A mountain range extends along almost the entire length of the island and there is enough rain to make most of Grenada verdant throughout the

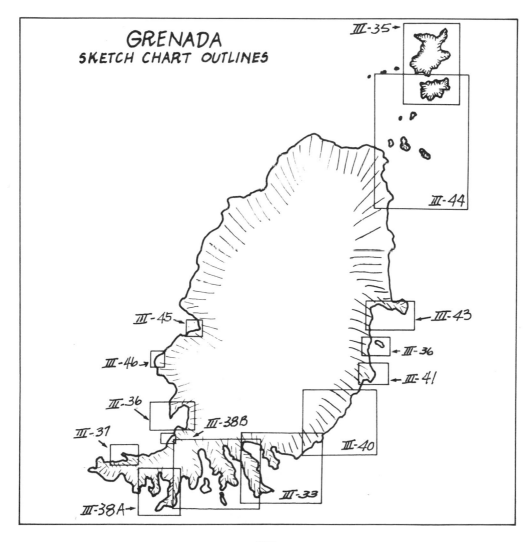

year. However, because the north and southwest ends are low, the island basically has three climates: The rainfall in the mountains is double that of the town of St. George's, while out toward the Point Saline, Prickly Bay, and Mount Hardman area, the rainfall is half that of town. This makes the south coast hard on farmers, but wonderful for the vacationer and yachtsman.

Grenada was originally settled by the French and taken over by the British during the eighteenth-century colonial wars, when spices had become as valuable as gold. The value the British assigned to this trade can be judged by the number of old forts now to be seen on the island. Fort George still stands today as it did in the early eighteenth century. A small fort on the top of the hill to the north of town was once reputedly connected to Fort George by an underground tunnel. On the hills east of town are Fort Frederick, Fort Lucas, and Fort Dalfas, with their large parade grounds out front. Dalfas has been a prison for many years. Fort Jeudy, on the south coast, was built to protect the entrance to Egmont Harbor.

A French colonial influence persists in the commercial habits of the island, in that everything revolves around the capital, St. George's. Produce grown throughout the island is shipped to the market at St. George's, where it is sold, loaded into carts, and trundled back out to the countryside. The market itself is a spectacle to behold. It is open six days a week, the best days being Wednesdays and Saturdays.

On any Saturday of the year, a profusion of cargo schooners and bright-red sloops can be seen lying peacefully at the waterfront, set off against the green hillsides, whose slopes are zigzagged by the narrow tracings of roadways. The market itself is piled high with wonderful collections of fresh fruits and vegetables, trussed-up chickens and hens, and squealing pigs and goats, and cluttered with hordes of small children underfoot. Brightly uniformed policemen gesticulate smartly to unsnarl the traffic through town. Colorful trucks from the countryside line the streets. The names emblazoned on their sides are eyecatchers: "Trust No Friend," "Fool's Paradise," "Happy Home."

These "mammy buses," as they're called, are big banana trucks that used to be converted to carry passengers when they weren't carrying bananas. During Maurice Bishop's People's Revolutionary Government days, most were replaced by minibuses, which are less colorful (though they still have names), but much more efficient. They run many routes until almost midnight.

A tour of the island may be had by rented car or taxi. The taxi drivers are courteous and honest, but on longer trips it is best to check out the fare beforehand. There are many taxi drivers who are favorites of yachtsmen, but one old faithful is Wilfred Lewis (2743). If you are interested in the flora and fauna, call Wilfred, who has a thorough knowledge of all the best places to visit in the botanical garden, spice estates, and rain forest.

An excellent day trip is to tour the island in the morning, then stop at Betty Mascal's Plantation Morne Fendue restaurant, La Belle Creole, St. Patricks (telephone: 9330). After an excellent two-hour West Indian lunch, go to one of the beaches at the north end of the island, and then drive home.

Grenada was for many years one of the wealthiest islands in the Eastern Caribbean. If one examines the *British West Indian Yearbook*, compiled by the British government throughout the nineteenth century and up to recent years, one finds that Grenada showed a favorable balance of trade and profit year in and year out (with the exception of an occasional bad year) from 1820 until 1955, when the island was devastated by a hurricane. It was the only island in the Eastern Caribbean that could claim this economic distinction. The bases of its economy have been cocoa, nutmeg, and other spices. Hence it has always been referred to as "The Spice Island."

Historically, Grenada has had the largest collection of small landowners of any of the islands in the Eastern Caribbean. Cocoa, nutmeg, and bananas are crops that small farmers with just three or four acres could cultivate and from which they could make a decent living. There were, of course, large estates, but most of the land was owned by Grenadian farmers. The Grenadian does not feel that he has been victimized by the big sugar planter or the banana producer, and this makes him easier for nonlocals to get along with than many people of other Islands.

Visiting yachtsmen are often surprised to discover that the day laborer varnishing his brightwork or painting his topsides owns his own plot of land, or sometimes three or four acres. And those men make up what is probably the best labor pool available in the entire Eastern Caribbean.

A word of warning, though: While many of these workmen are excellent, a few are terrible and should be avoided at all costs. Some of the worst are among the most enterprising, so do not use the first person who comes along. When at the Grenada Yachting Club, check with the local yachtsmen before hiring anyone; at Spice Island Marine Services and Grenada Yacht Services (GYS), be sure to check with the office before hiring anyone. This is extremely important, as both yards have some laborers hanging about whom they certainly would not recommend.

For all its historical prosperity, Grenada has suffered hard times in recent decades. The political disasters have been bad enough, but the first blow fell in 1955, when Hurricane Janet completely flattened the island. It needed massive aid from England to help rebuild. (Anyone who would wield a hammer was pressed into work. These days, the worst insult you can lay on a Grenadian carpenter is to tell him, "You're nuttin' but a Janet carpenter, mon.") The British government gave large disaster-relief loans to farmers and estate owners to help restore their nutmeg and cocoa crops. But a cocoa tree takes about seven years to mature, a nutmeg tree seven–ten years to bear and fifteen before it really begins to produce, so it has been a long pull for the farmers. Still, they have a lot going for them. Anything can be made to grow in Grenada, including, nowadays, onions and Irish potatoes—two crops that used to be imported because the agricultural "experts" maintained they could not be grown in the tropics.

Tourism began to take hold in the early 1960s, and by the early 1970s, Grenada had a rapidly expanding industry. The island had also become the center of yachting in the Southern Caribbean.

Then came the disastrous political troubles that reversed all the economic gains of the seventies. I don't want to dwell too long on politics in a cruising guide, but if Grenada resumes its place as the yachting capital of the Southern Grenadines, as I feel sure it will, it's important that visitors have some historical perspective on what's been happening there.

The U.S. intervention in October 1983 was merely the culmination of thirty years of political turmoil that began in the 1950s, when a young labor leader named E. M. Gairy returned from Aruba and formed GULP (Grenada United Labor Party). He organized the agricultural workers for the first time and was elected premier. Then began a period of such unbridled free-spending—known as the era of Squandermania—that the British actually sent in a frigate, landed troops, removed Gairy, and installed the opposition. This happened twice, in fact, and each time Gairy got himself reelected, the second time in 1969. (For a fictionalized picture of this period, read Alec Waugh's 1956 novel *Island in the Sun* or see the 1957 movie

of the same name, which starred Harry Belafonte. It is the thinly disguised story of Gairy and Grenada.)

Although a period of economic prosperity followed, Gairy established a tyrannical one-man rule, backed by the much-feared "Mongoose Gang," which many have compared to the *Tonton Macoute* in Haiti. Law and order broke down, and crime and violence were rife.

In 1973, Gairy won yet another suspicious election, and took it as a mandate to lead Grenada to independence. A general strike followed, during which, on Bloody Monday, Gairy sent in his goons, armed with 303 Enfields—which, fortunately, most of them didn't know how to use. They did, however, kill Rupert Bishop, father of the man who later became the leader of the People's Revolutionary Government.

Although most Grenadians didn't want independence (at least under Gairy), the British in 1974 acted on Gairy's wishes and removed Grenada from Associate State status and gave it independence. This put an intolerable financial burden on the island—as it did on all the other former colonies that had dropped out of the British West Indies Federation to become independent. (Now, all the former British Islands except Montserrat, the British Virgin Islands, and Anguilla are independent.)

Even in pre-independence days, the Islands, lumbered with top-heavy bureaucracies, could barely make ends meet. Now, with missions to London, Toronto, Washington, and the UN, plus raising and equipping defense forces, the barriers to solvency seem insurmountable.

Furthermore, there are only so many educated people in the Islands, and when a lot of them go off to the foreign service, it doesn't leave enough for government and business. Some of those jobs are inevitably going to be filled by people partially or altogether unqualified.

After independence in 1974 came another election, well managed by the Gairy government to ensure his reelection. But in a few more years, Gairy's ego and the oppression and confusion of his rule became so overwhelming that many Grenadians—including businessmen as well as politicians—decided something had to be done.

On March 13, 1979, an almost bloodless coup, extremely well organized by the New Jewel Movement and led by Messrs. Bishop, Radix, and Cord, overthrew the Gairy dictatorship. It was so neatly done that tourists wandered through the streets taking photographs of the revolution as it progressed. On the morning of the revolution, every-one was most impressed by Mr. Bishop's speech on Radio Montserrat. He stated that the people were justified in overthrowing the Gairy government and that the new government felt that foreigners were welcome to the island, that they had a right to stay on the island, and that their property would be protected. The next morning the newly created People's Revolutionary Government flew the American ambassador and the British and Canadian high commissioners to Grenada from Barbados. The new government took them on a tour of the island to show them that all was cool and calm, and requested these representatives to assure Grenada that their respective governments would not support Ex-Premier Gairy, who had appealed to their governments and the U.N. for money and materiel to invade the island.

Within twenty-four hours, the British and Canadian governments gave their assurances. However, the American government took a full ten days to do this. Although the U.S. did not flatly turn down the request by the new government for arms and aid funds, it certainly put the government off. Nor did the newly appointed U.S. ambassador distinguish herself by her understanding of and dealings with the new government.

The Cubans saw the opportunity, jumped into the breach, and supplied arms, ammunition, and instructors to turn the ragtag group of instant revolutionaries into a proper army. Cuba supplied medical aid in the form of doctors, equipment, and money for the hospital, all of which were sorely needed. Most important of all to the average Grenadian, Cuba promised to build a jetport to make possible night landings in Grenada, something every Grenadian had been dreaming about for the last fifteen years.

When Bishop's group took over, most of us didn't know whether they were Communists, Socialists, or what. And for a while things definitely improved. The Mongoose Gang was locked up, crime was curbed, and thieving in Grenada's harbors was nearly eliminated.

But the People's Revolutionary Government and its arm, the People's Revolutionary Army, turned out to be working not for the Grenadian people but for the Communist cause, and improvements in law and order were counterbalanced by suppression of individual freedoms. Those who opposed the administration ended up in prison, referred to as Mr. Bishop's Reeducation University. A power struggle developed between Cord, the radical, and Bishop, the moderate. The island

was flooded with Cubans, who not only built the promised airfield at Point Saline, but also dredged a twenty-foot channel into Egmont Harbor so they could off-load heavy equipment directly onto the military base.

The base was not for launching rockets at Washington (what's the point, when Cuba is closer?); it was to build an army that could immediately go to the support of a Communist revolt or coup on any of the neighboring islands.

Neither was the airfield a military installation, as President Reagan claimed in his verbal attacks on Grenada. (He was singularly ill-advised by his advisers.) The airfield was certainly not military, since all the fuel tanks were above ground. On the other hand, it *was* a perfect staging and refueling point for any Cuban or Russian planes that might have had business in the area. Remember the Russian plane loaded with arms that was seized in Brazil? Had the Grenada runway been completed at the time, that plane would almost certainly have refueled in Grenada and not been seized in Brazil. So to that extent the airfield had military value.

In October 1983, the feud between Cord and Bishop finally boiled over, and there was a bloody massacre at Fort George, where Bishop and an unknown number of his supporters were murdered. A general curfew rang out, and there was allegedly a list of some 5,000 people—out of a population of 90,000!—to be eliminated.

That is when Governor General Scoon and the heads of other Caribbean states asked the U.S. to intervene. (The U.S. dodged the stigma of aggression by calling the action, if you can believe it, a "vertical insertion"; the Grenadians refer to it simply as the "rescue" or "intervention.") The intervention used massive numbers of men and massive fire power, and was quickly accomplished despite incredibly bad planning and lack of information. The CIA had complete intelligence about the island, the Cubans and their gun emplacements, and so on. Various people had been contacted and were ready to advise the liberating forces about the lay of the land. But as a result of massive blunders, little of this help got to the military. Helicopters were even flying around without maps of the island!

Nevertheless, the troops behaved magnificently during the liberation, and continued to do so after the island was secured. They remained until April 1985; many Grenadians were sorry to see them go then, being firmly convinced that hard-core PRA types (with buried guns) will make trouble again sooner or later.

The performance of the U.S. State Department

and AID (American Investment Development) officers is another story. So unimpressive was their record that for the first time in my life I was embarrassed to be an American.

First of all, the U.S. government employees on the island drew *combat pay* for a long time after the liberation. They rented the most expensive homes, paid considerably above the market price, then stored the indigenous furniture at government expense and had all their fancy American amenities flown down from the States. At the same time, the Grenada government couldn't get AID to furnish a few second-hand trucks to carry water to parts of the island that had gone dry!

At one point, I met an OAS (Organization of American States) officer who after spending a few months checking the yachting scene on Antigua had come to Grenada to see what could be done to reestablish yachting there. (I admit that he got off on the wrong foot with me by stating that he'd never heard of this Street guide or the Imray-Iolaire charts.) His chief concern seemed to be how he could buoy the beaches so that water-skiing boats would not interfere with swimmers! I fear I ruffled his feathers by pointing out that there weren't more than three water-skiing boats in all of Grenada—and that two of them were probably broken down. So much for misdirected aid.

A U.S. embassy has been established, complete with ambassador and staff, but they don't issue passports or visas. You have to go to Barbados for those. What does the embassy do? I met the ambassador at a party on Spice Island several months after the invasion, and he told me in no uncertain terms that he worked from nine to five and that he didn't care how long I had lived on the island. He was not interested in talking about Grenada with me unless I got an appointment to see him in his office: our dedicated diplomats at work.

In general, although with great goodwill and enthusiasm Uncle Sam granted a massive aid program to repair battle damage and restore basic services, most local people feel that the amount of money constructively spent in Grenada bears little relation to the total stated amount of the aid program.

Nevertheless, things are finally moving ahead in Grenada. The airport is finished, and there are direct flights from New York and Miami and probably, by the time you read this, from London. There has been a massive road-resurfacing program and hotels are being refurbished and new ones built.

On the marine scene, there are plans for a total redevelopment of the whole lagoon area in St. George's Harbor, including the rebuilding of Grenada Yacht Services. The plan calls for bulkheading the whole lagoon for stern-to docking, and for completely rebuilding the Grenada Yacht Services dock—improvements that would provide some 400 secure, all-weather, in-the-water moorings. This many yachts would have a major impact on Grenada's economy. (The tax department of St. Thomas released a report stating that charter yachts alone contributed 14 percent of the tax dollars collected in St. Thomas!)

St. George's Harbor is slowly being expanded, partly to cope with the increased freight traffic caused by Grenada's reawakening economy, and partly to attract more cruise-ship business. The harbor department proposes widening the existing channel into the Lagoon to create a cruise-ship berth in front of the Grenada Yacht Club. This would be a mixed blessing, for though it would increase the number of cruise-ship visits, the widening of the channel might very well allow the winter ground swell to get into the Lagoon, thus destroying it as a totally secure anchorage. The loss of the potential yachting industry is too big a price to pay for a few more cruise-ship customers—who don't spend that much money in Grenada anyway.

My suggestion is to let the cruise ships continue to anchor off, but instead of taking the passengers ashore in little launches, provide big, power-driven catamarans that could carry 250 passengers at once. This plan would cater to the cruise-ship business, but would cost a lot less than building a cruise-ship berth in the Lagoon, and wouldn't destroy the Lagoon as a yacht haven.

With a thriving hotel and tourist business, a reestablished yachting industry, and revitalized agriculture, Grenada could again become the Caribbean's wealthiest as well as one of its most beautiful islands.

One last note that shows how a lot of Grenadians felt about their governments in recent years is the fact that somewhere around 50,000 of them left the island during the ten-year period following independence. As the saying goes, they voted with their feet. Among those who left were a tremendous number of well-trained and competent crew and shipyard workers. You'll run into Grenadian boat boys in Antigua, Tortola, Miami, and even Newport (but only in the summer—they don't like cold weather any more than the birds do). Almost to a man, the Grenadians who worked on boats were opposed to both the Gairy and Bishop governments.

Iolaire, incidentally, came through the liberation of Grenada almost unscathed—but was she lucky! She was moored at the end of the Grenada Yacht Services dock in St. George's, and during the attack, a rocket ripped a six-foot hole in the dock only twenty feet away from her starboard side; machine-gun bullets and shrapnel stitched holes in the dock behind her and up along her port side. (Meanwhile, the Street family's two houses, which had been occupied for three and a half years by the Grenadian military, were blown to smithereens by Uncle Sam's helicopters.)

After the liberation, we took *Iolaire* to St. Thomas on a fast starboard-tack sail, and not until we were smoothing over the dings on her topsides in Tortola did we discover that a piece of shrapnel had gone clear through the hull on the starboard side and lodged behind the icebox. Someday I'll buy a Purple Heart from a hock shop and mount it on the bulkhead!

We hope the yachts will be coming back to Grenada. Indeed, this is probably inevitable. From a yachtsman's standpoint, the island is almost ideal. Back in 1839, it was described in the old sailing directions as "the loveliest of our islands in the West Indies." Little has happened in the last 100 years to change that view. I have sailed in the Eastern Caribbean for a quarter century, and Grenada is still tops.

In St. George's you have a safe, secure anchorage in the lagoon within dinghy distance of markets, supermarkets, fish markets, telephone, cable offices, banks, and mariner and general hardware stores. The south coast of Grenada has a beautiful cruising climate and provides anchorages literally too numerous to mention. In short, if you miss Grenada, you are missing the best part of your Caribbean cruise.

Customs and Immigration for Grenada is found at Prickly Bay, at Grenville, and at St. George's. In the last named, tie up at the Grenada Yacht Services dock or moor to the north of the dock, hoist your "Q" flag, and send the skipper ashore to Customs and Immigration at GYS. At Prickly Bay, follow the normal "Q" flag, skipper-only-ashore routine.

Through an EEC grant, the buoyage of Grenada has been changed to the IALA system B, i.e., the U.S. system of red-right-returning. The harbor department has on its staff Mike Forshaw, a surveyor recognized by the leading Lloyd's underwriters, a good yachtsman, and former hauling boss at

GYS. I feel confident that the buoyage system will stay in fairly good shape for years to come. It is still in a state of flux, though, and so a complete buoyage system cannot be presented in this guide; I advise you to consult the *latest* Imray-Iolaire charts, which will be kept up to date as the Grenadian buoyage system develops.

ST. GEORGE'S
(II 1, B, B-3, B-32; Sketch Chart III-36)

There is no problem in entering. The ranges in the outer harbor are for large ships and may be disregarded. There is plenty of water all the way in. If you arrive at night, it is best to anchor in the northeast corner of the Carenage. The range lights shown on the chart may not be working, but there are no hazards, and you should have no trouble entering if you mind the charts. *All buoy lights must be regarded as unreliable.* The "official" yacht anchorage is in the northeast corner beyond a line drawn between the firehouse and the Texaco agency (dotted line, Sketch Chart III-36). Stay well up in the northeast corner to be clear of the maneuvering big ships. It is best to drop anchor in the shallows and then pay out into deeper water. The center of the harbor is 60 feet deep over a poor-holding, mud bottom. Yachts are not permitted to go alongside the main wharf unless they have made previous arrangements with the harbormaster. It is reserved for large vessels. (Many of these tie up stern-to with the wind holding them off.) It goes without saying that you should anchor clear of the fairway, but more than once I have seen yachts anchored at the mouth of the harbor right smack in the middle of the commercial channel.

St. George's Harbor looks a bit like a battlefield these days. As of May 1986, three steel freighters in the harbor were one step away from sinking, and five or six fishing trawlers were sitting there, unused. Inevitably someone forgets to pump the bilges and the boats go glug-glug, necessitating a salvage operation. The Lagoon has various wrecks, the most conspicuous of which is the *Aurora Borealis,* a 185-foot wooden World War II army freight boat, sunk right next to Grenada Yacht Services. Needless to say, Grenada is going to have trouble becoming a yachting center again if its main harbor is littered with wrecks.

There is always a great deal of activity in the Carenage, with water taxis and fishing boats shuttling back and forth all day long. These water taxis (bum boats) are the most economical way of getting from one side of the harbor to the other. They will

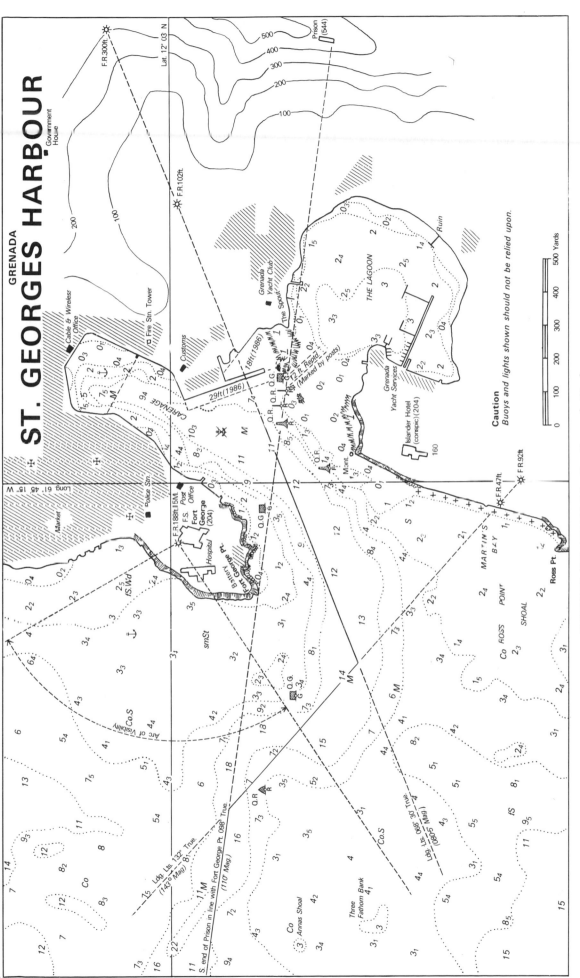

GRENADA

ST. GEORGES HARBOUR

SKETCH CHART III-36   St. George's Harbor

Range A: Two red lights ashore in line leads east of Anna's Shoal, 142-322 magnetic.
Range B: Two red-orange lights in line lead along Harbor Channel, 079-259 magnetic.
Range C: Harbor reef buoy under Government House leads clear of Ross Point Shoal, 060-240 magnetic.
Note: *Buoy lights are totally unreliable; some posts marking the channel have been knocked down and have not been replaced.*

also pick you up at Food Fair, where you can load all your groceries directly into the water taxi and be rowed directly to your boat. It is certainly a lot more pleasant to climb in a bum boat, sit with a beer in one hand and a book in the other, and have a leisurely, comfortable ride back to the Yacht Club, GYS, or your boat moored in the Lagoon than it is to bounce over the rough roads and fight traffic jams in a taxi and then have to carry your groceries the length (1400 feet) of the GYS dock! The only problem is that getting a water taxi from GYS or the Yacht Club into town is difficult. For fifteen years I've been urging GYS to organize the water taxis to regularly swing by three or four times a day; it would certainly make lying at GYS a much more attractive proposition.

Food Fair used to be one of the best places to stock for a cruise in the whole area. The variety was superb, and the management was willing to get what they didn't have if you asked for it. With the difficult times, however, Food Fair understandably declined, so that it stocks just the basics. Now it should upgrade again. Not only yachtsmen but also U.S. government employees would be willing to spend money on the best food if it were available. I suggest that Food Fair take advantage of LIAT's unlimited island-hopper fare and send a representative to visit the deli counters at the supermarkets of St. Thomas, Antigua, and Tortola. Then Food Fair should follow suit.

The recess south of the Carenage is known as the Lagoon. A narrow channel leads inside. No more than 12 feet can be carried through here at high water. Originally the channel into the Lagoon was marked by a row of posts along each side. Over the years, however, boats have run into the posts and knocked them down or bent them over, and they have not been replaced. So only half the posts are there. Be sure you line up those remaining and stay exactly in the center of the channel. In December 1978, the trimaran *Tri Star* was coming down the edge of the channel and impaled herself on one of the bent-over poles. This went through the center hull and emerged in the main cabin. Luckily she had enough buoyancy to float on her outer hulls. Now the channel is clearly marked by buoys, but the broken-off posts are still there on the edges. Make damn sure you stay absolutely in the middle. Also, remember that the Caribbean's water is lower in May, June, and July. Deep-draft boats are advised to check the depth of the channel by lead line from the dinghy before entering.

It is possible, although not recommended, to sail through this channel; the axis is 150 magnetic. If your engine is not working, it's best to arrange for a tow from Grenada Yacht Services inside the Lagoon. If you decide to anchor off the dock at GYS, bear in mind that the bottom is the softest mud and poor holding. This is the place to use your heaviest anchor and plenty of chain. The advantage of lying in the Lagoon is the easy access to town and the fact that you are out of the way of the heavy commercial traffic.

However, it does tend to be muggy at night and the water is too foul to swim in. If you are anchored in the Lagoon and want to swim, jump in the dinghy and go across to the flats southwest of the main channel where 2 or 3 feet can be carried. Anchor the dinghy right off the statue under the Islander Hotel. Here you will find clear water and a great place for a wake-up or end-of-the-day swim.

The best dinghy landings in town are off Food Fair, the Nutmeg restaurant, and the post office, which is readily accessible to Rudolf's restaurant and bar—but leave a stern anchor out to hold your dinghy off or it will try to bash itself to pieces against the sea wall. Or else tie your dinghy to the small dock at the Turtle Back restaurant.

Fuel, water, and electricity are available alongside the GYS dock. Cube ice is available at Claud's Marine Store, while Basil St. John, who lives across the street from GYS, supplies block ice and is also a refrigerator repairman. Across the Lagoon, at McIntyre's Garage, block ice from a relatively new ice plant is available; it should operate with a fair degree of reliability.

At the southeast corner of the Lagoon you'll find Lincoln Ross, who specializes in ironwork; it may not look polished and smooth when he's finished, but his work is strong and the price is usually right.

On the north side of the Lagoon is the Grenada Yacht Club, a long-established and most hospitable organization that has entertained yachtsmen from all over the world. The frequency with which it is visited by yachtsmen in proportion to its size puts it in the same league as the Island Sailing Club at Cowes.

The bar of the Grenada Yacht Club overlooks the harbor and is one of the most pleasant places in the world to enjoy a sundowner. Because you sit looking west, toward the setting sun, you have a wonderful perch to see the green flash. Half the year the sun sets in the slot between Fort George and the Islander Hotel. The green flash (a phenomenon reported on at some length in *Cruising World*, in August 1982 and July 1983, and in

Yachting, in August 1986) is sometimes seen just as the upper limb of the sun goes under the horizon—if you have a crystal clear sky with no haze on the horizon. The old saying goes that if you have not seen the green flash you have not met your true love. The club has showers and a phone that are available to members and visiting yachtsmen.

There is also a small hand-powered slip capable of hauling boats to about 35 feet. This provides probably the cheapest hauling in the Eastern Caribbean. Visiting yachtsmen are given guest privileges for two weeks. After that, they should take out temporary membership, which is one of the best bargains in the yachting world.

The club sponsors fleets of Lasers and Mirror dinghies, which provide an excellent training ground for up-and-coming yachtsmen of the future. The club also conducts races for larger boats. The two main regattas are the Carl Schuster Memorial Race and the Round Grenada Race, which take place during the first weekend in January; and the Easter Regatta, which comprises a race from Trinidad to Grenada, small-boat racing in St. George's, and a race to the south coast for the larger boats. During these regattas, the club is besieged by, among others, the fun-loving, hard-drinking, competitive Trinidadians, who race all day and party all night.

The Trinidad–Grenada Race and the Easter Regatta combine with either the Trinidad or Barbados three-day Race Week—they alternate years—to form the Southern Caribbean Ocean Racing Circuit. Unlike the regattas in the northern end of the Caribbean, this circuit has very low entry fees and lots of free parties. The racing is good, and tough, and while the races admittedly are not run with the expertise of the northern regattas, they are still a lot of fun, especially for the cruising division. It's a circuit worth taking in.

One of the nicest things about the Grenada Yacht Club is the fact that both the starting and finishing lines are ranges from the clubhouse; thus a spectator can see the entire small-boat course and the starting and finishing of all the cruising races right from a bar stool.

Although St. George's still offers such amenities as well as basic facilities, it has a long way to go to become the preeminent yachting center it used to be and should be again. As of May 1986, GYS had been bought by new owners, and they could do great things for yachting in Grenada.

First of all, GYS should be separated from the various real estate entities it has long been part of and run simply as a first-rate yachting headquar-ters. It should have a good marine store, a strong charter organization, and a powerful communications setup, both SSB and VHF, with a relay tower in the mountains. It must have carpentry, fiberglass, paint, machine, engine, refrigeration, electric, and electronic shops; and it has to have really good hauling facilities, with adequate sidetracking capacity so there won't be any waiting in line to get hauled. In short, the new owners of GYS have a tall order, and a great responsibility to yachting in Grenada.

The Coast Guard also has a challenge, because as more yachts come back to St. George's there's likely to be more "thieving" (pilferage as opposed to armed robbery). I have a suggestion for Captain Byers, commandant of the Grenadian Coast Guard and captain of the Coast Guard vessel *Tyrell Bay:* Instead of setting up an armed guard zooming around the harbor (who might inevitably make a nervous mistake and ventilate some happy yachtsman on his well-oiled way back to the boat), I recommend an *unarmed* guard drifting through the harbor in a gray or black dinghy. He should be equipped with a pair of 7 × 50 night glasses (I'll happily donate *Iolaire*'s spare pair), a very bright spotlight, and an old hand-cranked air-raid siren. If he sees something suspicious, he makes a lot of light and a lot of noise; if he flushes a thief, plenty of volunteers among the yachtsmen will give chase in their high-speed whalers or rubber duckies. Or, if you don't like the vigilante approach, an armed watch could be on call on the Coast Guard cutter based at GYS. It's a far-out idea, but I bet it would work—after thirty years in the Islands I think I know what will and what won't work!

In any case, the worst thing that could happen to Grenada from a yachting viewpoint is to let the thieving get out of hand as it did in Grenada in the 1970s and in Antigua in the early 1980s, when boats stayed away in droves.

During Grenada's heyday in the early seventies, several of us sat down once and figured that the yachting industry employed about one-third the number of people employed by the whole hotel industry, and that, since the Grenadians working in yachting got paid higher salaries than those in hotels, the overall dollar total of money in Grenadians' pockets was probably about the same in the two industries. In short, yachting had a tremendous amount to do with the healthy economy of the seventies. It could go a long way to rejuvenating that economy if private money and government assistance were forthcoming. Is anyone out there listening?

GRAND ANSE

If you tire of the Lagoon, it is possible to find a good anchorage fairly near town at Grand Anse. This is very good in the summer and somewhat variable in the winter, when the ground swell is up. At such times the best thing is to anchor bow-and-stern, stern- or bow-to the swell, whichever way your boat rides best. If you are approaching from St. George's, steer a course of about 250 magnetic from the harbor reef, which is marked by a buoy at the southeast corner of the harbor. This course will clear the shoal off Ross Point, after which a course may be steered further inshore, although you must be very careful of Dathan Shoal north of the Silver Sands Hotel, a white three-story building with porches on all floors. The shoal is about 350 yards offshore. Grand Anse beach is a full mile long, lined with hotels and palm trees; some consider it one of the most magnificent beaches anywhere. The most popular anchorage seems to be between the Silver Sands and Grenada Beach hotels. (Be careful of the shoals to the west of the Aquatic Club.) You would do well to dive down to inspect the set of your anchor, as it is all too easy to wrap a rode on a coral head here. During the winter there is always a good deal of activity on the beach. Small boats may be rented from Grenada Water Sports near the Grenada Beach Hotel.

MORNE ROUGE BAY
(Sketch Chart III-37)

This is west of Grand Anse and south of Long (or Quarantine) Point, and, draft permitting, is a far superior anchorage to Grand Anse. Feel your way in carefully and anchor in the mouth of the bay. Well offshore the bottom rises abruptly from 5 fathoms to 1½ and to 1 fathom. The bottom is hard sand with patches of grass. Shoal-draft boats can work their way in farther using the lead line or sounding pole. Long Point Shoal offers a good deal of protection from the ground swell hooking in from the west around Long Point. Normally a yawl with its mizzen up will lie stern-to the swell; she will hobbyhorse gently rather than pitch wildly.

The bays between here and Saline Point can be regarded as only lunch stops. There are several beaches along this stretch, but all of them are exposed to the northerly swell—good in calm weather only. When heading westward from Grand Anse to Point Saline, avoid the shoal extending northwest of Long Point. You may pass inside the shoal by placing the southwest corner of the warehouse on the dock at St. George's Harbor under Government House (Range A, course 062 magnetic). Or you may pass outside by placing the northwest corner of the same warehouse under Government House (Range B, course 069 magnetic).

Before the Cubans built the runway on Point Saline, yachts sailing out of St. George's could be becalmed under the point, then be knocked flat by the wind on the south coast; it blows unobstructed all the way from Africa. The lighthouse and hill that used to be on the point were removed when the runway was built, though, so now the wind whistles across the runway and gives you a pretty good idea ahead of time whether or not you should tie in a reef for the beat up the south coast. If you've any doubt, reef.

Don't approach the point too closely, because when they leveled the hill some large chunks of it fell into the sea; no close-inshore surveys have been done, so watch out.

South Coast

About 150 yards southeast of Point Saline and unmarked by the chart is a rock with 6 feet over it. I discovered this one the hard way during the Easter Sunday Race in 1973. *Iolaire* received a good thwack, although *Rosemary V*, following directly behind, passed safely by. It could be that we knocked the top of it off, but I mention it just the same.

Glovers Island, south of Point Saline, is seldom visited, except as a lunch stop in its lee. From here you can row ashore and explore the ruins of a Norwegian whaling station.

Hardy Bay used to be an attractive part-time anchorage, but the airport construction filled it in, and it's no longer of much use.

TRUE BLUE BAY
(Sketch Chart III-38A)

The water is not very clear and it shoals at the head. A protected anchorage can be had northwest of the point on the eastern side of the bay. The bay is easily spotted from seaward by a flagpole on the point and by several buildings that were build for an exposition in 1969. When entering, be careful of the reef off the west corner of the bay.

PRICKLY BAY (L'ANSE AUX ÉPINES)
(Sketch Chart III-38A)

East of True Blue, Prickly Bay (or L'Anse aux Épines, in French), is the most popular anchorage

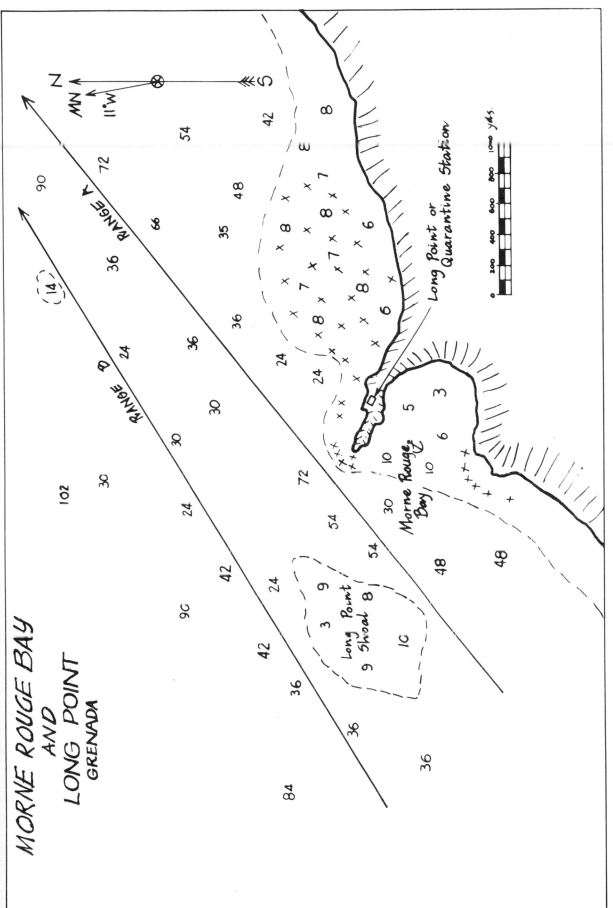

SKETCH CHART III-37   Morne Rouge Bay and Long Point

Range A: Southeast corner of the transit shed under Government House leads inside Long Point Shoal, 062-242 magnetic.

Range B: Northeast corner of transit shed under Government House leads northwest of Long Point Shoal, 069-249 magnetic.

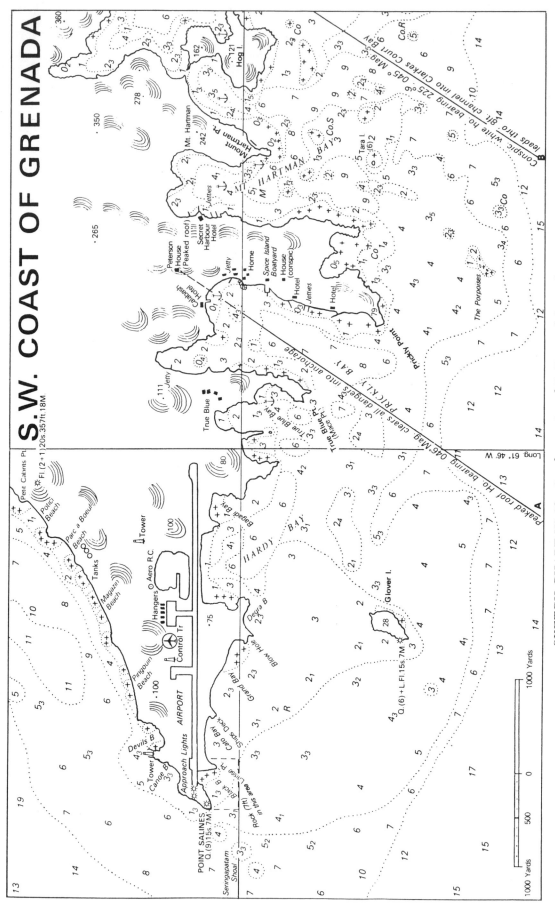

S.W. COAST OF GRENADA

SKETCH CHART III-38   Southwest A and B Coast of Grenada

Range A   Peaked roof house bearing 046-226 magnetic clears all dangers into anchorage.
Range B   Conspicuous white house bearing 045-225 magnetic leads through 8' channel into Clarke's Court Bay.

S.W. COAST OF GRENADA

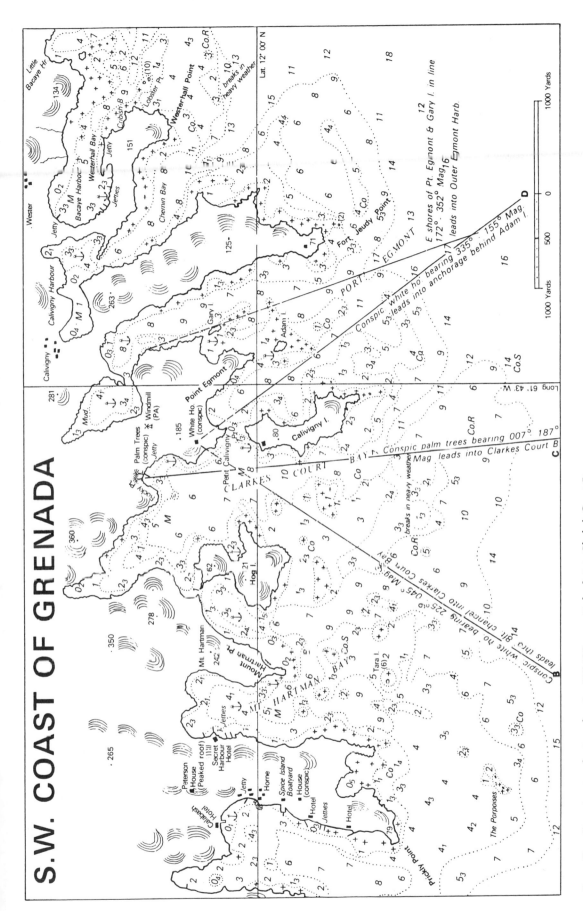

Range C Conspicuous palm trees bearing 007-187 magnetic leads into Clarke's Court Bay.

Range D Conspicuous white house bearing 155-335 magnetic leads into anchorage behind Adam Island.

Range E East shores of Point Egmont and Gary Island in line 172-352 magnetic leads into outer Egmont Harbour. Follow eerange until Port Jeudy Point is abeam to starboard then head up, follow the eastern side of the harbour to avoid reefs south of Gary Island—stand off and anchor in inner or outer Egmont Harbour.

on the south coast of the island. This is the home of the Calabash Hotel, the Horseshoe Bay Hotel (12° north), and Spice Island Marine Services (formerly the Spice Island Boatyard). At the head of the bay is a beautiful white-sand beach. The best anchorage is in the northeast corner of the bay. The bay many be roly during the winter, with the swell hooking around the point and piling up into the harbor. This is not a dangerous situation, only an inconvenience. Once you have cleared to windward of the shoals east of True Blue Point, bring the peaked-roof house (detail, Sketch Chart III-38A) to bear at 045 magnetic, which will take you clear to windward of the reefs west of Spice Island Marine Services. The harbor is a 4-mile drive from St. George's. Taxis can be found at Spice Island.

Spice Island Marine Services began in the mid-sixties, when Peter Spronk started his career as a catamaran designer and builder and convinced Gordon Brathwaite, who owned the L'Anse aux Épines estate and was starting a residential development, that a catamaran would be a nice thing to have. To build one, said Peter, you had to build a building to build it in; the building was built, and then Peter decided he wanted to haul his own boat, so he built a small railway. Others came and asked to be hauled; one thing led to another and the place slowly grew. *Blue Crane*, Peter's first catamaran, was launched, and then Bill Stevens of Stevens Yachts took over the establishment, and started building the Spice Island Boatyard. It was later sold to John Blunt, who, building on the basically good structures and ideas of Bill Stevens and aided by Dodd Gorman and Adrian Voleny, created what I have previously described as the "prettiest little boatyard in the Caribbean."

Needless to say, with the troubles under Gairy, followed by four years under the People's Revolutionary Government, everything went to hell in a handbasket. Then in 1985, Glen Evans, Jr. (known throughout the Caribbean as Junior), and backers bought out the yard. He, his wife, and younger brother Champy are in the midst of a massive renovation and expansion project. The whole yard has been rewired; an excellent restaurant has been built; in May 1986, the docks were being rebuilt and a 35-ton travel lift was due to arrive within the month. The commissary is being expanded, and Junior claims he is going to develop the store into a first-rate marine supply facility. (They presently stock the Street guides and the Imray-Iolaire charts.)

The laundry is still run with charm and efficiency by Merl, and Junior has achieved a major coup in getting direct bus service laid on from Spice Island to town and back, which makes lying in Prickly Bay a much more viable proposition than it used to be.

The government of Grenada seems to be doing its best to help reestablish yachting in Grenada. They have granted Spice Island Marine Services a ten-year exemption from import duty on sailcloth and all materials that have anything to do with sailmaking. This should allow Johnnie Phillips to really build up the sailmaking business. They have also allowed Spice Island to set up a duty-free bonded store for marine paints, which will be able to sell duty-free paint direct to the yacht. In the past, the only way one could obtain duty-free paint was to have it shipped from abroad and consigned direct to the yacht—a cumbersome procedure, and usually the minimum bill-of-lading charge used up any saving in duty. These two concessions alone should do much to attract yachts to Spice Island Marine Services.

There was one fly in the ointment as of May 1986: Spice Island was trying to collect a dinghy landing fee. For thirty years I have watched various organizations try to collect dinghy landing fees, and am convinced it is a waste of time and counterproductive. All it succeeds in doing is antagonizing potential customers and driving business elsewhere. "Why should I have to pay a dinghy landing fee when I'm coming ashore here to spend money in your boatyard, restaurant, and bar?" I hope Spice Island will see the light soon.

In contrast, during the winter of 1986 the Calabash Hotel was only too glad to have the yachtsmen use their beach and dock free of charge; they figured they would earn their money many times over in increased bar and restaurant traffic.

Within walking distance from the boatyard is the Red Crab, which is a delightful anachronism. Who would expect to find an English-style pub run on English hours by a Czechoslovakian ex–British Spitfire pilot in Grenada? Unfortunately, Julian Pianachez, who built the Red Crab, is no longer with us, but his Red Crab still is. (Not long ago I was walking barefoot down the blacktop road at noon, headed for the Red Crab, when I passed two boatboys sitting under a tree drinking beer. One shook his head, looked at the other, and said, "The Skip may look like a white man but he sure got black man's feet!")

Situated at the head of the bay, the Calabash Hotel has beautiful grounds, a beach bar that is most hospitable, and windsurfers and sunfish for rent on the beach; arrangements can be made for dinner ashore. It is only a short walk through the Calabash grounds to the Red Crab.

South of Spice Island Marine Services is the Horseshoe Bay Hotel, an extremely attractive small hotel originally built by John and Aggie Yarwood, now operated by the government of Grenada. One wonders how long the government will continue to run it or whether it will be turned over to private enterprise.

The Porpoises are a group of awash rocks three-quarters of a mile south-southeast of Prickly Point. There is deep water all around them, except that 40 yards north of the easternmost Porpoise is a rock under 6 feet. Although the chart didn't mark it, Bill Stevens of Stevens Yachts discovered this one by bouncing hard off it in a Hughes 38.

MOUNT HARTMAN BAY (SECRET HARBOR)
(Sketch Chart III-38A)

This is the next anchorage east of Prickly Bay. (The harbor on the point between it and Prickly Bay is shoal and for dinghy use only, despite what the charts show.) Making entry to Mount Hartman Bay requires a certain amount of reef-dodging. There are a number of ways to enter; the one I prefer is to hug the reef along the western shore. Pass through the break and continue on until the Secret Harbor Hotel comes into view; head directly for it and stand on into the harbor. An alternate approach is to stand east from Prickly Point until Mount Hartman Peak bears 022 magnetic; stand in along this line of bearing, bearing off when the hotel bears 330 (Range A). What the chart shows as an exposed sandbar is now a foot under water, and the reef to the south of it has built up to an island 6 feet high. Called Tara Island by the locals, it is no more than a heap of slab coral that was thrown up by the heavy seas of Hurricane Flora in 1963, and yet it abounds with sea life and appears to be growing in size all the time. The water is shallow and a strong current sweeps by it in such a way that there is no convenient lee in which to make a dinghy approach. If you go ashore, wear a pair of sneakers and take two light dinghy anchors along, one to hold the stern off and one to bury ashore.

Most charts (and most other guidebooks) are quite incorrect about this area, so be very careful not to rely on bearings taken from the charts unless you're using Imray Chart B-32.

The anchorage is good anywhere in Mount Hartman Bay; one that is guaranteed to be cool and bug free is behind the low saddle at the south base of Mount Hartman. The east breeze sweeping through this notch in the land is most refreshing. Nearby, the Secret Harbor Hotel, high on a hill on the western side of the harbor, offers excellent food and service. It is run by Barbara Stevens and is certainly one of the most beautiful hotel projects in the Islands.

HOG ISLAND
(Sketch Chart III-38A)

East of Mount Hartman Bay is an unnamed anchorage behind Hog Island, which is one of the finest spots on the south coast. To get there from Mount Hartman Bay, you have only to swing around the reef off-lying Mount Hartman Point along a wide semicircle. The shoals extending west of Hog Island must be eyeballed. You can anchor anywhere in the basin between the island and the mainland. I prefer a spot west of the north hill on Hog. There is a dinghy passage into Clarke's Court Bay between the island and mainland. It is possible to take a boat through here, but I hesitate to recommend it. For shoal-draft boats, I provide the following directions: Coming from the west, approach the gap favoring the starboard side of the channel; as the point on Hog Island is approached, veer to the left on 010 magnetic for a distance of 40 yards; then veer right and you are through. The controlling depth is 5 feet and the channel is 30 feet wide at its narrowest.

If you are approaching the anchorage behind Hog Island from seaward, you must eyeball it. The shoal due south of Mount Hartman Point is shallower than government charts let on; consequently you should continue east until the hill on Mount Hartman Point bears north magnetic; run in on this bearing, keeping your eyes peeled for reefs on either side. Slowly head up, working your way eastward behind Hog Island and into the anchorage.

CLARKE'S COURT BAY
(Sketch Chart III-38B)

This large harbor contains many coves and is one of the most attractive bays on the south coast. There are other bays that may have better anchorage, but none has so many in one single, sheltered bay. Twenty boats could anchor inside Clarke's Court Bay and still not feel crowded.

I fell in love with this bay early on in my visits to Grenada. In 1963, I bought a house and some land overlooking Clarke's Court Bay and expanded the house and built another for my in-laws, largely in anticipation of the development of a marina and boatyard in the harbor. This would enable me to have the yachtsman's dream: a house high on a ridge, cool and bug free, from which to look down on my boat, moored stern to the beach. Our view east was all the way to Westerhall Point, to the west as far as Point Saline. Our nearest neighbor was half a mile away. Alas, so much for a sailor's dream. The People's Revolutionary Government decided that would be a perfect spot for a military base, with a commanding position over the coastline. So they took over the whole point, walked into our house and at gunpoint chased out our maid and gardener, allowing them to take nothing from the house. The maid cleverly grabbed most of my charts (crammed with necessary navigational notes), and later we got Mr. Bishop to order the army to relinquish our double bed, which is now in Glandore, Ireland, and a Sodeberg etching of Star boats racing. Otherwise, everything in both houses was burned or used up. No one in the family was allowed ever to visit the place again.

The PRG partially compensated us for the houses; better still, they never transferred the titles of the houses in the register. So, although the U.S. helicopters that blasted the houses left us with only two concrete slabs, we do still own seven acres, hold the deeds, and pay the taxes. Someday we hope to rebuild. Certainly Calivigny Island and the neighboring point would make a fantastic site for a development. We'll wait and see what happens.

Calivigny Island forms the eastern side of Clarke's Court Bay, and one of the best anchorages in the area is between it and the mainland. You may sail right up to the shoal, throw your anchor on top, and back off. A stern anchor should be used overnight when the wind has died down and when the current has a tendency to swing you around. It is best to use a heavy anchor, as the bottom is grass.

In the center of the harbor, directly south of Rocky Point, is a large shoal spot with about 1 foot over it. Because this is extremely difficult to make out, I would strongly advise against going to the head of the bay unless the light is perfect.

There is another good anchorage in what I have come to call Saga Cove on the eastern shore of Hog Island. *Saga*, owned by Harry Disharoon, frequently anchored here, and he considered it one of the best anchorages on Grenada. Good swimming and snorkeling can be found here, and as this is on the lee side of the harbor, there is always a good breeze over calm water.

When entering Clarke's Court Bay, beware of the shoals, whose depths are significantly less than shown on the government charts. The way must be eyeballed in good light. It is possible to sail upwind across the shoals southeast of Hog. Range B on Sketch Chart III-38B, course 045 magnetic, will carry 7 feet—and no more—safely over the shoals. Certainly the safest way to enter is to stand eastward, taking care to avoid the 2-fathom shoal south by east of the hill on Hog. This frequently breaks in heavy weather. Continue east until Stevens Beach bears 005 magnetic (Range C). The beach may be identified by a line of palm trees, a cliff on either end, and a small stone dock in the center.

Five feet can be carried between Petit Calivigny and Calivigny Island. One must stay 50 feet off the Point Egmont shore and feel the way along with a sounding pole. The channel may be spotted by heading about 50 yards north of the point south of the conspicuous white house. As you approach shore, start curving south, following the shoreline around the point. Once around, head north, east, and then south to the Adam Island anchorage. It is advisable to test this route beforehand from a dinghy. Even so, you will save time over the long beat around to Adam Island.

ADAM ISLAND
(Sketch Chart III-38B)

The anchorage behind this island is a good deal better than the government chart indicates. The chart does not reflect the extent to which the small reef south of the island hooks to the west. If you tuck behind—northwest of—this reef, you will be sheltered at all times. From my house on Point Egmont I never saw it rough behind the reef. To enter from seaward, place the white house marked on Sketch Chart III-38B on a bearing of 335 magnetic (Range D). Put a man aloft and watch your course carefully, as there is very little room for error through here. Follow this bearing and round up immediately after passing the west reef; head in and anchor when the house on Adam Island bears southeast and the west reef closes with the south end of Calivigny Island. Between Adam Island and the mainland there is a dinghy passage with 18 inches of water.

GARY ISLAND
(Sketch Charts III-38B and 39)

There is a good shoal-draft anchorage behind this island that will carry no more than 4 feet. A deeper daytime anchorage (2 fathoms) can be found immediately south of Gary Island. It is well sheltered from normal trade wind weather, but open to winds from the south.

POINT EGMONT
(Sketch Chart III-38B)

The inner harbor here is the most protected harbor on the south coast of Grenada. Almost landlocked, it is surrounded by high hills on all sides. Even in the most violent hurricane, I cannot imagine a boat's incurring damage in Egmont. The entrance is simple as long as you proceed when the sun is high. Steer east offshore until the eastern end of Gary Island is in line with the eastern side of Point Egmont (Range E, 351 magnetic). Bear off, favoring the right-hand side, and continue on north into the harbor. The wind hooking around Fort Jeudy Point is likely to put you dead before it. As you approach the head of the harbor, watch out for the shoal along the western side and for an unmarked shoal north of the anchor mark on Sketch Chart III-38B. Both can be hazardous.

The inner basin and channel were always thought to be steep-to on both sides, and so they are—if you draw less than 9 feet of water. But there is a rock with a bare 9 feet over it on the south side of the entrance to the inner Egmont Harbor—we know this for sure, as Mike Jorrold's *Lily Maid*, a beautiful 1904, British-built cutter, bounced off it in the winter of 1978. With this exception, there is a minimum of 12 feet through this channel.

As mentioned earlier, the Cubans dredged the Egmont inner harbor channel to 20 feet, presumably so they could off-load military equipment onto the base in secrecy. They planned to put their dock in the southern bight of the inner harbor, but they evidently hadn't read Street's *Guide*, or they would have known about the rocks that *Lily Maid* hit. As it was, they were unable to dredge over to the south side because there was too much rock. Egmont Harbor is now deeper than before, but still an excellent hurricane harbor.

You may anchor anywhere in the inner harbor. It is so sheltered that there will be very little strain on the rode. The swimming and fishing are excellent, and the seclusion perfect.

In leaving, the wind will be dead against you, so that it is probably advisable to motor out and set sail under the lee of Fort Jeudy Point. As you leave, stay east of Range D until Prickly Point separates from the south tip of Calivigny Island. This will keep you from bearing off onto the shoals south of Adam Island.

CALIVIGNY HARBOR
(Sketch Charts III-38B and 39)

The next harbor east of Point Egmont, this is not to be confused with Calivigny Island. The old sailing directions speak highly of this harbor, inasmuch as the square-riggers could sail in without having to anchor first and warp their way up to the anchorage at its head. The outer entrance, to Chemin Bay, is very narrow. The shoals extending southwest of Westerhall Point are shallower than the government charts indicate. On the western side of the channel the 1¼-fathom spot extends quite far to the east and connects with the reef off Fort Jeudy Peninsula. This is a case for eyeball navigation in good light. The shoals on the starboard hand are more easily discernible than those to port. Favor the Westerhall Point side as you enter Chemin Bay. Stand right on up the harbor, keeping to the middle. You may anchor anywhere within the inner harbor. Some boats prefer to drop a stern anchor and sail right up to the sand spit, which is very steep-to. You can jump ashore and tie a line to a bush or bury a hook in the sand. There is abundant fishing among the mangroves on the western side. You will find a good dock on the Westerhall side of the harbor. Westerhall Point is a large, private development put together by Beres Wilcox. The houses are expensive and beautifully landscaped in this rather nice preplanned community, which is on the main road from St. George's, thirty minutes away by car. The guard at the entrance will probably allow you to use the phone to call a cab.

The western half of Calivigny Harbor has shoaled drastically. See newest corrected II charts dated after October 1985. In the eighteenth and nineteenth centuries, this arm of the harbor was the main port for the island of Grenada; it has shoaled up so much through the years that only a dinghy can get in there now.

BACAYE HARBOR
(Sketch Charts III-38B and 39)

North of Westerhall Point, Bacaye is an excellent anchorage, although seldom used because of

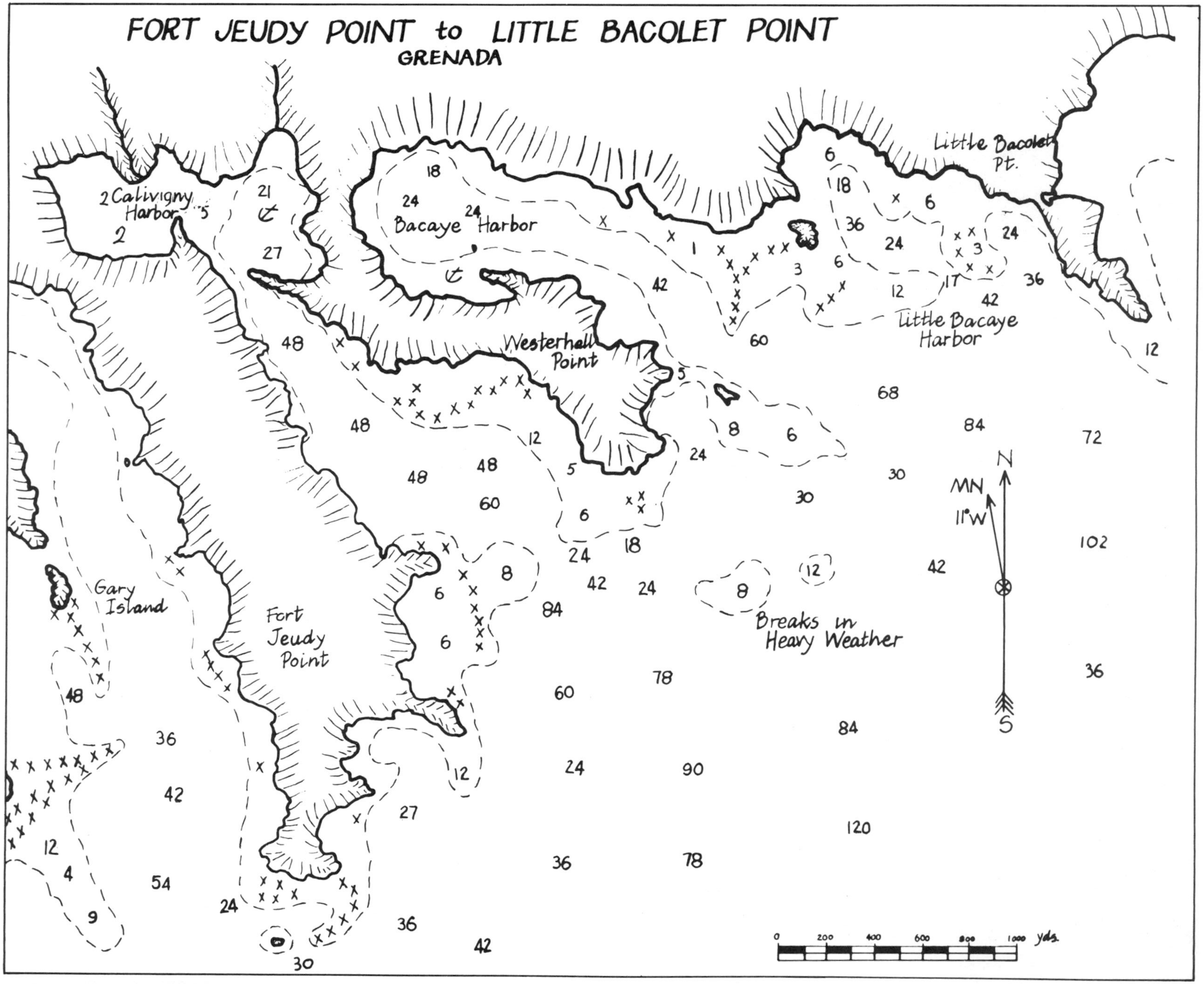

FORT JEUDY POINT to LITTLE BACOLET POINT
GRENADA
Calivigny Harbor
Bacaye Harbor
Westerhall Point
Little Bacolet Pt.
Little Bacaye Harbor
Gary Island
Fort Jeudy Point
Breaks in Heavy Weather
MN
11°W
N
S
0 200 400 600 800 1000 yds.

SKETCH CHART III-39 Fort Jeudy Point to Little Bacolet Point

the gross inaccuracy of the government charts. The deepwater passage shown between Lobster Point and the small island east of it has shoaled. The 2- and 3-fathom spots noted farther southeast have become shallower. The 3-fathom spot breaks in heavy weather, and the 2-fathom spot has no more than 8 or 9 feet and breaks continually in heavy weather. Give both spots a very wide berth.

Access to the harbor is through Westerhall Bay along an east-west axis; it should not be entered after 1300 or the sun will be in your eyes. The depth sounder will not substitute for careful eye-balling, since the reefs are steep-to and would not show up on the dial before you were hard on them. The best anchorage is in the cove on the south side of the harbor in 9–10 feet of water. The bottom is soft mud, so be sure to use a good, heavy anchor.

The best time to leave is after noon and under power. At 0900 the sun will be directly on your line of bearing, making an exit difficult if not impossible. Many years ago, I ran aground in 4 feet of water trying to tack out in the early morning, having misjudged the end of the reef on the north side of the harbor. No damage was done, thanks to a full-length lead keel; with the aid of a strong anchor windlass I managed to kedge off.

Southeast Coast

ST. DAVID'S HARBOR
(Sketch Chart III-40)

Few yachts venture to anchorages east of Westerhall Point, although there are a number to choose from. St. David's Harbor is very good, as long as the wind is not in the south. Follow all the way up to the head of the bay and anchor on the eastern side close ashore. I would suggest a bow-and-stern mooring along a north-south axis in anticipation of the swell that tends to hook around St. David's Point. Stand eastward as you enter until St. David's Point bears 010 magnetic; then bear off and run in a course due north, watching for the detached rock on the western side of St. David's Point and for the 8-foot spot on the western side of the harbor entrance.

LA SAGESSE BAY
(Sketch Chart III-40)

The only anchorage is on the eastern half of the bay, west of Marquis Point. A beautiful white beach always has some surf on it. The bay is easily identified by an old estate house on the northeast corner of the beach. This is a popular spot with the Grenadians on weekends and it is a good lunch stop for the visiting yachtsman, but it's not for overnight use.

LASCAR COVE
(Sketch Chart III-40)

This heretofore unnamed cove was sounded by Bill Gould and myself aboard his *Lascar*, hence the name. It is a beautiful spot, located between Marquis Point and Petit Trou Point, with a small, first-rate anchorage in its northeast corner. There is a slight roll in the northwestern corner, where a small stream enters. The cove is difficult to spot from seaward. A small white building that looks like a church and is marked on the British chart as a courthouse will come into view as you work eastward. Bring this to bear at 355 magnetic and it will lead you directly to Lascar Cove. Entrance should be made in good light, as the reefs impinge closely from either side. The opening is no more than 100 yards. Once inside, head for the beach in the northeast arm of the bay and anchor off in 2 fathoms. Stay to the west of the reef on the starboard side. Another reef projecting south breaks the harbor into eastern and western halves. There is enough room to round up and anchor, but I would advise using a Bahamian moor, especially if there is more than one boat inside. The diving and fishing are very good in here.

In December 1977, I talked to a Dutch couple who, with their small baby, had sailed across the Atlantic, and after a stay in Barbados had cruised on to Grenada. After reading my 1974 *Cruising Guide*, they decided to anchor in Lascar Cove. As soon as the anchor went down, a man came out in a rowboat, welcomed them to the harbor, and said they were only the third yacht ever to stop in Lascar Cove.

"What can we do to help you?" people asked the couple. "Could we look after the baby while you explore ashore?" The couple stayed in the cove for three or four days, and during this time they were brought fruit, vegetables, fish, and lobster by the local people. They couldn't speak highly enough of the cove, the fishing, and the marvelous people. This is how yachting used to be twenty-five years ago, and it's heartwarming to think experiences like this still occur.

PETIT TROU
(Sketch Chart III-40)

There is a pretty, deserted beach here, but the shelter is not good, so that I can recommend it only for daytime use in settled weather.

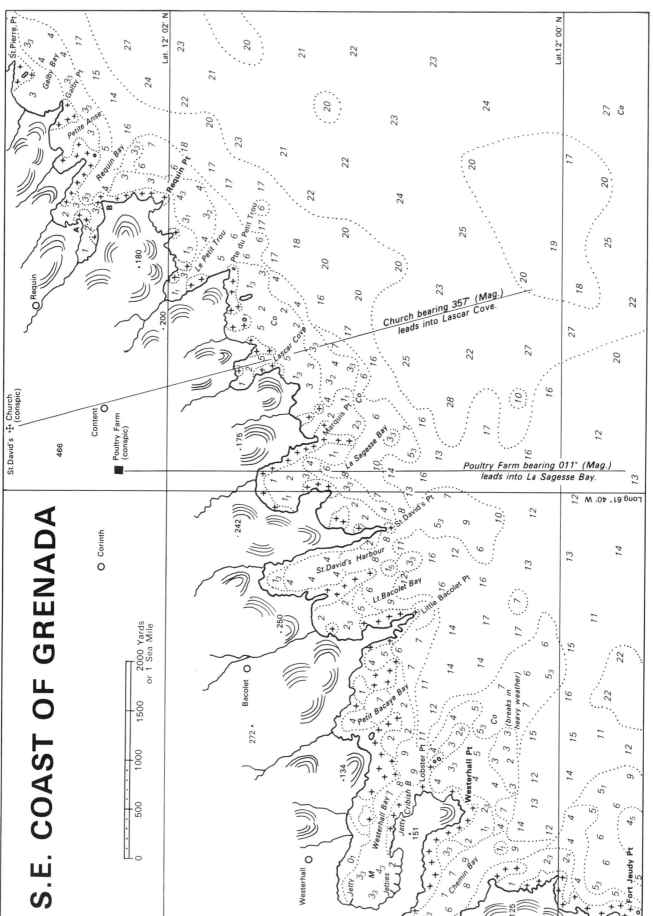

S.E. COAST OF GRENADA

SKETCH CHART III-40 Southwest Coast of Grenada

Range A: The church, labeled "Court House" on the British chart, brought to bear 335 magnetic leads

REQUIN BAY
(Sketch Chart III-40)

This bay may be hard to make out; a pair of rock arches marks the next bay east of it, from which you should count back one bay to Requin. Once Requin has been identified, stand to the northeast until point A appears from behind point B (Sketch Chart III-40). Bear off to a course of roughly 335 magnetic, which leads up to the white-sand beach on the northeast arm of the bay. This is a dogleg channel requiring eyeball navigation. The reef extends from the eastern point of the bay farther than the chart shows. Once you have cleared the eastern reef on starboard tack, head up until you are past the other reef on your port side. Then bear off and run down into the western arm of the bay. The best anchorage is south of point A, since farther west the bottom becomes grassy and poor holding. Eight feet may be carried all the way to the dock on this western arm. The eastern arm has a slight roll most of the time. There is a fine beach ashore where the Little Requin River empties, but it's the old story of the good beach that seldom gives a good anchorage. Beware of the turtle nets as you enter. They are used all along the southeast corner of Grenada. Their buoys are almost flush with the water, set wide apart, and difficult to spot.

Between Requin Bay and Marquis Island there are a number of bays that I have not investigated, but that seem to have possibilities. La Tante Bay has a good beach but poor shelter. The bays to either side of Menere Point look promising. Behind Crochu Point looks very good indeed. Great Bacolet Bay (Sketch Chart III-41) is probably not a good anchorage, but it has a beautiful beach.

MARQUIS ISLAND
(Sketch Chart III-42)

Anchorages may be had behind the island or between the western tip of the island and the

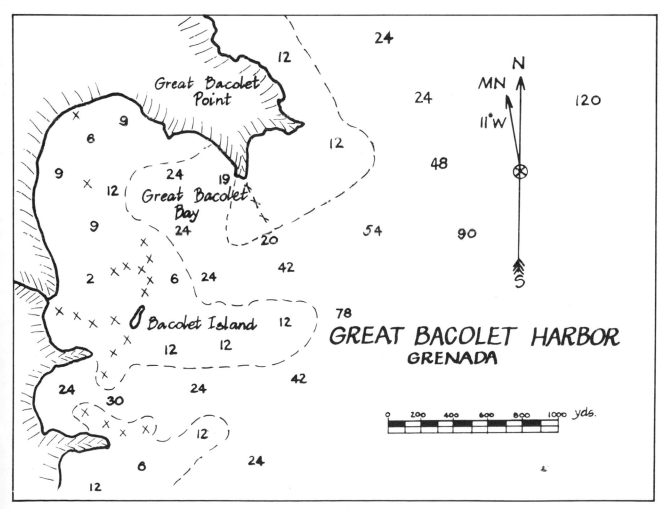

SKETCH CHART III-41 Great Bacolet Harbor

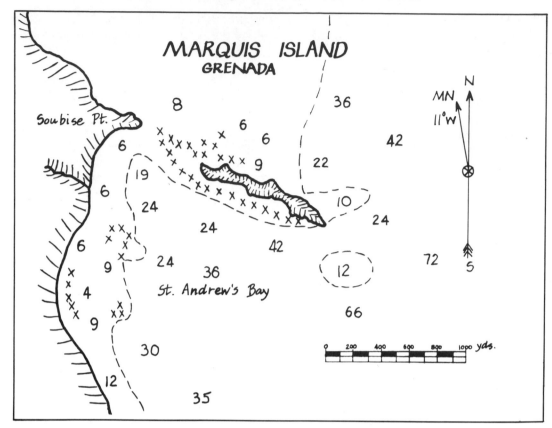

SKETCH CHART III-42   Marquis Island

mainland. The former is the more protected, although a double moor is required, as the wind looping over the top of Marquis will waltz you in every direction. It is not a particularly good shelter.

GRENVILLE HARBOR

(Sketch Chart III-43)

The only port of entry on the east coast, Grenville is the second largest town on Grenada. Food supplies are available, but in nowhere near the quantity as at St. George's. The windward reef affords total shelter, while the wind blows in to make the place cool. There are two beautiful old churches, many buildings, and an altogether pleasant atmosphere ashore.

The town is best visited on Fridays or Saturdays. The small sloops from Carriacou come down on Friday nights for the Saturday market, while the schooners come in from Trinidad the same afternoon. The harbor is crowded with local vessels, whose crews spend the night making merry. In the morning they all depart. The sailing of a West Indian cargo vessel has to be seen to be believed.

A large crew and a heavy cargo, complete with deck load, put the vessel right down to her marks. Yes, they do have plimsoll marks, but whoever places them has an optimistic view of the weather. They are just below the sheer line. On top of the deck load a few goats and chickens will be tethered, and you will notice a number of the crew's girlfriends going along for the ride, and occasionally passengers as well. Sails go up slowly; first the main, then the fore, amid the squealing of blocks (no West Indian seaman would dream of greasing a block). Then the anchor chain comes in. Usually the windlass won't work, so a tackle is hitched to a chain, which is always old, rusty, and corroded. The anchor comes home accompanied by much shouting, groaning, and singing. Headsails are hoisted, backed, and sheeted home, again amid shouting, confusion, and contrary orders, while the schooner threads its way among the vessels moored in the harbor, seldom, if ever, fouling another boat. As it leaves the harbor, you will notice one person quietly standing at the wheel, saying nothing, observing all, handling the boat beautifully, and completely ignoring the antics of the rest of the crew. He is the skipper. Photographs of a West Indian schooner leaving port miss

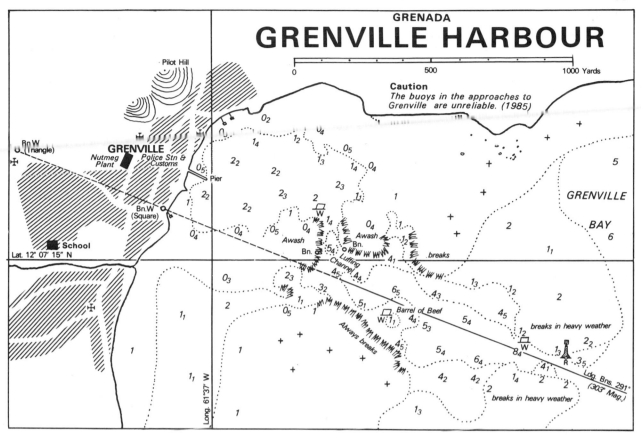

SKETCH CHART III-43   Grenville Harbor

the best part. Only a tape recorder could catch the true flavor of the show.

Grenville Harbor is sheltered, but its entrance and exit are not easy, and the buoys have in the past been unreliable. The last time I was there, there were no range marks, and the outer two buoys were missing. We were informed that "de range mark fall down and de buoy is sunk and we is negotiatin' for a replacement." However, pilotage is cheap. One bottle of Barbados rum seems to be the right price. You will note from the chart that there is either plenty of water or none at all, so you don't have to worry about the pilot running you over shoal spots. The American chart does not have the detailed insert of the harbor that the British one has. Sketch Chart 43 is more up-to-date than either.

If you are entering on your own, you should stay outside a line drawn from Great Bacolet Point to Telescope Point until the south end of town bears 300 magnetic. Then you may turn inshore, but keep a man aloft to spot the reefs or whatever buoys happen to be in place. If the sun is in the west, it will be practically impossible to spot buoys or reefs, so do not try to enter after 1400. You

should be able to pick up the two small outer buoys marking the reef on the north side of the channel. The range to the outer channel is a forward square, white mark atop a piling lined up with a white triangle onshore. The triangle looks just like the eaves of a house and may be very difficult to spot. Look for a large, square, stone building, the old nutmeg factory and now a school. North of this school is a green-painted store under a huge, green shade tree (*Ficus benjamina*). Between the store and the tree you will spot the elusive triangle. If you still can't find it, line up the outer range with the Catholic church. The church is misplaced on the Admiralty chart; it is actually on a hill in back of town.

Leaving to starboard the two outer buoys that mark the entrance to the channel, run down this range; alter course slightly northward to pass the 1¼-fathom spot (marked "Barrel of Beef" on Sketch Chart III-43) to port. (The local sailors will also refer to the eastern group of rocks flanking Luffing Channel as "Barrel of Beef," so be sure not to confuse the two.) As you enter Luffing Channel, round up, heading roughly north and favoring the east side of the channel. This will put you on the wind for a space of 50 yards. Then bear off into the basin and anchor where you see fit. Ten feet of water can be carried through Luffing Channel, and the basin has ample water in its northern half.

Mike Forshaw has told me that the buoys for Grenville Harbor are going to be fixed up and the range marks rebuilt in the same yellow-and-orange color scheme used on the range marks in St. George's. He says there will be an outer, lighted bell buoy and new channel buoys. (The previous Grenville sea buoy, given to the Grenada government by the U.S. Coast Guard, couldn't cope with the winter swell and turned turtle!)

These changes may have been made by the time you read this (in spring of 1986 they were still in the planning stage), and it will make Grenville much easier to enter. And then again, they may not have. Navigate with an up-to-date Imray-Iolaire chart, and be careful.

In May 1986, the U.S. Navy "Seals" had some fun and created a hell of a bang. The fishermen loved it because the harbor was littered with dead and stunned fish; the schooner skippers loved it because Luffing Channel is now considerably wider and slightly deeper.

Motoring out of Luffing Channel is advisable. Sailing out can be extremely difficult without a very competent crew. Keeping the range in line over the stern while tending sheets and short-tacking is a complicated procedure, especially at the outer end of the channel, where the gaps in the reefs are no more than 70–100 yards wide. It is best to motor out after 1000, when the sun is no longer in your eyes. If your engine is out, it is easy to arrange for a tow.

Between Grenville and Bedford Point there are no harbors, and none on the northeast coast of Grenada. When proceeding north, beware of the rock west of Range E, Sketch Chart III-44, which breaks in heavy weather. If the ground swell is down, a good anchorage can be had in the lee of Sandy Island or Levera Island.

SANDY ISLAND
(Sketch Chart III-44 and detailed insert II B-32)

One may anchor due west of the house on Sandy Island in 2 fathoms. The tide is very strong here, requiring a Bahamian moor. The wind will be from the east, while the tide will be setting northwest-southeast, which is the axis your boat should lie to. Make sure that both anchors are securely set. The snorkeling is good on the reefs west of Sandy Island, as is the shelling on the reef extending from the south tip. The lovely sand beaches are rarely visited by anyone.

GREEN ISLAND
(Sketch Chart III-44 and detailed insert II B-32)

The best anchorage due west of the hill is made difficult by 40- to 60-foot depths and a very strong reversing tide. A Bahamian moor will be necessary with about 275 feet on each rode. If you are willing to make this effort, you can enjoy good snorkeling off the south coast and some beautiful beaches.

LEVERA ISLAND
(Sketch Chart III-44 and detailed insert II B-32)

To the west of Sandy and Green islands lies Levera Island, called Sugar Loaf by the locals. The best anchorage is roughly west of Sugar Loaf Peak. Here the water is not particularly deep, but the tide is extremely strong and will reverse itself east and west. Anchor accordingly. This is the best of the small-island anchorages and usually has the least amount of swell. Care must be taken in entering from the west, as the 1¾-fathom shoal has grown shallower over the years. Entering or leaving, you should eyeball the deep water. The tide runs anywhere from 1 to 3 knots, and this should be taken into account in planning any swimming expeditions.

Sailing the north and west coasts of Grenada, the sailor gapes at countless miles of sand beaches off which there are practically no anchorages. It can be a frustrating experience, yet there is really no point in putting in to shore unless you want to turn your insides out. It is, at least, fairly easy sailing along the north and west coasts, with few off-lying hazards. The only danger on the north coast is the 7-foot shoal, six-tenths of a mile west of Levera at 305 magnetic. The shoal is probably more shoal than the charted depth, and it breaks continually in heavy weather. David Point—locally called Tangle Angle—can be rounded close aboard. The west coast of Grenada presents no difficulties. The shore is steep-to, the water very deep, and the winds usually from the east.

HALIFAX HARBOR
(Sketch Chart III-45)

This is the only proper harbor north of St. George's on the west coast of Grenada. Known

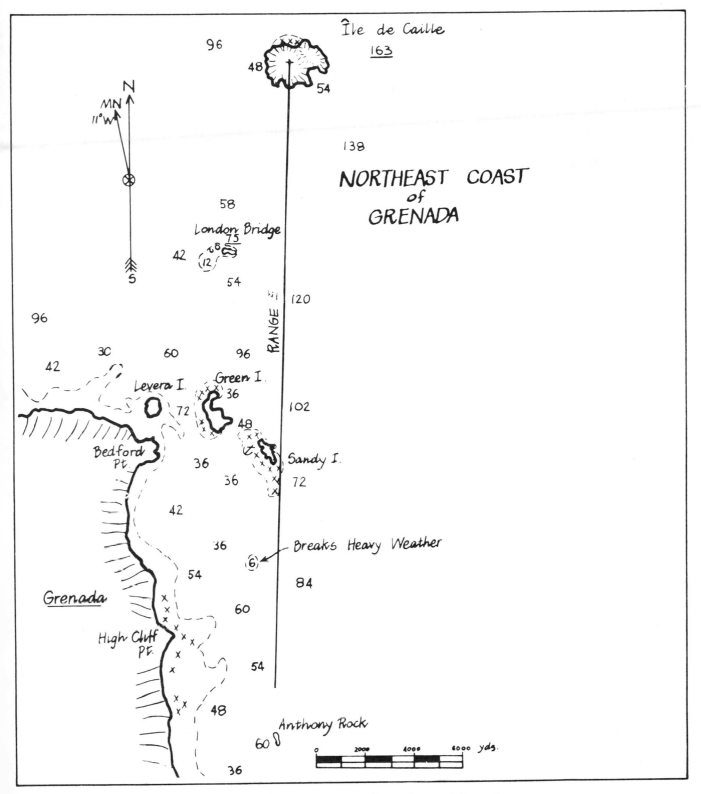

SKETCH CHART III-44 Northeast Coast of Grenada

Range E: Stay outside a line drawn from the high land of Île de Caille along the east coast of Sandy Island to Anthony Rock (010-190 magnetic). This will clear the shoal south-southwest of Sandy Island.

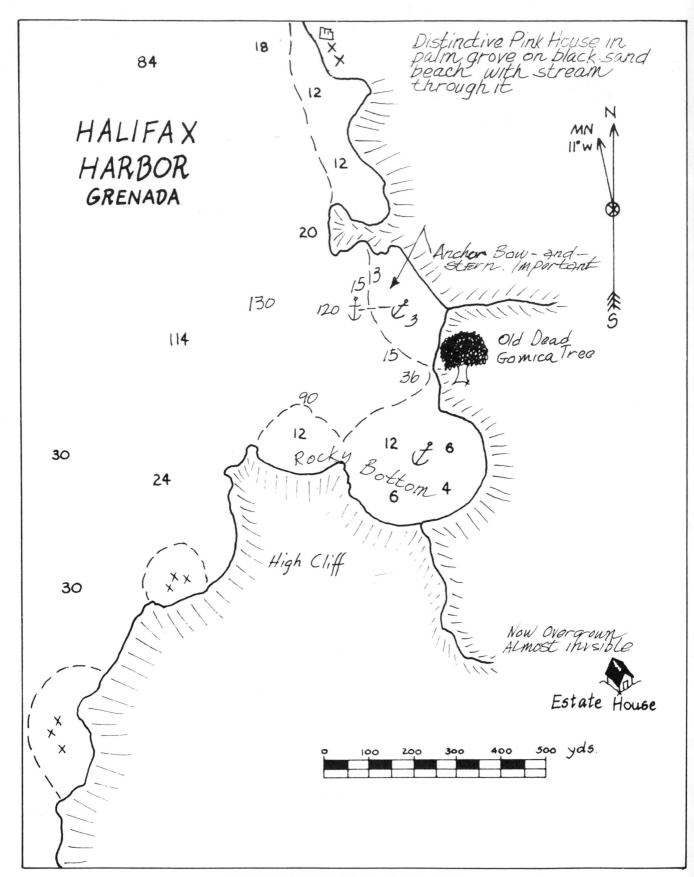

84

18

12

**HALIFAX
HARBOR
GRENADA**

Distinctive Pink House in
palm grove on black sand
beach with stream
through it

12

N
MN
11°W
S

20

Anchor Bow-and-
stern. Important

130

15 13

120 ⚓ — ⚓ 3

15

114

36

Old Dead
Gomica Tree

90

30

12

Rocky
Bottom

12   ⚓ 6

24

6   4

High Cliff

30

Now Overgrown
Almost invisible

Estate House

0   100   200   300   400   500 yds.

SKETCH CHART III-45   Halifax Harbor

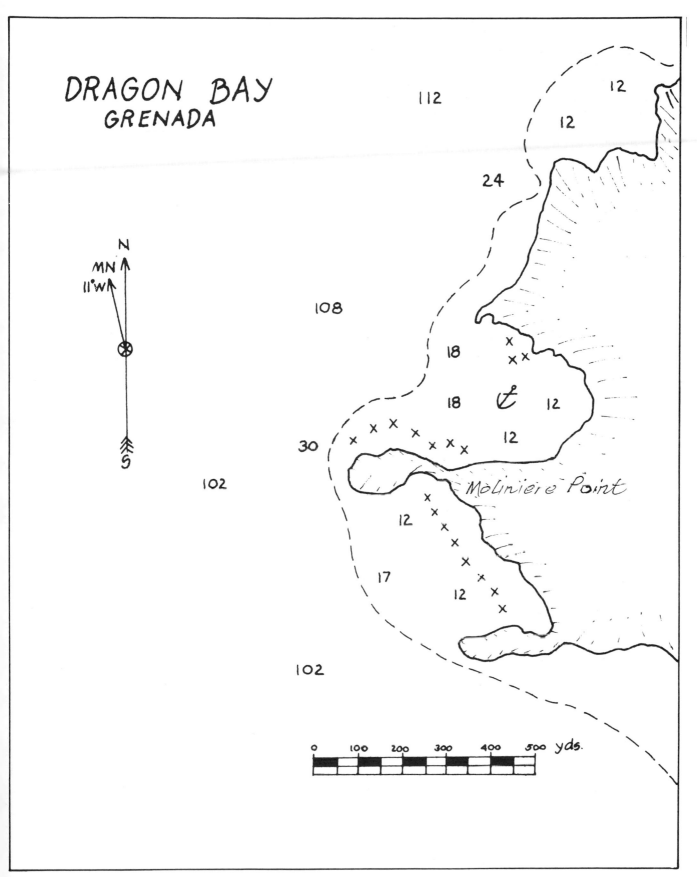

SKETCH CHART III-46   Dragon Bay

locally as Black Bay, it used to be located by the buildings on the Perseverance estate, set well back in the hills. The Perseverance estate, like many others, was semi-abandoned during the troubles and became largely overgrown and barely visible through the trees. If the estate is renovated and the foliage cut back, it will again stand out as the sailor's landmark for Halifax Harbor.

Another landmark in the region of Halifax Harbor is a square, pink concrete house right down at the water's edge, south of which is a grove of palm trees and a black-sand beach with a stream running through it. Roughly a quarter mile south of this beach you will find Halifax Harbor. When heading north, if you see this landmark you'll realize you've gone past Halifax and can turn around and go back.

One fair anchorage is in the southeast corner, with Perseverance bearing southeast. This part of the harbor is roly in any sort of swell. Feel your way in to a suitable depth and drop anchor in soft mud. Make sure you anchor bow and stern, as the wind dies at night and you will swing around beam to the sea and roll your guts out. Do not anchor off the southwest corner of the harbor, as that area is very rocky and you are guaranteed to foul your anchor.

Most of the time, the best anchorage is in the northeast corner of the harbor. (The government charts are not reliable here. See Sketch Chart III-45.) The bottom comes up quickly from really deep water to 2 fathoms and then shoals to 3 feet. This 3-foot shelf extends about 200 yards offshore.

Drop a stern anchor with 40 feet of line; as soon as you feel the anchor set, feed out line until you get to the 3-foot shelf. Then walk or row the anchor well onto this shelf and set it hard. Don't attempt to lie to a single anchor.

I think this harbor is a bit overrated, because the swell can at times make it almost untenable. But when it's good, it's very good. An interesting exploration, especially for photographers, is a dinghy ride up the coast around the northwestern point. There are fascinating rock formations, including one with a hole right through it.

DRAGON BAY
(Sketch Chart III-46)

Just north of Molinière Point, Dragon Bay is fast becoming a popular anchorage. It is a place to escape the press of St. George's Harbor without having to go all the way to Halifax. This is a confined anchorage, and the way in must be carefully sounded. Once in, you must be prepared to leave on short notice, especially in the winter, when the swell can make up in a dangerously short time. However, from June to October in settled weather it is safe and comfortable. At night, when the wind dies down, you may swing around unpredictably, so that a Bahamian moor will be required.

Grenada offers many anchorages whose possibilities have barely been discovered. For this reason, it is an inviting alternative to the popular anchorages on the islands farther north. The Grenadines are becoming a virtual thoroughfare, and in years to come, perhaps, boats will be seen rafted ten across in formerly deserted places like the Tobago Cays. This catastrophe is not foreseeable along the coasts of Grenada, where a week or two can be spent in relative seclusion visiting the anchorages I have discussed, or exploring the unexplored.

NOTES

NOTES

NOTES

NOTES

NOTES

9

Trinidad and Tobago

II B, D; DMA 24402, 24403, 24404; BA 483, 493, 505, 508

Trinidad and Tobago form one independent state within the British Commonwealth. It was discovered by the Spanish on Columbus' third voyage. At the head of a small fleet, Columbus entered the Gulf of Paria through Serpents Mouth and anchored. A minor volcanic eruption evidently caused a tidal wave or bore to sweep through the gulf, inflicting considerable damage to his fleet. He then moved north across the gulf and anchored under the south coast of Peninsula de Paria. This was the first stop by a European on the South American mainland. The actual anchorage was most likely at Ensenada

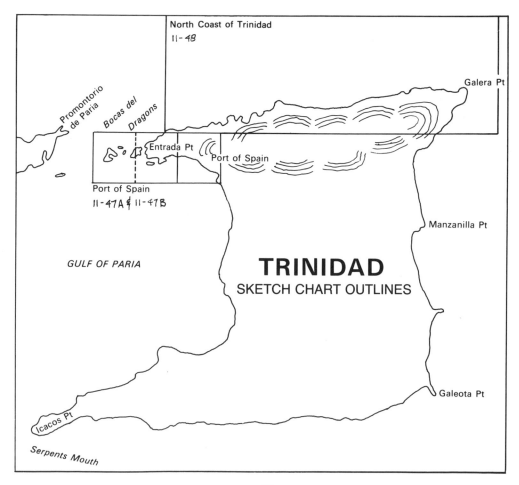

Cariaquita, as Dr. Camejo of Sargasso has maintained, although this view is disputed by Admiral Morison's biography of Columbus. Columbus all but ignored the island of Trinidad; the first settlement was not made on the island until much later, in 1552.

Trinidad

Unlike most of the South American colonies, Trinidad did not prosper. By 1780, the population was a scant 300 people. In that year, the colony was opened to settlement by all nations, and by 1797, when the island surrendered to the British without a fight, the population had grown to 18,000. The island remained in British hands for almost two centuries, administered by a governor appointed by the Crown. In 1962, a few years after the British tried unsuccessfully to set up a West Indies Federation, Trinidad and Tobago were granted independence.

In 1970, there was a rebellion by the Trinidad and Tobago Army Regiment that briefly disturbed the peace. The matter was handled judiciously by the government, the leaders being given jail sentences and subsequently freed on appeal. This was a far less bloody solution than that which befell the rebellion in 1837 by the black recruits in the West Indian Regiment. The leader, Donald Stewart, was tortured and put to death along with a number of other rebels. Now the only organized civil disturbance occurs during Carnival.

The Trinidadians are a raucous, hard-living people. This is no land for the timid; the number of people who are done in each year by car or motorcycle accidents, stabbings, shootings, or drownings is simply horrendous. Not surprisingly, the police force on Trinidad was the first among former British colonies to be armed with pistols. A swagger stick is apparently not enough.

Each island has its own accent: Trinidad's is a particularly pleasing one. The language has its own peculiarities. For instance, a Trinidadian's boat has an outhaul rather than a haulout. (I always ask whether the morning after is cursed by an overhang.) Trinidad's population is made up of a far-flung blend of English, Chinese, Spanish, East Indians, and Africans—a combination that has produced some of the most beautiful women in the world. They may not be as beautifully dressed or as chic as the women of Martinique, but if you visit the island during Carnival, I am sure you'll agree with me that Trinidad's women are beautiful indeed.

Trinidad is the main transshipment port for the Lesser Antilles. The commercial congestion in the harbor is quite beyond belief, second only to the inefficiency that it gives rise to. It may take a month or more to have goods transferred through Port of Spain to points north. If I have important gear being shipped to me through Port of Spain, I usually sail down and pick it up myself.

Trinidad's weather is, for the most part, governed by the easterly trades. When the island cools off at night, there is usually a calm in the Gulf of Paria. An easterly breeze springs up in the mornings, building to anywhere from 10 to 20 knots by the afternoon and dying down at sunset. From time to time, during periods of light winds and very hot days, the island will heat up and a column of warm air rising overland will draw in a wind from the west. The resulting southerly or southwesterly breeze is a cause for great confusion among the weekend racers.

Approaching Trinidad from the north, there are no off-lying hazards. The mountainous north coast gives ample warning of approach to land. Both Trinidad and Tobago are well lit and may be approached at night, although the actual entry into harbors should be made in daylight. As you approach Trinidad from seaward, bear in mind that the main light on Chacachacare Island is visible for more than 26 miles. It is 4½ miles to leeward of the easternmost *boca* (mouth). Do not head directly for it, as the current will most likely be setting you strongly to the west. If you do not take careful bearings, you will end up well to leeward, leaving you a rough beat east against wind and current.

If you happen to be approaching Trinidad from the southeast, do not enter the Gulf of Paria through Serpents Mouth. This would put you hard on the wind for 35 miles up to Port of Spain, and the first part of this trip would be complicated by the many offshore oil rigs. I would advise rounding the island to windward and entering from the north. The distance may be greater, but the effort will be far less.

You can enter the Gulf of Paria through any of four northern openings, or *bocas*. From the west they are Boca Grande, Boca de Navios, Boca de Huevos, and Boca de Monos, which is recommended. The normal flow of current is from the Gulf of Paria into the Caribbean, with the current running strongest during the ebb and less fast, though in the same direction, during the flood. You should plan on using your engine through the *bocas*, no matter what the current. If you have no engine, Navios and Grande are easier to sail through—but then of course you're farther to leeward of Port of Spain.

Proceed directly up to Port of Spain and anchor off the Customs wharf, the easternmost small wharf, or tie bow and stern to the small wharf just west of where all the small commercial freighters are offloaded—it is a small finger pier jetting southward from the terminal for the Trinidad and Tobago ferry. Take your papers to the easternmost pier, to the tide surveyor's office—that's what the Trinidadians call the Customs officer—who will give you preliminary clearance and send you to the other people with whom you must check in. This may be a long and difficult operation; undertake it with patience because there is nothing you can do to make it better. Apparently the Customs and Immigration people are even more unpleasant to local yachtsmen—so be glad you're merely a visitor.

Trinidad does not allow any Rhodesians or South Africans ashore; if by chance they do go ashore, they are promptly put into jail until the boat is ready to leave.

This led to a light moment before the 1977 Trinidad–Grenada Race. We had sailed down for the race, and were in the process of entering when the officer pointed out that my secretary, who was traveling on a British passport, was born in Umtali. He said she was Rhodesian and could not go ashore. I protested that as she had a British passport she was British. "No," he insisted, "she was born in Rhodesia and therefore must be Rhodesian." This went on for a while and and then I said, "Wait a minute. If a cat has kittens in the oven, does that mean they're biscuits?" Roaring with laughter, he stamped her passport and said, "You've got me there, skipper. Have a good time." Another time, after they'd had a fire in the Customs building, Customs and Immigration were spread from one end of Port of Spain to the other. I staggered into the Customs office, hot, tired, and thirsty, got my final piece of paper for clearance, and asked, "Where is the nearest bar I can buy a cold beer?" The Customs officer looked at me and said sadly, "I'm afraid it's about a mile away from here, sir." "I don't think I'll make it," I replied, and he said, "You're in luck. In my little refrigerator here I have two cold Heinekens. How about we sit down and have an afternoon drink?" Customs officers in Trinidad aren't all bad!

There are various navigational problems in Port of Spain. Don't attempt to sail up to the Customs dock after dark, as the harbor is littered with sunken wrecks, most of which are unmarked. Also, there are dozens of small freighters in various states of repair and disrepair anchored at the eastern corner of the harbor and manned by crews of all nationalities whose honesty leaves a lot to be desired. Thievery in this area is absolutely rife. In fact, there has been at least one murder of a yachtsman and possibly more. The harbor police absolutely cannot guarantee your safety; yet they insist on impounding not only your firearms but also your flare pistol—but they don't tell you how to defend yourself against marauders. With the amount of thieving in the harbor of Port of Spain, and considering the amount of illegal arms on the loose in Trinidad, I think it's a mistake for the authorities to take the firearms from yachts.

In 1968, Customs did it differently in Trinidad. They placed our automatic in an accessible locker, sealed with a light wire, and said, "If someone comes aboard and you need the gun, break the seal and use it. Then report to us immediately. If we later find the seal broken and you haven't reported to us, you're in serious trouble. By the way, if you have to use the gun, please shoot straight. And have a good time in Trinidad."

Nowadays, if you have to spend the night in the eastern part of the harbor, I advise you to keep an all-night anchor watch. If it's Carnival and you want to stay downtown to watch the fun, the best thing is to raft five or six boats together, keep all dinghies alongside, and take turns standing anchor watch. Also, make sure to display an anchor light, because the police sometimes decide to enforce the anchor-light rule during Carnival, and this has cost some yachts a bit of money in the past.

Trinidad used to be a good place for mechanical repairs, but unfortunately, both the Swan Hunter and Tugs and Lighters boatyards have gone out of business. There are still good repairmen and excellent availability of parts, though.

About the only place you can lie alongside while repairs are made is at the Trinidad Yacht Club, which is in Cumana Bay, halfway between Port of Spain and Carenage Bay, near an area shown on some charts as Coco. You can also get fuel, ice, and water here. The Yacht Club's slip will haul boats up to 6-foot draft.

Another source of yacht service is north of the fueling dock at Pointe-à-Pierre in the southeast corner of the Gulf of Paria. Here is a hospitable yacht club, once run by the Texaco Oil Company, and taken over in 1986 by the government. Prior arrangements to use its facilities should be made through Arthur Spence, Texaco, Pointe-à-Pierre.

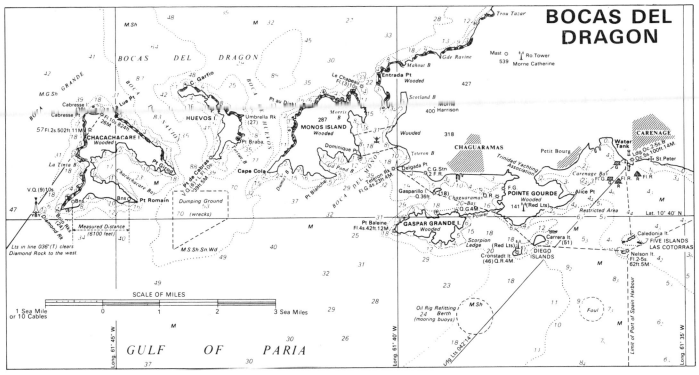

SKETCH CHART III-47A Bocas del Dragon

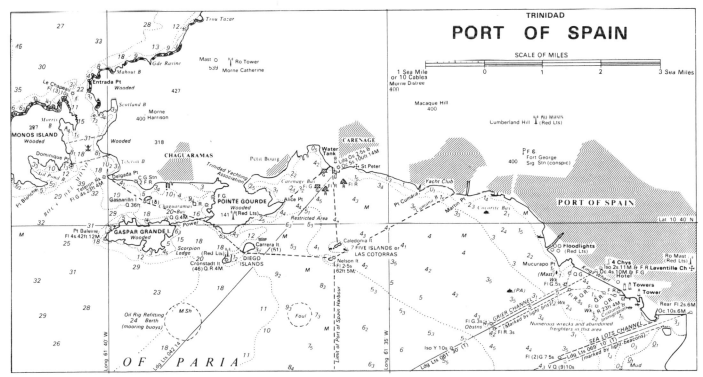

SKETCH CHART III-47B Port of Spain

Eight feet can be carried to the old jetty just south of the club. The channel lines up with the jetty and should be sounded with the lead line.

The third yachting center is the Trinidad Yachting Association, located in Chaguaramas in Carenage Bay. The Association has a clubhouse, moorings, launch service, travel lift limited to fifteen tons, and so on. There is no charge for staying there, but there is a Catch-22 problem. You have to clear Customs before mooring at the Association, but you have to have an invitation from the Association before Customs will clear you to go there. So, what you do is take a bus from downtown to Chaguaramas, introduce yourself to the club manager and to some members, get invited to moor there, and then go back to Customs. The number of the Association is 634-4376.

Under the influence of the Trinidad Yachting Association, yachting has grown tremendously in Trinidad over the last dozen or so years. Marine supplies are now available for boats up to 50 feet from Peak and Company, 177 Western Main Road, St. James, Port of Spain. This is near Westmall. They stock Imray-Iolaire charts and Street guides.

Imray-Iolaire charts are also available from Landry and Company, Brenton Hall, Stanmoor Avenue, Port of Spain (Box 615). Landry and Company caters to the commercial ship market, so it is one of the few places in the Eastern Caribbean where you can get charts for Europe, the Panama Canal, and the Pacific.

Fuel is available not only at the Trinidad Yacht Club and the Texaco facility (but not the Trinidad Yachting Association), but also at Island Home, near the old Swan Hunter boatyard in Chaguaramas Bay.

Across the street from Customs and Immigration is the Seaman's Mission, which has all sorts of facilities: bank, swimming pool, showers, etc. Unhappily, the last I heard was that they have stopped letting yachtsmen use the Mission—only those with seamen's cards were allowed in. It's worth a try to see if the policy has changed again.

In the spring of 1985, prices in Trinidad had gone sky high. One old stand-by Chinese restaurant, Shey Shey Chiens, though, was still reasonable. The portions are huge; the best plan is to gather about fifteen people, go to the restaurant (any taxi driver will find it for you), set up a big table, order fifteen quarter-portions of different items, put them in the center of the table, and dig right in. Now, of course, with the devaluation of the Trinidad dollar, meals should be cheap in Trinidad.

For those with wooden boats, Dougie Myer, easily contacted through the Association or the Port of Spain pilot station, reports that Trinidad now has an excellent supply of timber.

Willie Pincero, the Ulmer agent at 40 Beechwood Drive, Goodwood Gardens, Trinidad (telephone: 632-0559), not only has conventional sails but also repairs the esoteric materials—Kevlar, Mylar—as well.

PORT OF SPAIN
(II D; Sketch Chart III-47B)

It is possible to go into Port of Spain and lie alongside the Customs dock, but this is not something I would want to do for more than a short while. Go in, clear, and move out to either the Trinidad Yachting Association or the Trinidad Yacht Club. Port of Spain is crowded, rough, and filthy. The same holds true of the anchorage at Pointe-à-Pierre.

CUMANA BAY
(II B)

Here you'll find the Trinidad Yacht Club, about 2 miles west of downtown Port of Spain. It's an open, bouncy anchorage, but the Yacht Club has sunk a couple of wrecks to make a breakwater, and now there's a marina inside that provides excellent shelter against the afternoon breeze and bobble. There is supposed to be 12 feet of water inside the breakwater, but silting may have made it less. If you've a deep draft, you had better send the dinghy in first to take some soundings.

Contact the Yacht Club on channel 68. Fuel, ice, and water are available. Outdoor showers used to be, too, but some French sailors, in town for Carnival, took showers stripped to the buff. The showers are in full view of the dining room. They have been disconnected.

If you want to lie alongside to have work done on the boat, you must, of course, make arrangements with the club. Contact the manager, Richard Taitt, Trinidad Yacht Club, Baphore Cocorite, Port of Spain, Trinidad (telephone: 637-4260 or 637-7945).

By law, the Trinidad Yacht Club is not allowed to sell drinks except to club members, so visiting yachtsmen must take out temporary memberships. If visiting yachtsmen do not get the red-carpet treatment here, incidentally, it is completely understandable, because foreign yachtsmen descend on Trinidad each year for Carnival and their behavior has been known to be less than gentlemanly. One year they tore apart the Trinidad Yacht Club with overenthusiastic parties, and recently the club found itself stuck after Carnival with $1,000 worth of bills for overseas phone calls not paid for by the visitors. As has been said elsewhere, quotation marks must often be put round the word "yachts-man."

CARENAGE BAY
(Sketch Chart III-47B)

The Trinidad Yachting Association is here, on the western side of Carenage Bay, just west of the former navy seaplane hangar, now used by the Trinidad government for storage and helicopter landings.

The Association has excellent sailing facilities, showers, launch service, ice, water, and electricity, but no fuel.

The anchorage isn't too good, since the afternoon breeze picks up in the Gulf of Paria and in turn kicks up a lot of bumpy water. Getting in and out of the launch or a dinghy can be tricky. As of May 1986, they were hoping to obtain a couple of old freighters and sink them across the mouth of the cove to form a breakwater.

The Association has an extensive sailing and racing program. The racing season lasts from November through May; in the summer they cruise up to the Grenadines, train racing crews, and work on their boats. An excellent junior program is run in the summer by two Canadians, who also teach adults.

Their fleet ranges from tiddlers to red-hot IOR, high-tech boats such as Dougie Myers' *Legacy*, a Soveril 43 that Doug built himself in Trinidad. The cruising class includes *Iolaire*'s old rival, *Rosemary V*, and an ex-8 Meter, *Lara*.

The Association is devoted strictly to sailing. No motorboats are allowed. Only sailboat-owners can vote in the Association's meetings—it doesn't matter if it's a windsurfer or a 60-footer, but you have to own a sailboat. That's how they ensure that any proposals for tennis courts, swimming pools, or fancy restaurants invariably get voted down.

Otherwise, there is very little to recommend the Gulf of Paria. It is shallow, muddy, and, during summertime, full of jellyfish. No yachtsman wants to linger in this area unless he has business to conduct or friends ashore. There are, however, a few good anchorages scattered through the area. The cove on the south side of Gaspar Grande is attractive and well sheltered. On Monos Island are two good all-weather anchorages. These are Morris Bay and Grand Pond (or Dehert) Bay. On the east shore of Boca de Monos is Scotland Bay, which is listed as restricted but is nonetheless used by local yachtsmen without anyone's fussing.

Relatively little cruising is done in the Gulf of Paria, even though there are some excellent anchorages on the Venezuelan Peninsula de Paria. Venezuela requires clearance at Punta Guiria, which is time-consuming and out of the way. Besides, the port captain can be downright hostile to yachtsmen. Most Trinidadians prefer the Grenadines and points north for their cruising grounds. The east coast is not suitable for overnight cruising. It is a lee shore with no viable anchorages.

North Coast

This area is seldom visited by yachts, as it is completely exposed to the northerly ground swells during the winter months, from late October through April. It is visited by fishermen, who tuck themselves in behind various headlands for some respite from the wind and sea.

During June and July, though, there are certainly some spots on Trinidad's north coast where you could find shelter while working your way east to Tobago.

A problem is that there are no detailed charts of this coast. DMA 24404 goes as far as Chupara Point, 20 miles east of Boca de Monos; DMA 24400 picks up ten miles or so east of that, but shows almost no detail. The BA chart is helpful but has little detail. The best thing is to get topo maps in Trinidad at the Ministry of Agriculture, Lands, and Survey, corner of Richmond and Queen streets, Port of Spain. Without a topo map, it's pretty hard to figure out where you are on this relatively featureless coast.

If you're going from Trinidad to Tobago, I advise you to use the easternmost *boca*, Boca de Monos, just as the tide begins to fall, then work your way east along the coast. For two or three hours there should be an easterly-going current. The obvious course is to short-tack as close to shore as you dare; the coast is rather steep-to, with a few off-lying rocks, best shown on the topo maps.

One problem in navigating this coast is that the Trinidadians have one name for a bay or an island, the U.S. chart has another name, and the topo map has yet another. Ten miles east of Boca de Monos is Maravaca Island, also called Saut d'Eau

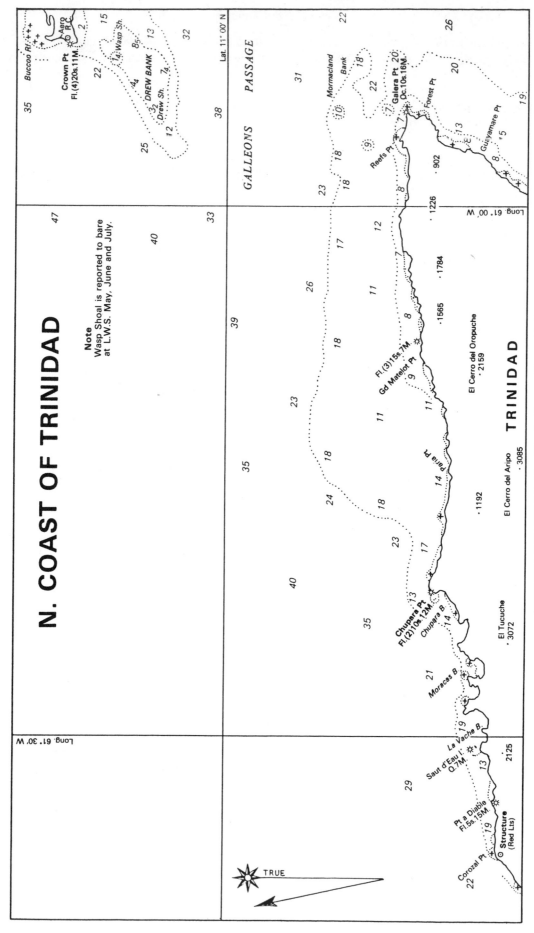

N. COAST OF TRINIDAD

Note
Wasp Shoal is reported to bare at L.W.S. May, June and July.

SKETCH CHART III-48   North Coast of Trinidad

TRINIDAD

GALLEONS PASSAGE

Long. 61° 30′ W.

Long. 61° 00′ W.

Lat. 11° 00′ N.

Buccoo Rf.
Crown Pt
Fl.(4)20s.11M.
Aero
R.C.
DREW BANK
Wasp Sh.
Drew Sh.

Mormacland
Bank
Galera Pt
Oc.10s.16M.
Forest Pt
Reefs Pt
Guevamare Pt

El Cerro del Oropuche
.2159
El Cerro del Aripo
.3085
El Cerro del Aripo
.1192

Fl.(3)15s.7M.
Gd Matelot Pt

Paria Pt

Chupara Pt
Fl.(2)10s.12M.
Chupara B.

El Tucuche
3072

Moracas B.

La Vache B.
Saut d'Eau I.
Q.7M.

Pt a Diable
Fl.5s.15M.

Corozal Pt

Structure
(Red Lts)
.2125

TRUE

Island, locally referred to as Sadau Island; do not try to pass between this island and the mainland. A bow-and-stern anchorage can be had in calm weather behind Medine Point, and there's good diving in the area, plus all sorts of caves at water level. The island is a birdwatcher's dream, as it is a protected area.

MARACAS BAY

During June and July, this provides good shelter and good beach. Best anchorage is, of course, in the southeastern corner referred to on the topo map as Tyrico Bay. With the high land to the east, the wind will come from all directions. The shore is quite steep-to; moor bow and stern. The south side of the bay has a great, long white-sand beach produced by the winter ground swells.

LA CUEVAS BAY

This bay is easily spotted from offshore by its long white-sand beach with two white houses on the beach, which are lifeguard huts; this is a very popular surfing bay during the winter, and obviously not a winter anchorage. In summer, though, you should be able to find good shelter from the sea behind Abercromby Point. Ease your way in with the aid of a lead line or depth sounder, and anchor bow and stern because of the variable wind.

CHUPARA BAY

This bay should provide shelter in summer. Again, a bow-and-stern anchorage, with a very small beach that should be partially sheltered by a reef that extends west from Chupara Point for half a mile. Give the point a wide berth if you are sailing into the bay or short-tacking up the beach.

East of Chupara Point there is no possibility of stopping before Matelot, a possible anchorage 14 miles away. Watch out for Machapure Rock, half a mile offshore off the eastern entrance to Blanchisseuse, which is spotted by the village of the same name.

MATELOT BAY

According to the *British Admiralty Pilot* book, L'Islette is joined to the coast by a small causeway or low sandspit and provides a sheltered anchorage for small craft to the west of the island off the town of Matelot. This anchorage is not shown on the Admiralty or DMA charts and can be found only with the aid of the topo maps.

GRAND RIVIÈRE BAY

With the wind south of east in the summer, an anchorage should be possible off the village of Grand Rivière, six miles east of Matelot. It's the next to last anchorage before one goes off to Tobago.

TOCO

Toco, seven miles east of Grand Rivière Bay, is the easternmost village in Trinidad. It has a small jetty, and before the roads were built, it was connected to civilization by a coastal freighter, which anchored off and put supplies ashore, winter and summer. I am told that the boatmen, all from Carriacou, were the finest surf seamen in the world. In summer there might possibly be a half-decent anchorage off the town of Toco; it is a case of feeling your way in, as there are no charts.

Remember that you can use the whole north coast only from late April to October, and even then only when the wind is south of east. You should be prepared to up anchor and get out if the wind goes north of east; and it can go all the way around to the north even in the summer months.

Tobago

Discovered in 1498 and settled in 1639, Tobago was neither zealously colonized nor jealously held; the island changed hands roughly thirty times before the British ultimately established control in 1814. In 1962, along with Trinidad, Tobago was made independent. Lacking good, deep-water harbors, it has never prospered commercially.

In 1963, the year after independence, a hurricane went through Tobago, knocked everything flat, and completely destroyed the agricultural economy that existed at the time. Relatively few of the planters tried to reestablish the farming economy, which they figured was going to die with independence anyway, since the Trinidad government looked to the oil industry as the salvation of Trinidad and Tobago: They dreamed of building an industrial nation with the profits from the oil industry.

In the years of high oil prices, this dream had a chance of coming true, but now, with the fall

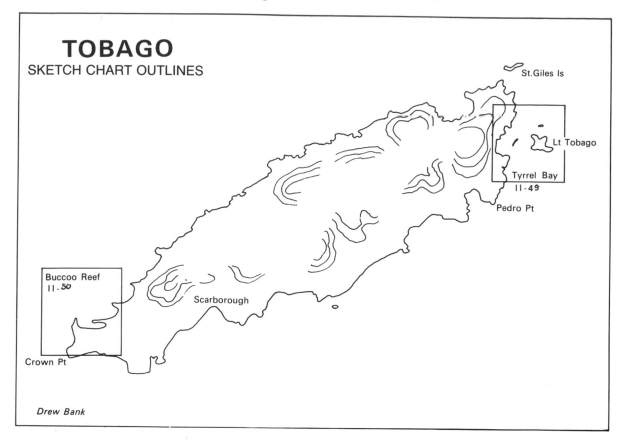

TOBAGO
SKETCH CHART OUTLINES

St.Giles Is

Lt Tobago

Tyrrel Bay
11-49

Pedro Pt

Buccoo Reef
11-50

Scarborough

Crown Pt

Drew Bank

in prices, Tobago's salvation seems to be in the field of tourism. The island is well suited for this, with its beautiful beaches, fair number of hotels, and superb scenery. It also has more birds than any other Eastern Caribbean island; the island was never plagued with poisonous snakes and thus escaped mongoose infestation. Mongooses were imported to other islands to eliminate the snakes; once the mongooses got rid of the snakes they started on the birds. Hence the relatively low bird population in most of the Caribbean Islands.

One of our nicest outings in recent years was in Tobago, where we rented a van and drove around the island. Well, almost; the road from Bloody Bay to within a few miles of Charlotteville and Man of War Bay is unpaved, and just before Man of War Bay the road was blocked by a fallen tree and a small washout. This was discouraging because the tree had been down for four months and the road still had not been cleared. It would have taken only a jeepload of road workers no more than a day to clear the whole road.

Tobago is very seldom visited by cruising yachtsmen because for most cruisers it is so difficult to reach.

The trans-Atlantic yachtsman who has made his landfall in Barbados, on the other hand, is all set:

He has an easy, broad reach of about 140 miles. However, he had better do his navigation very carefully as he approaches Tobago, since the current runs northwest at 2 to 3 knots; if allowance is not made for the current, he will find himself west of Tobago and may possibly miss the island altogether.

This northwesterly flow of the current is true not only around Tobago, but extends up the eastern side of the lower end of the Lesser Antilles as well. In March 1985, when we were heading from Martinique to Tobago, we were doing 7 to 7½ knots through the water, but with the current on the nose we were making only 5 knots over the bottom. It was not one of *Iolaire*'s fastest passages.

If you are in the Lesser Antilles and are trying to get to Tobago, head north or south to Martinique, go around to Ste. Anne, then take off from there on a course of about 175 magnetic, if you can average 7 knots, or more to the east if you are slower.

If you are sailing from Trinidad to Tobago, you have a long tough haul. Even the sports fishermen think it is a rough run. For many years the sail from Trinidad to Tobago was seldom attempted—the Lazzari brothers of *Draconius* were among the few Trinidadian yachtsmen who had successfully made the trip. With the advent of the modern IOR type cruising boat, yachtsmen have fought their way up to Tobago more regularly; in fact, for two years they had Spring Regattas in Tobago, although some yachtsmen objected on the grounds that it was too hard to get there.

If the wind is in the southeast, it is possible to stop along the north coast of Trinidad, especially from the end of March through mid-October, when the northerly ground swells are seldom encountered. (See the previous section for notes on the north coast of Trinidad.)

When heading for Tobago from Galera Point on Trinidad, it is imperative to avoid Drew Bank and Wasp Shoal. I am told by Jim Young and other divers who have dived on both shoals extensively that they are considerably shoaler than the charts show. Jim claims that at low-water springs in May, June, and July, when the water is lower in the Caribbean than it is in the winter, the coral heads on Wasp Shoal actually break water. Yet the British Admiralty and U.S. charts show a minimum depth over them of 12 feet. During the winter, when the wind is blowing hard, the entire area can be a seething mass of breakers. Under no circumstances should you allow yourself to get onto Drew Bank or Wasp Shoal; pass to windward or leeward of them, but do not cross them.

At this point, a discussion of the Tobago charts is in order. The new metric editions, 14 and 15, of the U.S. chart 24402, and the 14th edition of 24403, are definitely not nearly as accurate or useful as the charts they replaced. The soundings were switched from fathoms and feet to metric, many soundings were deleted, and the large-scale insert of Tyrrel's Bay was eliminated. An examination of the new charts makes one wonder what is happening in Washington, as supposedly these charts were compiled from information from the earlier editions, yet they are full of discrepancies. If you are sailing to and exploring Tobago, try to obtain the old 13th edition. Or else get BA chart 508 of all of Tobago, and 505, harbor plans of Tobago, although the old plan for the Little Tobago–Tyrrel's Bay area has been omitted and the Buccoo Reef area is singularly inaccurate. For these two areas, use the sketch charts in this book. By the time you read this book, a new Imray-Iolaire chart covering Tobago might be available.

All the U.S., British Admiralty, and Imray-Iolaire charts are basically drawn from the British Admiralty surveys of 1864 and 1865 plus colonial surveys of 1920 and 1955; as such, they must be viewed cautiously.

The only point of entry is Scarborough, and foreign yachts must go into Scarborough even if they are coming from Trinidad.

SCARBOROUGH
(BA 508, 505; DMA 24402, 24403)

When approaching Scarborough, be very careful of the shoals in Rodney Bay to the west of Scarborough harbor, which now because of the ferry has been well buoyed; the buoys do not show on the U.S. chart, but are on the hand-corrected BA chart. Scarborough is not a particularly good anchorage, to say the least. The inner harbor is used by the Trinidad and Tobago ferry and local freighters and is therefore unavailable for yachts. Anchor among the fishing boats southeast of the harbor; moor bow and stern as far inshore as possible to stay clear of the entrance channel of the ferry—you'll be told in no uncertain terms if you are anchored too close to its route.

Once ashore, leave the dockyard and turn left: 600 to 800 yards to the west, just across the small river, you will find the Immigration office; you have to go back to town to clear Customs. I must say that in March 1985, the Customs officers were less than friendly. They insisted that our flare pistol be brought in from the boat and locked up in the police armory. (What were we supposed to do if we had a problem and needed to fire a distress flare?) They also announced that we were allowed to go to only Milford Bay and Man of War Bay; we could not visit the other bays on the north side of the island because the authorities could not guarantee our safety. Very puzzling for an island whose chief salvation is tourism.

Scarborough is not one of the great scenic towns of the Eastern Caribbean. You can do your shopping in one of the three small supermarkets in the village, or go to a new big Hi-Lo on the western end of the village, where you'll also find an ice plant (cubed ice only, no blocks). There is an excellent open-air market in the same area. Water is free—when you can get alongside the dock after the ferry leaves. Fuel is strictly a case of jerry cans.

Scarborough is a town to visit, enter, and then depart as soon as possible.

South Coast

Numerous small coves on Tobago's south coast can be visited by a small yacht drawing 4–5 feet and piloted by a good reef navigator. Like Anguilla, Tobago lies on a northeast-southwest axis, so that if the wind is in the southeast, most of the harbors on the south coast are uncomfortable or untenable, whereas those on the north coast are okay—and vice versa. This means, generally, that in the winter months, when the wind is from the north and the ground swell is prevalent, you should visit the south coast; in spring and summer, spend your time basically on the north coast.

Interestingly, Pinfold Bay, behind Smith Island, was the original harbor and settlement on the island.

The anchorage behind Richmond Point, inside Richmond Island, might be worthwhile to visit to see the old Strong estate. Water for the estate's waterwheel was provided by an aqueduct more than a mile and a half long. It led back into the hills to various pools that were dammed up to provide water during the dry season.

KINGS BAY
(DMA 24402)

This is the first real anchorage on the southeast coast. It is described in the *British Admiralty Pilot* as the most secure anchorage in all of Tobago; the wind would have to go all the way to the south and blow hard to make it uncomfortable. The one problem is that the bay is very deep, so I would strongly advise a bow anchor on the beach and a stern anchor holding you off.

The tourism industry in Tobago has a long way to go, and the hotels could use some upgrading; but from the yachtsman's standpoint, the island has at least one very nice outstanding feature: On every beach we visited along the coast of Tobago we found little kiosks with bathrooms and showers. Kings Bay has such beach facilities, and, also, after a short walk up the river, a very nice waterfall, which is featured on almost all Trinidad and Tobago postcards.

The south equatorial current that pours up against Tobago at the rate of 3 to 4 knots splits offshore of Pedro Point. One leg bends north around Cape Gracias de Dios and in between Little Tobago Island and the mainland. The other branch swings west by Queens Island, then southwest along Richmond Island and down the south coast of Tobago. Note that in heavy weather Great River Shoal off Goldsborough Bay is covered with breakers; give the shoal a very side berth.

TYRREL'S BAY; GOAT ISLAND; LITTLE TOBAGO
(BA 508, 505; DMA 24402 and discontinued DMA 2440; Sketch Chart III-49)

This area is extremely interesting, but you must be prepared for a very strong current that runs north inside Tobago Island at a solid 4 knots and causes heavy tide rips and overfalls off the north end of Little Tobago Island. The best approach is from the south, between Middle Rock and the mainland, where you probably have a 2-knot current under you. At this point you have three anchorages to choose from: in Anse Bateau off the Blue Waters Inn; or under the lee of Goat Island in Tyrrel's Bay; or, if you draw 6 feet or less and are a good reef navigator and conditions are perfect, inside the reef out of the tide in the small cove on the west side of Little Tobago Island.

Anse Bateau off the Blue Waters Inn is an easy entrance. Bear off and sail under Goat Island. Study the coastline with binoculars and you will discover a large waterwheel north of Speyside; sail north to the Blue Waters Inn, then run downwind into the cove. This is strictly eyeball navigation; round up and anchor in 12 feet of water, completely out of the current.

Jim Young, who owns the Dive Shop down in Pigeon Point on the southwestern coast of Tobago, has a boat permanently stationed here and runs dive trips out of the Blue Waters Inn. He can be contacted via the hotel if you wish to arrange diving trips.

If you are anchored in Anse Bateau northwest of Goat Island (Sketch Chart III-49), it is worth taking a walk over to the next bay to see the ruins of an old huge undershot waterwheel (perhaps a hydraulic engineer can explain to me why one builds an undershot rather than an overshot wheel); it is a magnificent piece of machinery built by W. A. Smith and Company, Glasgow, in 1871. Obviously the plantation economy was still going strong long after the end of slavery in 1839; otherwise, who would have spent a huge amount of money to build canals, aqueducts, and a very expensive waterwheel to grind sugar? Historians who claim that sugar became unprofitable immediately after the freeing of the slaves apparently don't know that there is old sugar-making equipment scattered throughout the islands with dates showing that the equipment was installed from the 1870s through the 1890s.

GOAT ISLAND
(Sketch Chart III-49)

Under the lee of Goat Island, an anchorage can be had right off the large white house. It is very deep water and the beach is steep-to; you will have to drop a stern anchor, power on into the beach, and literally jump from the bow of the boat onto the sand and bury your anchor. Most of the time

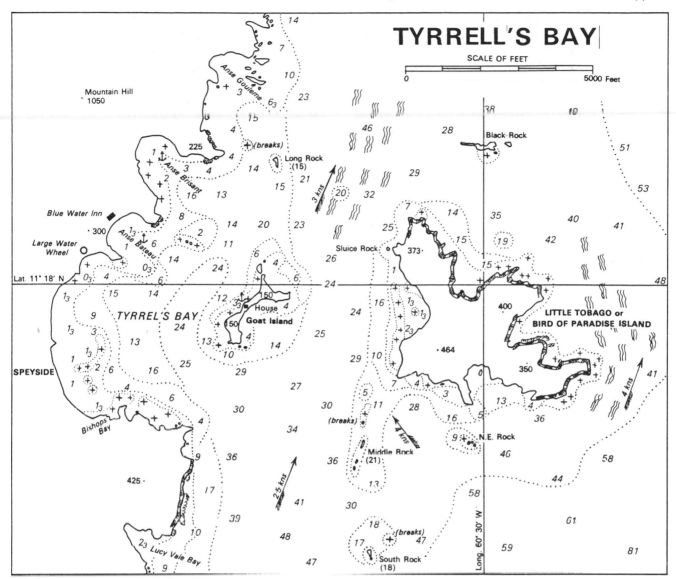

SKETCH CHART III-49   Tyrrel's Bay

the house is unoccupied, and I am told that the owners do not object to yachtsmen mooring bow-on to this beach. If yachtsmen behave themselves we will probably be welcome; let's hope a few don't ruin it for everybody else.

LITTLE TOBAGO ISLAND
(Sketch Chart III-49)

Little Tobago Island is of great interest to the ornithologist because it used to be the only home in the Western Hemisphere of birds of paradise, which had been imported from Varuna Island, off the coast of Borneo, in the early twentieth century. The chap who imported them also installed a couple of caretakers on the island to protect the birds.

Upon the owner's death, the island was sold and

resold and has finally ended up in the hands of the Trinidad and Tobago government. Now the birds of paradise have apparently died out completely—I am told that the last birdwatcher who came looking for them spent six months on the island and never saw one. However, it is still a beautiful island and very much worth exploring.

When passing north out of Tyrrel's Bay, favor the Long Rock side of the channel to avoid the heavy tide rip from overfalls off the northwest tip of Little Tobago. If you're going north, I would strongly advise passing outside of St. Giles (Melville) and Marble islands. Do not pass between those off-lying islands and the mainland.

If by any chance you are approaching Tyrrel's Bay from the north (which I advise against), remember that you will be bucking a 4-knot current if you go south between Goat Island and the mainland. I would strongly suggest you not try it unless you have an engine and the boat is capable of doing 6 knots over the bottom. We did succeed in getting through with *Iolaire* but it put more than a few gray hairs in my beard. I urge that you pass fairly close to Long Rock to avoid the above-mentioned tide rip, and then run between Goat Island and the rocks to the west. Run in and anchor off the Blue Waters Inn.

Coming from the north and trying to anchor behind Little Tobago Island is almost impossible under sail because the island throws a considerable wind shadow. If you have an engine, hug the Little Tobago shore, use eyeball navigation, and pass between the north end of the reef and the shore; feel your way south behind the reef to the anchorage. This should be attempted only by very good reef navigators with boats drawing 6 feet or less under ideal light conditions.

West and North Coasts

When heading west from Scarborough, pass south of Bulldog Shoal off Rockley Bay, now well buoyed as of March 1985. You'll encounter a strong west-flowing current, but off Crown Point close inshore there is a strong east-going eddy; swing well clear of Crown Point and anchor at the south end of the beach between Pigeon Point and Sandy Point. Off the north end of the beach you will see signs for the cable that brings power to Tobago from Trinidad.

Anchor fairly far offshore here, as the fishermen shoot their nets early in the morning. Incidentally, anytime you are anchored in the vicinity of fishermen shooting their nets, do not use a Herreshoff anchor, as the fluke sticking out of the bottom is bound to catch a net; instead, anchor with the Danforth-type, Bruce, or plow anchor; then the net may drag across the top of your anchor and anchor line with a fair chance of not fouling.

In Milford Bay, anchor bow and stern; otherwise when the wind dies, the current will swing you beam to wind and you will rock and roll all night. Milford Bay is open to the ground swell, which can be encountered anytime from October to mid-March and occasionally through mid-April or early May.

Ashore, you will find the beach crowded on the weekends. Glass-bottomed boats excursion boats anchored off the beach will take you for a tour of Buccoo Reef. Roadside shops sell beer, *roti*, hamburgers, etc. Three large hotels will cater to every-

one depending on how much money you want to spend. Cars are for rent, and a good idea is to hire one and do a tour of the island, as we did; we put a big icebox in the back loaded with beer and wine and sandwich materials and drove off.

On the north end of the beach is Jim Young's Dive Shop. Jim is an experienced diver with an interesting heritage—he is part Chinese, part Carib Indian. He will be most happy to take you down by Buccoo Reef or anywhere along the north coast of Tobago. Your diving area, of course, will be determined by your experience.

BUCCOO REEF
(BA 505, 508; DMA 24402 [definitely use the 13th edition of the DMA chart]; Sketch Chart III-50)

Despite what the 14th edition of the DMA chart shows, Buccoo Reef forms an excellent harbor. You can enter through the northernmost of the two entrances. Twenty feet of water can be carried well inside the reefs, where it shoals rather rapidly to about 8 feet. How far east you go to anchor depends on the time of year and your draft. When messing around in the Buccoo Reef area, remember that at spring tides there is roughly a 3-foot rise and fall of tide.

Once inside the reef, if you head approximately 150 magnetic, you will reach halfway to Sheerbird Point; then eyeball and zigzag until you get to Sheerbird Point, where you can anchor bow and stern off a white-sand beach. With care at high water 7 or 8 feet can be carried all the way in to the inner lagoon. Once off Sheerbird Point or in the lagoon, you'll have approximately 20 feet of water. When threading your way through the shoals inside Buccoo Reef, you will see white flags staked out on various reefs—a privately maintained buoyage system.

On the east side of the bay inside Buccoo Reef is Nylon Pool. I don't know why it is called that, but it is famous for the fact that it is about 4 feet deep and the water gets so heated up by the sun that it is practically the warmest water in the Caribbean.

Needless to say, the Buccoo Reef area provides extremely good snorkeling inside the reef for the inexperienced outside, the reef drops off suddenly and provides good snorkeling and diving for the more experienced.

Behind Pigeon Point there is an almost marina— I say "almost marina" because it seems that before independence in 1962, the swamp area was dredged out to build a large marina; then just before they

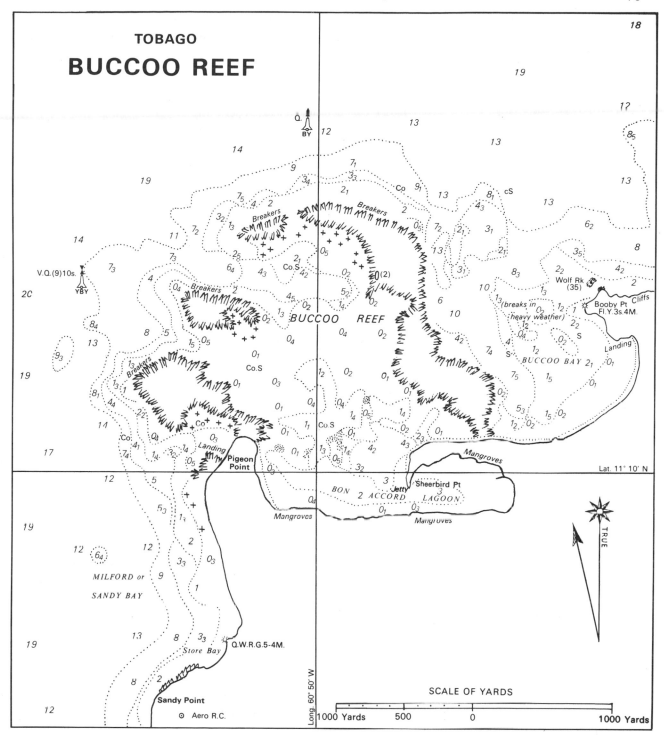

SKETCH CHART III-50 Buccoo Reef

broke through, the newly independent government of Trinidad and Tobago decided there should not be a marina in Tobago. This certainly hurt tourism severely. It is interesting to think about what would have happened had a large marina been built in Tobago in the early sixties.

BUCCOO BAY

(BA 505, 508; DMA 24402; Sketch Chart III-50)

Buccoo Bay has miles of white-sand beach, but it is strictly a May-to-October anchorage; ground swell from the north makes it completely untenable. Basically, this is true for all the bays, except possibly Man of War Bay, on the north coast of Tobago. When entering Buccoo Bay, favor the Buccoo Reef side of the bay; using eyeball navigation, come south along the reef, then swing east in behind the shoals that extend west from Booby Point and anchor where you want.

IRVING BAY

Anchorage is available in behind Rocky Point. This is an excellent, steep-to beach, with nothing much ashore; use eyeball navigation, and anchor bow and stern.

PLYMOUTH
(BA 505, 508; DMA 24402, and discontinued DMA 2440)

Plymouth is reputed Tobago's second town, but it looks more like a village. A small gun battery sited on Courland Point hardly fits its description as a fort, but it provides a good view of the harbor. Best anchorages are in the northeast end of the harbor. Watch out for the shoals extending southwest from Courland Point. The nice white-sand beach has a hotel on it. West of Hawks Bill there is possibly a small daytime anchorage in calm weather, right under the Trinidad and Tobago golf course, which has an excellent reputation.

CASTRA BAY
(BA 508; DMA 24402)

Summer-only, bow-and-stern anchorage off the beach. Check immediately upon anchoring as to where the fishermen are likely to be shooting their nets. Shower and bathing facilities are ashore; there is a small village, but no charter boats.

ENGLISHMANS BAY
(BA 508; DMA 24402)

Three streams run into Englishmans Bay; if you follow the middle stream 10 minutes' walk, you find a very nice waterfall, which is great for showers and bathing. As with other bays on this coast, check with the fishermen upon anchoring to make sure you will not foul up their fishing.

PARLATUVIER BAY
(BA 508; DMA 24402)

Despite what the chart shows to the contrary, there is a shelf here, and you can anchor bow and stern. Be wary of the reef on the north side of the bay. There's a beautiful white-sand beach, very little civilization, and excellent diving on both sides of the bay.

BLOODY BAY
(BA 508; DMA 24402)

A distinctive bay in that there is a white-sand beach in the northeast corner of the bay and a black-sand beach on the south side. We were told that during the wars between the British and the French in the late eighteenth and early nineteenth centuries, there was a naval battle off Bloody Bay. The bodies of those killed ended up on the beach of what they call Dead Mans Bay on the western side of the harbor; somehow or other, due to the current, all the blood got washed over to what is now called Bloody Bay. The chart shows a rather large river, but when we saw it in dry season it was a mere trickle.

When sailing east from Bloody Bay to Man of War Bay, stay well clear of the Brothers and the Sisters, as they both appear to be improperly charted.

MAN OF WAR BAY
(BA 505, 508; DMA 24402 and discontinued DMA 24401)

This was a favorite stopping place for British ships in the West Indian fleet before World War II. Life was more relaxed then, and whenever a ship came in, parties would be organized by the various estate owners for the officers and crew. One of the high points of the pre–World War II social scene was the arrival of HMS *Hood*, later sunk by the *Bismarck* in a famous naval battle.

Today, Man of War Bay is a big empty harbor with plenty of fishermen. The best anchorage is up in the northeast corner, tucked in behind North Point, an area locally referred to as Privateers Bay. The new DMA Chart 24402 shows three small islands on the eastern side of the harbor, but they are not there. This is a bow-and-stern anchorage. Charlotteville is a small village with shops that can supply the most essential supplies. You'll also find Jane Boyle, a scuba diver who runs a diving establishment from Turpin Cottages on the western side of the bay; she is easily spotted riding around on her small motorbike.

If you're going east from Man of War Bay, do not try to pass between St. Giles Island and the mainland; go north of Marble Island to avoid the worst of the westward-setting currents.

In sum, Tobago is well worth a visit, especially during the summer months, when the winds are lighter, the danger of northerly ground swells minimized, and the danger of hurricanes almost non-existent (there have been only two hurricanes there in recorded history). Customs officials may be difficult, but the people are extremely friendly.

NOTES

NOTES

NOTES

Bibliography

Cruising Guides

Buzby, V. M. *Virgin Island Sailing Directions.* 1952. Privately printed by the Coast Guard Auxiliary in the early 1950s.

Carey, Charles, and E. A. Raiwhold. *Virgin Anchoraging.* A superb collection of aerial photographs.

Chubb, Percy, III. *Cruising Guide to the Windward and Leeward Islands of the Eastern Caribbean.* 1961. Privately printed.

Eggleston, George Teeple. *Virgin Islands.* 1959; reprinted, Huntington, N.Y.: Krieger, 1974. Available at Palm Passage Bookstore, St. Thomas.

Eiman, William J. *St. Maarten/St. Martin Area Plus St. Kitts and Nevis Cruising Guide.* Copyright 1983 by Virgin Island Plus Yacht Charters, Inc. Also covers Anguilla, St. Barts, Saba, and Statia.

Forbes, Al. *Virgin Islands Cruising Guide.* Hollywood, Fla.: Dukane Press, 1970.

Kelly, Tom, and Jack Van Ost. *Yachtsman's Guide to the Virgin Islands.* 1968. Now Van Ost, John R., and Harry Kline. *Yachtsman's Guide to the Greater Antilles.* Coral Gables, Fla.: Tropic Isle, 1979.

Mitchell, Carleton. *Islands to Windward.* New York: Van Nostrand, 1948. Now out of print, this classic yarn of Mitchell's cruise from Trinidad to Nassau on board the *Carib* in 1946 is the first cruising guide written for the area.

Street, D. M., Jr. *Cruising Guide to the Virgin Islands.* 1963. Privately printed. No longer available.

———. *Yachting Guide to the Grenadines.* Hollywood, Fla.: Dukane Press, 1970.

———. *A Cruising Guide to the Lesser Antilles.* New York: Norton, 1964, 1974.

Stevens Yachts of Annapolis, *A Cruising Guide to the Windward Islands,* Annapolis, Md.: 1979. A picture and text guide.

Wilensky, Julius M. *Yachtsman's Guide to the Windward Islands.* 2nd ed. Stamford, Conn.: Wescott Cove, 1978.

General

Fenger, Frederic A. *The Cruise of the Diablesse.* New York: Yachting, Inc., [1926]. A description of cruising through the islands in 1915. Possibly back in print. If not, try the library. A truly great book on the Lesser Antilles.

———. *Alone in the Caribbean.* Belmont, Mass.: Wilmington Books, 1958. A description of cruising through the Islands in a decked canoe in 1911. Another great book on the Lesser Antilles.

Mitchell, Carleton. *Islands to Windward.* Washington, D.C.: National Geographic Society, 1967. A description of the author's second cruise through the islands in 1965 aboard the *Finisterre.*

Robinson, William. *Where the Tradewinds Blow.* New York: Charles Scribner's Sons, [1963]. A collection of stories about various cruises by the editor of *Yachting.*

History

Kay, Francis. *This—Is Grenada.* St. George's, Grenada: Carenage Press, [1971]. An excellent description of Grenada and a must for anyone who loves it.

Lewisjohn, Florence. *Divers Information on the Romantic History of St. Croix.* Hollywood, Fla.: Dukane Press, [1963?].

———. *Tales of Tortola and the British Virgin Islands.* Hollywood, Fla.: Dukane Press, 1966.

———. *St. Croix under Seven Flags.* Hollywood, Fla.: Dukane Press, 1970.

Mann, Zane B. *Fair Winds and Far Places*. Minneapolis: Dillon Press, 1978. Excellent account of a successful executive who chucks it all and runs away to the Lesser Antilles. An honest appraisal of the joys and sorrows involved. Required reading for anyone thinking of doing the same.

Morison, Samuel Eliot. *Admiral of the Ocean Sea*. Boston: Little, Brown, 1942. Superb biography of Columbus with vivid descriptions of the men, ships, islands, and sailing. Voluminous and interesting footnotes.

————. *Christopher Columbus, Mariner*. Boston: Little, Brown, 1955. A condensed version of *Admiral of the Ocean Sea*, and infinitely more readable.

O'Neill, Edward A. *Rape of the American Virgins*. New York: Praeger, 1972. A must for anyone who wishes to understand the problems of the U.S. Virgin Islands.

Thomas, G. C. H. *Ruler in Hiroona*. [Port of Spain], Trinidad, [1972]. Novel of a mythical island, but an all-too-apt description of the typical West Indian situation.

Waugh, Alec. *Island in the Sun*. New York: Farrar, Straus and Cudahy, [c. 1955].

Westlake, Donald E. *Under an English Heaven*. New York: Simon & Schuster, 1972. Provides valuable historical insight into island governments throughout the Lesser Antilles. A must for anyone who wants to understand the islands.

Humor

Wibberley, Leonard. *The Mouse That Roared*. Boston: Little, Brown. Side-splitting description of the invasion of Anguilla, with local island characters very thinly disguised.

Wouk, Herman. *Don't Stop the Carnival*. New York: Doubleday, 1965. A perfect description of St. Thomas in the late 1950s.

Flora and Fauna

Chaplin, C. G. *Fish Watching Guide*. New York: World.

Collins, James Bond. *Birds of the West Indies*. 2nd ed. Boston: Houghton-Mifflin, 1971.

Devas, Father Raymond. *Birds of Grenada, St. Vincent and the Grenadines*. Grenada: Carenage Press.

Groome, J. R. *A Natural History of the Island of Grenada*. Privately printed. Available at Sea Change Book Stores, St. George's, Grenada.

Hargreaves, Dorothy, and Bob Hargreaves. *Tropical Blossoms of the Caribbean*. Kailua, Hawaii: Hargreaves, 1960.

Mognotte, Sony. *Shelling and Beachcombing in the Southern Caribbean Waters*.

Murray, Dea. *Birds of the Virgin Islands*.

Randall, John E. *Caribbean Reef Fishes*. Neptune, N.J.: T.F.H., 1978.

Among the most readable books for those wishing to know about the Eastern Caribbean's colorful past are the novels and nonfiction works of Dudley Pope. His knowledge and research are impeccable. The following are highly recommended.

Dudley Pope: Nonfiction

The Black Ship. Philadelphia: Lippincott, 1964. The story of the worst single-ship mutiny in the Royal Navy. On board the *Hermione*, in 1797, between Hispaniola and Venezuela, the captain and all the officers were murdered.

The Buccaneer King. New York: Dodd, Mead, 1978. The first third of this biography of Sir Henry Morgan gives a wide-ranging introduction to the early days of the Eastern Caribbean.

Dudley Pope: Novels

Governor Ramage, R.N. New York: Simon & Schuster, 1973. Covers the U.S. Virgins and Culebra.

Ramage and the Freebooters. London: Weidenfeld & Nicolson, [1969]. (In the United States, *The Triton Brig*. New York: Pocket Books, 1978.) Covers Grenada and St. Lucia.

Ramage and the Rebels. Describes how the island of Curacao was handed over to the British—and captured by them when the Dutch changed their mind.

Ramage's Diamond. London: Fontana, 1977. Describes the capture by the British of Diamond Rock, off Fort-de-France, Martinique.

Ramage's Mutiny. London: Secker & Warburg, 1977. Set in English Harbour, Antigua, and then in Venezuela.

Ramage's Prize. New York: Simon & Schuster, 1975. Covers the Lesser and Greater Antilles.

Index